John Howard Cromwell

A treatise on belts and pulleys. Embracing full explanations of fundamental principles; proper disposition of pulleys; rules, formulas

John Howard Cromwell

A treatise on belts and pulleys. Embracing full explanations of fundamental principles; proper disposition of pulleys; rules, formulas

ISBN/EAN: 9783337156947

Printed in Europe, USA, Canada, Australia, Japan

Cover: Foto ©Andreas Hilbeck / pixelio.de

More available books at **www.hansebooks.com**

A TREATISE

ON

BELTS AND PULLEYS.

EMBRACING

FULL EXPLANATIONS OF FUNDAMENTAL PRINCIPLES; PROPER DISPOSITION OF PULLEYS; RULES, FORMULAS, AND TABLES FOR DETERMINING WIDTHS OF LEATHER AND VULCANIZED-RUBBER BELTS AND BELTS RUNNING OVER COVERED PULLEYS; STRENGTH AND PROPORTIONS OF PULLEYS, DRUMS, Etc.

TOGETHER WITH

THE PRINCIPLES OF AND NECESSARY RULES FOR ROPE-GEARING AND TRANSMISSION OF POWER BY MEANS OF METALLIC CABLES.

BY

J. HOWARD CROMWELL, Ph.B.,

AUTHOR OF A TREATISE ON TOOTHED GEARING.

NEW YORK:
JOHN WILEY AND SONS.
1888.

Copyright, 1885,
By JOHN WILEY & SONS.

PREFACE.

IN the manufacture of modern machinery, which in the great majority of cases embodies a vast deal of careful study and precise calculation, there is probably no one element which enters as largely into the calculations and forms as important a part in the daily operations in the machine-shop as the endless belt for the transmission of power. The lathe, the drill, the planer, the shaping-machine—in short, almost without exception, all machine-tools—are commonly driven from the shop-shaft by means of belts and pulleys; and we can scarcely glance into a shop or factory of any description without encountering a mass of belts which seem at first sight to monopolize every nook in the building and leave little or no room for anything else.

Notwithstanding the countless thousands of belts for transmission in use and constantly being replaced in the shops and factories of America; notwithstanding the fact that many thousands of dollars are consumed every year by the rapid wear and destruction of our machine-belts, and the immense field thereby opened for the practical study and application of the principles of economy in this connection—there is no branch of machine-construction which is to-day in as crude and unsatisfactory a state of development as this all-important transmission by belt and pulley. Strange as it may seem, it is nevertheless true, that there is scarcely a machine-shop in America which can definitely and correctly calculate the proper width of a leather belt which will safely transmit a given horse-power. Nor are the manufactures of machine-belting in any degree in advance of the shops, for I have never yet seen the manufacturer who has any better solution for this apparently simple problem than his own "judgment."

Having taken the pains to write to a large number of the best-known machine-shops and belt-manufacturers throughout the country, asking for information concerning belting, and in every case having received an answer to the communication, I am compelled to assert that among all the letters received not a single one contained any definite information on the subject. As specimen answers to these letters I may quote the following extracts:

"We have no particular method of calculating widths of belts aside from tables found in books of reference." "There is no rule for the width of belting that we know of: it is always determined by the width of the pulley upon which it is to run." "We determine the width of belts more by experience than by any fixed rule." "We always try and make the strain as light, in pounds per inch of width, as possible, and when we are limited for room we use double belts. 100 pounds per inch of width is about the ultimate strength of transmission, and if you can reduce the working strain to 50 pounds, it means long life to the belt." "It is difficult to give any positive rule about belting that would apply to all cases." From one of the largest and best-known belt-manufacturing concerns in the country comes the following: "We have no rules or formulas for estimating the power of belts other than those given in works on mechanical engineering, nor do we apply these strictly. It is very much a question of judgment. . . . You will consider this letter very indefinite, but we do not know how to make it less so." Here are extracts from a letter received from another well-known belt-maker: "We wish to express the fear that what we have to say will be disappointing to you, to say the least. . . . As to the horse-power, we have no rule. . . . We have made no tests of the tensile strength of leather, for the reason that we do not consider it a matter of any importance. . . . We have made no efforts to obtain the coefficient of friction. . . . When we can obtain a homogeneous material which will be easily workable and a perfect substitute for leather, the manufacture, sale, use, and study of belting may begin to be a matter of satisfaction; in the meanwhile they are puzzling, if not indeed exasperating."

These extracts (many more of similar nature might be given) show almost no knowledge at all, on the part of our great belt-manufacturers and machine-shops, concerning the subject; and worse still in some cases, that little or no effort has been made to obtain any knowledge other than that of rough guesswork and rule of thumb. Small wonder is it, then, that the ordinary mechanic's practical knowledge of the subject is infinitely small. Several of the parties above referred to state that they use the rules found in the various books of reference; let us look over some of these works and endeavor to reach fair conclusions concerning the rules and formulas in common use to-day.

Arnold, in his "Mechanical Principia," gives the rule for belt-widths: "Multiply 36000 by the number of horse-powers; divide the amount by the number of feet the belt travels per minute; divide this quotient by the number of feet in length of belt contact with the smaller drum or pulley, and divide this by 6: the result is the required width of belt in inches."

Professor Reuleaux offers the formula $b = 18 \sqrt{P}$, b representing the width of the belt in millimetres and P the force in kilograms transmitted by the belt.

Unwin, in "Elements of Machine Design," gives the formula $\beta = \dfrac{2P}{f}$ in which β is the belt-width in inches, P the force transmitted in pounds, and f the safe working tension per inch of width, which he takes at 70 pounds for a belt $\frac{7}{32}$ of an inch thick. The formula is to be used only when the belt embraces about 0.4 of the smaller pulley-circumference.

In Nystrom's Mechanics we find $b = \dfrac{7500H}{da}$, b denoting the belt width in inches, H the horse-power transmitted, d the diameter of the smaller pulley in inches, and a the number of degrees occupied by the belt on the circumference of the smaller pulley.

Let us now assume an example which will serve to determine the variations in the results of calculations from the above rules and formulas. Suppose we wish to determine the proper width for a belt which will transmit a force of 25 horse-power; the smaller pulley having a diameter of 5 feet = 60 inches, and the velocity being 10 feet per second = 600 feet per minute. The belt embraces 0.4 of the pulley-circumference = 0.4 × 15.7 = 6.28 feet = 360 × 0.4 = 144 degrees. For the force transmitted, in pounds, we have $P = \dfrac{550 \times 25}{10} = 1375$ pounds.

With these quantities as data, Arnold's rule, given above, gives us for our required belt-width $\dfrac{36000 \times 25}{600 \times 6.28 \times 6} = 39.8$ inches. If we divide the force 1375 pounds by 2.2, we obtain 625 kilograms, and Reuleaux's formula gives $b = 18 \sqrt{625} = 450$ millimetres = 450 × 0.04 = 18 inches. From Unwin's formula we

PREFACE.

obtain $\beta = \frac{2 \times 1375}{70} = 39.3$ inches, and from the formula of Nystrom $b = \frac{7500 \times 25}{60 \times 144} = 21.7$ inches. Haswell in his "Engineer's and Mechanic's Pocket-book," gives a rule by which our belt-width would be 42 inches. Summing up our results will show that, for the same belt, under the same circumstances, the width is according to the authorities named as follows:

Haswell	42 inches.
Arnold	39.8 "
Unwin	39.3 "
Nystrom	21.7 "
Reuleaux	18 "

Of these different values the greatest is 2¼ times the least. Probably Arnold, Haswell, and Nystrom are in use in our shops more than the others, and these give results, for the belt-width in question, differing from each other by more than 20 inches. According to a list of prices for double, white-oak-tanned belting, which is before me, the *difference in cost* for the above-calculated belt, supposed to be double and 100 feet long, between Nystrom and Haswell would be *six hundred and sixteen* dollars, to say nothing of the difference in the cost of the pulleys, shafts, etc.

These great differences between the results from the rules of different authors are apparently due to the difference of opinion concerning the value of the coefficient of friction, which is taken all the way from 0.22 to 0.40, and to the fact that each writer on the subject has striven to obtain simple rather than accurate rules. At best we are dealing with an uncertain material when we attempt to déduce rules for the strength of leather belts, and if the elements of belt-thickness, method of lacing or fastening, etc., are entirely or partially neglected, the uncertainty of accurate results must be very greatly increased. In the matter of joint-fastening alone, a glance at the table on page 110 will show that a 20-inch leather belt $\frac{7}{32}$ inch thick running over two equal cast-iron pulleys will transmit a force of over 1800 pounds with a riveted joint or 1250 pounds when fastened with a double raw-hide lacing, while with a single leather-lacing the same belt will transmit but 976 pounds. In other words, to transmit a force of 1000 pounds over two equal cast-iron pulleys by means of a leather belt $\frac{7}{32}$ inch thick we will need a belt-width of 12 inches for riveted joint, 16 inches for double raw-hide lacing, and 22 inches for single leather-lacing.

I believe that it is utterly impossible for any man to write an *entirely simple* work on the subject of belting, which will be of any practical use to the mechanical world. The subject is complicated by difficulties far greater than are ordinarily met with in dealing with mechanical questions, and to attempt to simplify it beyond a reasonable limit is simply to omit certain necessary considerations, and thereby render the investigation worthless. My object in writing this work on belts and pulleys is, therefore, to present to the mechanical public a small yet comprehensive and, above all, an accurate book on the subject. I have constantly endeavored to have due regard for simplicity, yet when I have found it necessary to sacrifice either simplicity or accuracy, I have invariably chosen the former. All measurements and dimensions are given in English units in order to avoid the confusion sometimes resulting from the use of the Metric System, and I have endeavored by numerous simple examples throughout the book to fully illustrate the use of the various rules and formulas. In translating the part devoted to metallic cables from Reuleaux, the formulas and tables have been transformed from the metric system into English measures, which will, I trust, satisfactorily explain the unusual numbers which have resulted in a few instances.

In the hope that my humble endeavors to furnish accurate information on the subject of belt-transmission to those whom it may concern may be in a measure, if not entirely, successful, and trusting that in the present instance I may receive from mechanical men the same generous support and encouragement that have attended my previous efforts in the field of mechanical literature, I present to the public my " Treatise on Belts and Pulleys."

J. H. C.

NEW YORK, May 1, 1885.

TABLE OF CONTENTS.

SECTION I.

PAGE

Introduction—Absence of early Mechanical Records—Uncertain Origin of the Belt and Pulley—Probable Origin.............. 1

SECTION II.

Fundamental Principles—Direction of Rotation—Relations between Circumference, Diameter, and Radius—Velocity—Revolutions—Power—Horse power............................ 9

SECTION III.

Rules for the Proper Disposition of Pulleys—Axes which coincide geometrically—Parallel Axes—Axes which intersect each other—Axes which cross without intersecting................ 28

SECTION IV.

Transmissions by Belts without Guides—Half-crossed Belt—Conditions necessary for maintaining the Belt on the Pulleys—Distance between Pulleys........................... 29

SECTION V.

Transmissions by Belts with Pulley-guides—Half-crossed Belt with Pulley guide—Half-crossed Belt with Movable Pulley-guide—General Case of Crossed Arbors—Arbors at Right Angles... 32

SECTION VI.

Length of Belts—Open Belt—Open Belt, approximate Formula—Crossed Belt—Belts with Guides and intricately arranged..... 45

SECTION VII.

Speed-cones—Stepped Cones—Open Belt—Crossed Belt—Graphical Method—Continuous-speed Cones........................ 51

SECTION VIII.

Materials used for Belting—Leather—Vulcanized Rubber—Intestines of Animals—Rawhide—Hemp and Flax—Leather and Metallic Wire... 65

SECTION IX.

Lacing and other Modes of Fastening—Shortening—Single and Double Lacing—Belt-hooks—Cleat-fastening................. 68

SECTION X.

Strength of Leather Belts—Resistance to Slipping—Coefficient of Friction—Tensions on Belts—Breaking-strength—Width for Different Kinds of Fastening—Width necessary to transmit certain Powers... 75

SECTION XI.

Leather Belts over Leather-covered Pulleys—Coefficient of Friction—Tensions—Width for Different Kinds of Fastening—Width necessary to transmit certain Powers..................... 115

SECTION XII.

Vulcanized Rubber Belts—Number of Layers of Duck—Thickness—Breaking-strength—Coefficient of Friction—Width for Different Kinds of Fastening—Width necessary to transmit certain Powers—Rubber Belts over Leather- and Rubber covered Pulleys.. 140

SECTION XIII.

Rim, Nave, and Fixing-keys for Pulleys—Rounding of the Rim—Flanged Rim—Rim of Pulley for Belt with Circular Cross-section—Split Pulleys—Approximate Weight of Pulleys...... 159

SECTION XIV.

Arms of Pulleys—Oval Cross-sections—Number of Arms—Strength of Arms—Straight Arms—Single and Double Curved Arms.. 166

SECTION XV.

Shafts—Safe Shearing Stress—Steel—Wrought-iron—Cast-iron—Diameter necessary to transmit certain Powers............. 171

SECTION XVI.

The Tightening-pulley—Fast and Loose Pulleys—Reversing by means of Fast and Loose Pulleys—Fast and Loose Pulleys for Belts with Circular Cross-sections.... 179

SECTION XVII.

Rope-belts—Tension almost entirely due to the Weight—Pulley for several Rope-belts—Proper diameters for Rope-belts—Diameters of Pulleys for Rope-belts........................... 185

SECTION XVIII.

Jointed Chain-belts—Rouiller's Chain-belt—Metallic Belt of Godin—Jointed Chain-belt of Clissold—Coefficient of Friction—Dimensions.. 192

SECTION XIX.

Tensions of Metallic Cables—Number of Strands and Wires—Coefficient of Friction.. 196

SECTION XX.

Calculation of Diameters of Cables—Formulas and Tables of Diameters of Cables for Different Numbers of Wires............ 200

SECTION XXI.

Deflections in the Cable of a Horizontal Transmission—Deflection of Cable in Motion—Deflection in a State of Repose—Deflection in the Driving and Driven Parts..................... 207

SECTION XXII.

Transmission by Cable with Increased Tension—Increased Diameters of Cable and Wires....................... 212

SECTION XXIII.

Transmission by Inclined Cable—Tensions in Inclined Cables—Deflections—Height above the Ground...................... 217

SECTION XXIV.

Method of Tracing the Curves of Cables—Approximately Parabolic Curves.... 221

SECTION XXV.

Transmission by Cable with Pulleys near together—Small Value of S_1.. 222

SECTION XXVI.

Rim of Cable-pulleys—Single Cable—Several Cables upon one Pulley.. 223

SECTION XXVII.

Arms and Nave of Cable-pulleys—Number of Arms—Oval Cross-sections—Flanged Cross-sections—Straight Arms—Curved Arms—Reserve Cables....................................... 226

SECTION XXVIII.

Pulley-supports and Intermediate Pulleys—Stations at the Extremities—Intermediate Stations—Changing the Direction of the Cable.. 230

SECTION XXIX.

Dimensions of Pulley supports—Ratio between the Radius of the Pulley-support and Diameter of the Wires............... 234

SECTION XXX.

Pressure upon Axes of Pulley-supports—Weight of Large Pulleys 235

SECTION XXXI.

Station Pillars—Brick and Stone Piers—Pedestals—Two Pulleys side by side... 238

APPENDIX I.

Experiments for determining various Coefficients of Friction—Leather over Cast-iron Pulleys—Leather over Leather-covered Pulleys—Vulcanized-rubber Belts over Cast-iron and Covered Pulleys.. 243

APPENDIX II.

Special Applications of Principles of Belts and Pulleys—Devices for changing Motion and Direction of Rotation—Increasing and Decreasing Speeds—Intermittent Motion—Different Methods of arranging Principal Pulley and Shop Shafts in Mills... 252

BELTS AND PULLEYS.

§ 1. *Introduction.*

Says Thomas Ewbank in his famous " Hydraulics and Mechanics :" " Tradition has scarcely preserved a single anecdote or circumstance relating to those meritorious men with whom any of the useful arts originated ; and when in process of time History took her station in the temple of Science, her professors deemed it beneath her dignity to record the actions and lives of men who were merely inventors of machines or improvers of the useful arts; thus nearly all knowledge of those to whom the world is under the highest obligations has perished forever. . . . A description of the foundries and forges of India and of Egypt, of Babylon and Byzantium, of Sidon and Carthage and Tyre, would have imparted to us a more accurate and extensive knowledge of the ancients, of their manners and customs, their intelligence and progress in science, than all the works of their historians extant, and would have been of infinitely greater service to mankind.

"Had a narrative been preserved of all the circumstances which led to the invention and early applications of the lever, the screw, the wedge, pulley, wheel and axle, etc., and of those which contributed to the discovery and working of metals, the use and management of fire, agriculture, spinning of thread, matting of felt, weaving of cloth, etc., it would have been the most perfect history of our species—the most valuable of earthly legacies. Though such a work might have been deemed of trifling import by philosophers of old, with what intense interest would it have been perused by scientific men of modern times, and what pure delight its examination would have imparted to every inquisitive and intelligent mind!"

Rollin, writing of "The Arts and Sciences of the Ancients" many years ago, finds fault with the world for neglecting the great inventors and admiring the military heroes of antiquity. "Of what utility to us at this day," he asks, "is either Nimrod, Cyrus, or Alexander, or their successors, who have astonished mankind from time to time? With all their magnificence and vast designs they are returned into nothing with regard to us. They are dispersed like vapors and have vanished like phantoms. But the *inventors* of the *arts* and *sciences* labored for *all ages*. We still enjoy the fruits of their application and industry; they have procured for us *all the conveniences of life;* they have converted all nature to our uses. Yet all our admiration turns generally on the side of those heroes in blood, while we scarce take any notice of what we owe to the *inventors of the arts*."

In like manner, Robertson, in his work on India, laments the loss of, or rather absence of, early records concerning the useful arts and sciences. He says: "It is a cruel mortification, in searching for what is instructive in the history of past times, to find the exploits of conquerors who have desolated the earth, and the freaks of tyrants who have rendered nations unhappy, are recorded with minute and often disgusting accuracy; while the discovery of useful arts and the progress of the most beneficial branches of commerce are passed over in silence and suffered to sink into oblivion."

The origin, age, first application, and use of the mechanism known to us as the "endless belt and pulley" are entirely unknown; as far back into the history of the ancients as we can see by means of the earliest mechanical records, we find the endless belt running continuously around the pulley precisely as it does to-day. We may theorize, and assume a probable origin; we may bring up, in support of our assumption, all the reason and logical conclusions at man's disposal; we may even convince mankind that we have correctly traced and explained the path over which the mechanism has come down to us from the dim ages of the past. But here we must stop; we can go no farther: and the fact will yet remain that the real age and origin for which we are searching are still undiscovered and unknown. If, however, we cannot know with certainty the real age and origin of belts and pulleys, it is nevertheless a satisfaction to us to be able to trace out, by analogy, by reason, and by the known existence of things which must have necessitated the use of pulleys, what seems to us to have been the origin, the successive modifications, and the line of improvement by which this most useful contrivance has been handed down to us.

In searching for an uncertain origin or beginning of anything, we most naturally start by determining upon the very simplest and most rudimentary form (knowing that simplicity almost always precedes complexity, and that a thing must of necessity have a skeleton before it can have a form), and then strive to fix upon its exodus from the conception to the tangible thing itself. In order then to trace the growth of the thing in question from its origin to its present much altered and improved form, we strive to imagine the slightest possible change, in the right direction, which can be given to the original. Having successfully achieved the first transformation or alteration, we continue to pick out each slight alteration and improvement in proper order, until we have reached the present most improved form.

If we assume, as is claimed by some writers, that the mechanism of the belt and pulley was among the first mechanical contrivances of primitive man, we must search for its origin among what we judge to be the first necessities of the human race and the modes of obtaining these necessities. Although many claim that the human race, in the beginning, passed through a fireless period,—that men lived without the use of fire or artificial heat,—we must nevertheless conclude that this element was one of the first necessities of human life, and that the first effort made by prehistoric man in the line of invention was for the purpose of producing fire. It is very generally admitted that the first "fire-machine" (Reuleaux concludes that this was the first machine of any description. See Kenedey's English translation " Kinematics of Machinery," London,

1876, p. 204) consisted of an upright piece of wood, having one end pointed. This, fitted into a hollow in another piece of wood and being twirled rapidly backwards and forwards with the hands, generated sufficient heat to set fire to some small fragments of dry wood or other combustible material (Fig. 1). Here we have the first belt and pulley—hardly recognizable, it is true, but none the less the probable origin. The upright piece of wood here constitutes the pulley and

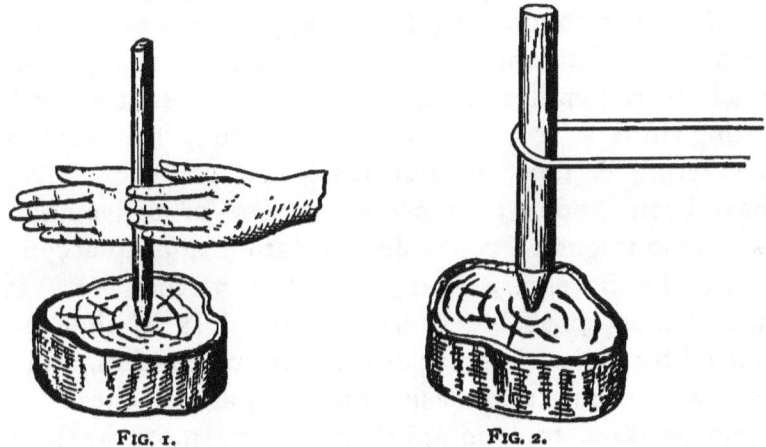

FIG. 1. FIG. 2.

the human hands the belt. The first transformation seems to have been the substitution of a cord wound several times around the upright piece (as shown in Fig. 2) in place of the direct application of the hands.

This rude contrivance, though it produced only an oscillating motion, was used for other purposes than that of producing fire; the primitive drill, lathe, potter's wheel, etc., were driven to and fro in this manner, the work being done only on the forward turn, and the backward turn serving only to place the work in such a position that the operation of cutting could be again continued. The change from this contrivance to the rope and pulley used for drawing water from deep wells, and for lifting the vast blocks of stone, columns, etc., used by the ancients in building, was indeed slight, and may reasonably have taken place not long after the first introduction of the improved form of "fire-machine."

For how long a period this oscillating motion sufficed for the rough manufacturing purposes of the age, or at just what era in the life of man the change was made to the endless belt, which transformed the oscillating into a continuous rotary motion, is indeed a mystery. Whole generations—even centuries—may have been needed to impress upon the primitive mind the advantages of continuous rotation and to accomplish the necessary change in the mechanism. It seems most probable to us that the loss of time incurred by the useless backward motion in lathes, drills, etc., and the natural desire on the part of these ancient artisans to accomplish more and more work in less and less time, must have led to the adoption of the two pulleys and the endless belt. Gradually, very gradually, the slight but all-important change was made. Some early thinker—now unknown even in the uncertain histories of the past ages—connected the loose and separated ends of the single cord, passed the now endless cord over two cylindrical sticks, fitted roughly into a frame to hold them apart, and caused both to rotate by turning one with a crank. Next some primitive inventor obtained the friction necessary for the transmission of considerable forces by winding the cord several times around each pulley; and so in process of time, in his attempts to obtain and transmit greater powers, the man of the ages long since forgotten at last discarded the round cord for the broad flat band or belt of the present era. Reuleaux says "the crossed belt appears to be the older;" but to us it seems most probable that the flat band was first used in its simplest form,—i.e., open,—and that the crossed belt was afterwards introduced in order to prevent (by its additional embracing of the pulleys) slipping, and to produce a rotation of the driven pulley in a direction contrary to that of the driver.

As to the material of the primitive cord and belt, we can prove nothing: it is, however, reasonable to suppose, since the skin of wild animals was the easiest material to obtain, and since, from the earliest records of history, skins have been used for clothing, bowstrings, etc., that the material of the primitive belt differed from the leather of to-day only in that it was untanned and unfinished, and perhaps taken from a different animal. Doubtless the fixing together or lacing of the ends of belts was the source of considerable difficulty to the ancients, for in all cases where such a belt could be made to perform the necessary work, round cords tied together at the ends seem to have been used.

It is supposed, and very reasonably, from certain known circumstances, that the first idea of continuous rotary motion which was developed in the mind of man took the form of an undershot water-wheel, driven by the current of a stream or river. The Chinese have doubtless used these water-wheels, for purposes of irrigation and drawing water, for many centuries, and, according to tradition, they were also used at an early date in ancient Assyria, Mesopotamia, and other countries of Asia Minor. These pristine water-wheels consisted of a rough axle and two or more long blades, usually built up of sticks and bamboo, sometimes with rough buckets formed out of mud or clay. It is not at all unlikely that the first attempts to con-

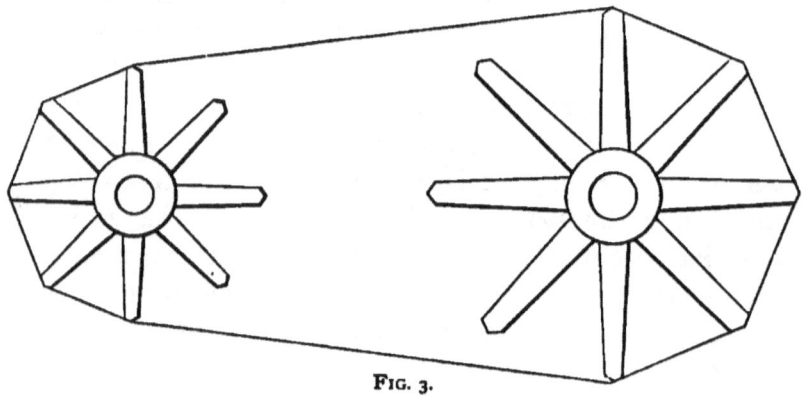

Fig. 3.

struct large pulleys were founded upon the principles of construction seen in the water-wheels, and that the pulleys were used without rims, as shown in Fig. 3. From the fact that wagon-wheels with entire rims and fellies are known to have been in existence in the earliest Greek and Egyptian times, we may very fairly conclude that the use of the complete wooden, if not also iron, pulley reaches far back into antiquity, and that its advent into the world probably took place not long after the discovery of the endless belt.

History informs us that the ancient city of Nineveh

was surrounded by a massive stone wall over 100 feet high, and that the city was fortified with 1500 towers, each 200 feet in height. Babylon, "the noblest city ever built by man," had a fortified wall which reached to the incredible height of 360 feet, and her famous hanging-gardens were built of "flat stones of amazing size." The Tower of Babel is said to have been "40 rods square at the bottom, and upwards of 600 feet high." These gigantic structures—supposed to have been built about the year 2200 B.C.—could not have been erected without the aid of strong ropes and pulleys, or similar contrivance. Thus for over four thousand years have been known and used successfully the cord and pulley which we use to-day. For how many centuries in the unknown ages of the prehistoric period men toiled and labored with their crude "fire-machines," perhaps even lived and died without reaching that much of "the machine," we must leave for future investigation and development to decide.

§ 2. Fundamental Principles.

The mechanism known in modern mechanics as the "endless belt and pulleys" is, primarily, a device, the object of which is to transmit a continuous rotary motion from one shaft or arbor to another parallel shaft, and the first fundamental principle of the mechanism may be clearly expressed as follows: If two drums or pulleys be placed in certain positions relative to each other, each being allowed the motion of rotation about its fixed axis, and no other, and if an endless band be passed tightly over the circumferences of the pulleys as represented in Fig. 4; then, if a continuous rotary motion be given to one of the pulleys, the friction between it and the band will cause the latter to move around the circumference, and the second pulley will

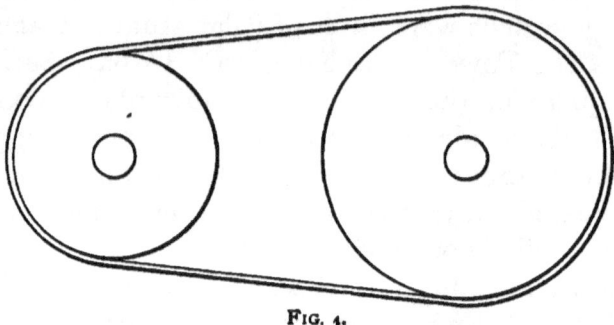

FIG. 4.

(because of the friction between it and the band) therefore be caused to rotate continuously about its fixed axis—that is, the continuous rotary motion of the driving-pulley will be directly transmitted through

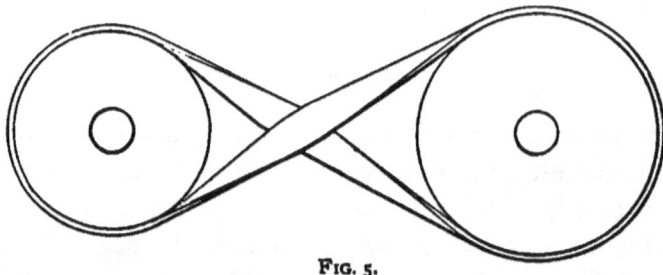

FIG. 5.

the endless band to the second pulley. In this definition it is presupposed that the friction between the band and pulleys is sufficiently great to overcome the resistance of the pulleys; otherwise the driving-pulley will simply slide around upon the band without causing it to move, and consequently the second or driven pulley will remain motionless.

(*a*) *Direction of Rotation.*—Belts may be either open, as shown in Fig. 4, or crossed, as in Fig. 5: in the former case the two pulleys rotate in the same direction, while in the latter case the driven pulley rotates in a direction contrary to that of the driver.

(*b*) *Relations between Circumference, Diameter, and Radius.*—The circumference C of a circle, the diameter of which is represented by D, is given by the expression

$$C = \pi D, \quad \ldots \ldots \quad (1)$$

in which π represents the constant quantity 3.14159.

RULE.—To determine the circumference of a circle in inches or feet, multiply the diameter in inches or feet by the constant 3.14159.

Since the radius of a circle is equal to one half its diameter, if we denote the radius by R, we shall have $R = \dfrac{D}{2}$, or $D = 2R$, and formula (1) becomes by substitution

$$C = 2\pi R. \quad \ldots \ldots \quad (2)$$

RULE.—To determine the circumference of a circle in inches or feet, multiply the radius in inches or feet by the constant $2\pi = 6.28318$.

From formula (1), by transposing the quantities, we may write

$$D = \frac{C}{\pi}. \quad \ldots \ldots \quad (3)$$

RULE.—To determine the diameter of a circle in inches or feet, divide the circumference in inches or feet by the constant 3.14159.

In a similar manner from formula (2) we may obtain

$$R = \frac{C}{2\pi}. \quad \ldots \ldots \quad (4)$$

RULE.—To determine the radius of a circle in inches or feet, divide the circumference in inches or feet by the constant $2\pi = 6.28318$.

If we let C and C' denote the circumference of two circles, D and D', R and R', the respective diameters and radii, we shall have, from formulas (1) and (2),

$$C = \pi D = 2\pi R, \quad \text{and} \quad C' = \pi D' = 2\pi R';$$

and we may write the proportions

$$C : C' :: \pi D : \pi D' :: 2\pi R : 2\pi R'.$$

in the form of an equation,

$$\frac{C}{C'} = \frac{\pi D}{\pi D'} = \frac{2\pi R}{2\pi R'}$$

which, by cancelling the equal constants in numerator and denominator, becomes

$$\frac{C}{C'} = \frac{D}{D'} = \frac{R}{R'}. \quad \ldots \ldots \quad (5)$$

RULE.—The ratio of the circumferences of any two circles is equal to the direct ratio of their diameters or radii.

(c) *Velocity.*—The circumferential velocities of two pulleys which are connected by one and the same belt (supposing there is no slipping of the belt on either pulley) must obviously be the same, each being equal to the velocity of the belt. For the belt must unroll from the driving-pulley just as fast as it is developed from the pulley-circumference; it must also roll upon the circumference of the driven pulley with the same velocity, else the belt would constantly tend to become tighter on one side and looser on the other, and sliding or rupture would necessarily ensue.*

The circumferential velocity of the driven pulley and the velocity of the belt are entirely independent of the pulley-diameters, and depend solely upon the circumferential velocity of the driving-pulley. Thus, if the circumferential velocity of the driver is 10 feet per second, 10 feet of circumference, and no more or less, can be developed per second upon the belt, be the driver ever so large or ever so small. In the same manner, just 10 feet of belt can roll per second upon

---

* The tensions on the two sides (or parts) of the belt are not the same (as will be seen farther on); consequently the circumferential velocities of the two pulleys are not absolutely the same. According to Professor Reuleaux, if v and v' denote the circumferential velocities of the two pulleys, t and T the tensions on the two parts of the belt, E the coefficient of elasticity of the belt, and S the strain on the driving part of the belt, the true velocities will be given by the expression $\dfrac{v' - v}{v} = \dfrac{1 - \dfrac{t}{T}}{1 + \dfrac{E}{S}}$. Reuleaux says, "The loss of velocity due to the sliding has for a mean value about ¼ per cent; it is accompanied by a loss of work, which is transformed into heat and produces wear of the belt and pulleys."

the circumference of the driven pulley, without reference to its size or diameter.

(*d*) *Revolutions.*—Since the circumferential velocities of any two pulleys, which are connected by one and the same belt, are the same without regard to the diameters of the pulleys, and since the circumferences of the two pulleys are directly proportional to their diameters (formula 5); if one of the pulleys has a diameter equal to twice that of the other, the circumference of the former will also be equal to twice that of the latter, and the former will need just twice as much time in which to perform one entire revolution as the latter. In other words, the larger pulley will make just one half as many revolutions in a given time as the smaller. In a similar manner, if the diameter of the larger pulley is three or four times that of the smaller, the former will need three or four times as much time for each revolution as will the latter, or the larger pulley will make only one third or one fourth the number of revolutions in a given time as the smaller. In formula, denoting by n and n' the numbers of revolution of the two pulleys, and by C and C', D and D', and R and R' the respective circumferences, diameters, and radii, we shall have

$$\frac{n}{n'} = \frac{C'}{C} = \frac{D'}{D} = \frac{R'}{R}. \quad \ldots \quad (6)$$

RULE.—The ratio of the numbers of revolutions of two pulleys, which are connected by one and the same belt, is equal to the *inverse* ratio of their circumferences, diameters, or radii.

FUNDAMENTAL PRINCIPLES

If we represent by n the number of revolutions per minute, by v_m the velocity *in feet per minute*, and by R_f and C_f, respectively, the radius and circumference of the pulley *in feet*, we shall have for the velocity the expression

$$v_m = 2\pi R_f n = C_f n. \quad . \quad . \quad . \quad . \quad (7)$$

RULE.—To determine the velocity, *in feet per minute*, with which a pulley rotates, multiply the circumference of the pulley, *in feet*, by the number of revolutions per minute.

If R and C denote respectively the radius and circumference of the pulley *in inches*, we shall have, between R and R_f, C and C_f the relations $R_f = \dfrac{R}{12}$ and $C_f = \dfrac{C}{12}$. These values, substituted in formula (7), give

$$v_m = \frac{2\pi R n}{12} = \frac{C n}{12} = 0.5236 R n. \quad . \quad . \quad (8)$$

RULE.—To determine the velocity of a pulley *in feet per minute*, multiply the circumference of the pulley *in inches* by the number of revolutions per minute, and divide the product by 12, or multiply 0.5236 times the radius *in inches* by the number of revolutions per minute.

Let v represent the velocity of the pulley *in feet per second;* we shall then have the expression

$$v_m = 60v$$

and formula (8) becomes, by substitution,

$$60v = \frac{2\pi R n}{12} = \frac{Cn}{12},$$

which reduces to

$$v = \frac{Cn}{720} = 0.00873 Rn. \quad . \quad . \quad . \quad (9)$$

RULE.—To determine the velocity of a pulley *in feet per second*, multiply the circumference of the pulley *in inches* by the number of revolutions per minute, and divide the product by 720, or multiply 0.00873 times the radius *in inches* by the number of revolutions per minute.

If we substitute the value $v_m = 60v$ in formula (7), we shall obtain the expression

$$60v = 2\pi R_f n = C_f n,$$

which reduces to

$$v = \frac{C_f n}{60} = 0.1047 R_f n. \quad . \quad . \quad (10)$$

RULE.—To determine the velocity of a pulley *in feet per second*, multiply by the circumference of the pulley *in feet* by the number of revolutions per minute, and divide the product by 60; or multiply 0.1047 times the radius *in feet* by the number of revolutions per minute.

FUNDAMENTAL PRINCIPLES.

By transposing formula (7), we may obtain, for the number of revolutions per minute, the formula

$$n = \frac{v_m}{2\pi R_f} = \frac{v_m}{C_f}. \quad \ldots \quad (11)$$

RULE.—To determine the number of revolutions per minute with which a pulley turns, divide the velocity of the pulley *in feet per minute* by the pulley-circumference *in feet*.

In a similar manner, by transposing formulas (8), (9), and (10) we may obtain the following formulas for the number of revolutions per minute:

$$n = \frac{12v_m}{C} = \frac{v_m}{0.5236R}. \quad \ldots \quad (12)$$

RULE.—To determine the number of revolutions per minute, divide 12 times the velocity *in feet per minute* by the circumference of the pulley *in inches*, or divide the velocity *in feet per minute* by 0.5236 times the radius of the pulley in inches.

$$n = \frac{720v}{C} = \frac{v}{0.00873R}. \quad \ldots \quad (13)$$

RULE.—To determine the number of revolutions per minute, divide 720 times the velocity *in feet per second* by the circumference of the pulley *in inches*, or divide the velocity *in feet per second* by 0.00873 times the radius of the pulley *in inches*.

RULE.—To determine the number of revolutions per minute, divide 60 times the velocity *in feet per second* by the circumference of the pulley *in feet*, or divide the velocity *in feet per second* by 0.1047 times the radius of the pulley *in feet*.

The numbers of revolutions per minute of two or more pulleys, which are fixed upon one and the same shaft, must plainly be the same, for the shaft at each revolution will carry each and all of the pulleys just once around without reference to the diameters of the pulleys. If, therefore, we denote by n the common number of revolutions, and by v and v' the circumferential velocities of two pulleys, which are fixed upon one and the same shaft, we shall have, from formula (9), the equations

$$v = \frac{Cn}{720} = 0.00873Rn,$$

and
$$v' = \frac{C'n}{720} = 0.00873R'n,$$

C, R, C', and R' denoting respectively the circumferences and radii of the two pulleys. From these two equations we may write the proportion

$$v : v' :: \frac{Cn}{720} : \frac{C'n}{720} :: 0.00873Rn : 0.00873R'n.$$

By cancelling out the equivalent quantities, and writing the proportion in the form of an equation, we have

FUNDAMENTAL PRINCIPLES.

RULE.—The ratio of the velocities of two pulleys which are fixed upon one and the same shaft is equal to the direct ratio of the pulley circumferences, radii, or diameters.

(e) *Power.*—By the *power* of a pulley we mean the force with which the circumference of the pulley turns: it is equal to that force which, if applied to the pulley-circumference in a direction opposite to that in which the pulley rotates, would be just sufficient to stop the

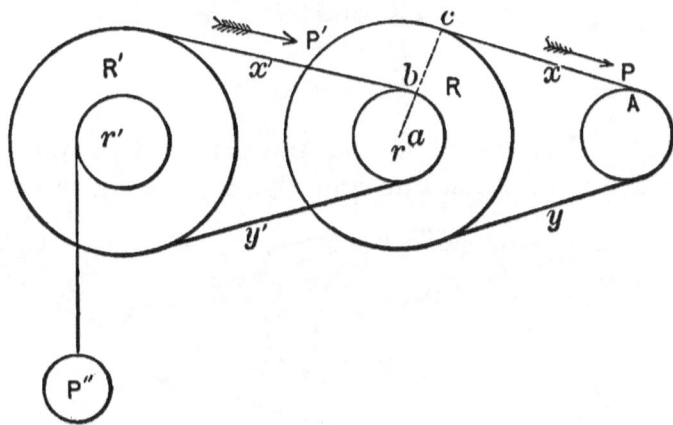

FIG. 6.

motion of the pulley. The powers of two pulleys which are connected by one and the same belt are equal; for the driving-pulley transmits all its circumferential force to the belt, and the belt in turn transmits the same force to the driven pulley (less a very slight amount which is consumed in the stretching of the belt).

Let the circles of which the radii are R, R', r, and A (Fig. 6) represent four pulleys, connected by belts as shown in the figure, A being the driving-pulley and R

and r being fixed upon one and the same shaft. The power P of the driving-pulley is transmitted directly to the pulley R through the belt xy. We may consider the imaginary line abc as a simple lever, the fulcrum of which is at the point a, and the arms of which are ac and ab. If now we let P' represent the power of the pulley r, which is transmitted directly to the pulley R' through the belt $x'y'$, we shall have, from the principles of the simple lever, the relation

$$PR = P'r,$$

or $\qquad \dfrac{P}{P'} = \dfrac{r}{R}. \qquad \ldots \ldots (16)$

RULE.—The ratio of the powers of two pulleys which are fixed upon one and the same shaft is equal

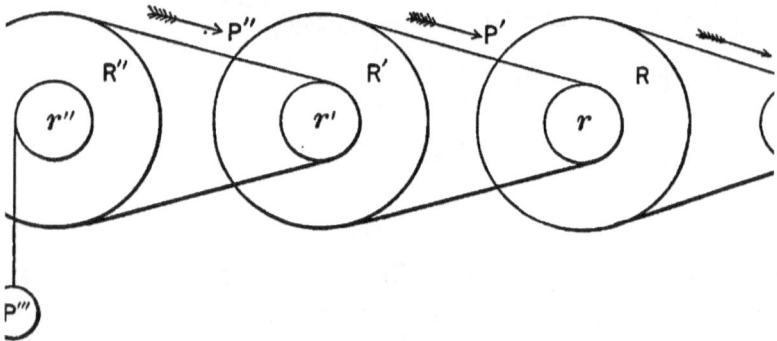

FIG. 7.

to the inverse ratio of the pulley-radii (diameters or circumferences).

Let the circles of Fig. 7 represent a number of pulleys, connected by belts as shown in the figure, and together constituting a "pulley-train." Let A be the driving-pulley, and let r'' be arranged to lift the weight

P''' by means of a cord wound around its circumference, as shown in the figure. From formula (16) we shall have the expression

$$\frac{P}{P'} = \frac{r}{R}, \quad \text{or} \quad P' = \frac{PR}{r}.$$

Also, we shall have

$$\frac{P'}{P''} = \frac{r'}{R'}, \quad \text{or} \quad P'' = \frac{P'R'}{r'}.$$

Substituting, in the last-found equation, the value of P' determined above, gives

$$P'' = \frac{PRR'}{rr'}.$$

From formula (16) again we may write the equation

$$\frac{P''}{P'''} = \frac{r''}{R''}, \quad \text{or} \quad P''' = \frac{P'R''}{r''};$$

and by substituting in this the last-found value of P'', we shall finally obtain the formula

$$P''' = \frac{PRR'R''}{rr'r''}. \quad \ldots \quad (17)$$

Then, inversely, $\quad P = \dfrac{P'''rr'r''}{RR'R''}. \quad \ldots \quad (18)$

RULE.—To determine the power of an *increasing* pulley-train (one in which the powers of the pulleys constantly increase from the driver), multiply the power of the driver by the continued product of all the larger pulley-radii (diameters or circumferences) except that of the driver, and divide the result by the continued product of all the smaller pulley-radii (diameters or circumferences) except that of the driver. To determine the power of a *decreasing* pulley-train (one in which the powers of the pulleys constantly decrease from the driver),* multiply the power of the driver by the continued product of all the smaller pulley-radii (diameters or circumferences) except that of the driver, and divide the result by the continued product of all the larger pulley-radii (diameters or circumferences) except that of the driver.

From formula (15) we know that the circumferential velocities of two pulleys which are fixed upon one and the same shaft vary directly as the pulley radii, diameters, or circumferences. We may therefore obtain, by combining formulas (15) and (16) and denoting the circumferential velocities of the pulleys R and r (Fig. 6) by V and v respectively,

$$\frac{P}{P'} = \frac{v}{V}. \qquad \ldots \ldots \quad (19)$$

RULE.—The ratio of the powers of two pulleys which are fixed upon one and the same shaft is equal

---

* If the pulley-train represented in Fig. 7 were a decreasing instead of an increasing train, the "direction" of the train would be reversed. That is, the pulley R'' would be the driver and the pulley A the one which lifts the weight.

to the inverse ratio of the circumferential velocities of the pulleys.

A glance at formula (19) will show that the increased power which we obtain by means of an increasing pulley-train necessitates a loss of time corresponding to the gain in power. For since the power varies inversely as the velocity, if we increase the power two, three, or four fold we necessarily decrease the velocity two, three, or four fold also. Thus, if by means of the train represented in Fig. 7 we can lift a weight of 1000 pounds with a circumferential force on the driving-pulley amounting to say 200 pounds only, we will need just $\frac{1000}{200} = 5$ times as much time as if we apply the force of 1000 pounds directly to the pulley which lifts the weight. Nevertheless there is a real gain represented in the increasing pulley-train; because, without it or a similar contrivance, we might tug, with our 200 pounds of power, for a lifetime, and still be unable to lift the 1000-pound weight one inch from its resting-place.

(*f*) *Horse-power.*—The term "horse-power," as commonly used, is equivalent to 33,000 foot-pounds: it is that amount of force or power which will lift a weight of 33,000 pounds one foot high in one minute, or a weight of one pound 33,000 feet high in one minute. If we represent the horse-power of a pulley by H, and the circumferential force or power in pounds by P, then $H \times 33,000$ pounds lifted one foot high per minute will represent the power of the pulley. If therefore we denote by v_m the circumferential velocity of the pulley in feet *per minute*, we shall have, for the power in pounds, the expression

$$P = \frac{33000H}{v_m}. \quad \ldots \ldots (20)$$

And inversely, $$H = \frac{Pv_m}{33000}. \quad \ldots \ldots (21)$$

RULE.—To determine the power of a pulley in pounds, divide 33000 times the horse-power by the circumferential velocity of the pulley in feet *per minute:* to determine the horse-power, multiply the power of the pulley in pounds by the circumferential velocity in feet *per minute* and divide the product by 33000.

If v denote the circumferential velocity of the pulley in feet *per second*, we shall have the relation $v_m = 60v$, and formula (20) becomes, by substitution,

$$P = \frac{33000H}{60v},$$

or $$P = \frac{550H}{v}. \quad \ldots \ldots (22)$$

Inversely, $$H = \frac{Pv}{550}. \quad \ldots \ldots (23)$$

RULE.—To determine the power of a pulley in pounds, divide 550 times the horse-power by the circumferential velocity in feet *per second;* to determine the horse-power, multiply the power of the pulley in pounds by the circumferential velocity in feet *per second*, and divide the product by 550.

The size of a pulley is usually given in terms of its diameter: thus a "36-inch pulley" is a pulley the diameter of which is 36 inches; a "4-foot pulley" is one the diameter of which is 4 feet.

Example 1.—The diameter of a pulley is 10 inches; it is required to find the circumference. From formula (1) we have $C = \pi D = 3.14159 \times 10$ or $C = 31.4159''$. Also we have $R = \dfrac{D}{2} = 5''$, and formula (2) gives $C = 2\pi R = 6.28318 \times 5$ or $C = 31.4159''$.

Example 2.—The circumference of a pulley is $C = 314.159''$; it is required to find the diameter. We have, from formula (3), $D = \dfrac{C}{\pi} = \dfrac{314.159}{3.14159} = 100''$.

Example 3.—The diameters of two pulleys, which are connected by one and the same belt, are $D = 30''$ and $D' = 10''$; the larger pulley makes $n = 120$ revolutions per minute. It is required to determine the number of revolutions per minute of the smaller pulley. From formula (6) we have $\dfrac{n}{n'} = \dfrac{D'}{D}$ or $\dfrac{120}{n'} = \dfrac{10}{30}$. From this, $n' = \dfrac{30 \times 120}{10} = 360$.

Example 4.—A pulley, the radius of which is 2 *feet*, makes 100 revolutions per minute; it is required to determine the circumferential velocity in feet *per minute*. We have, from formula (7), $v_m = 2\pi R_f n$, or $v_m = 6.28318 \times 2 \times 100 = 1256.6$.

Example 5.—The radius of a pulley is 24 *inches*, and the number of revolutions per minute 100; it is required to determine the circumferential velocity of the pulley in feet *per minute*. From formula (8) we have $v_m = \dfrac{2\pi R n}{12}$ or $v_m = \dfrac{6.28318 \times 24 \times 100}{12} = 1256.6$.

Example 6.—The radius of a pulley is 24 *inches* and the number of revolutions per minute 100; it is required to determine the circumferential velocity of the pulley in feet *per second*. Formula (9) becomes, by substituting the numerical data, $v = 0.00873 \times 24 \times 100$, or $v = 20.95$.

Example 7.—The circumferential velocity of a pulley is 1256.6 feet *per minute*, and the radius 2 feet; it is required to find the number of revolutions per minute. From formula (11) we have $n = \dfrac{v_m}{2\pi R_f} = \dfrac{1256.6}{6.28318 \times 2} = 100$.

Example 8.—It is required to determine the number of revolutions per minute of a pulley of which the radius is 24″, and the circumferential velocity, in feet *per second*, 20.95. From formula (13) we have $n = \dfrac{v}{0.00873 R} = \dfrac{20.95}{0.00873 \times 24} = 100$.

Example 9.—A shaft which makes 100 revolutions per minute bears two pulleys of which the radii are $R = 36$ inches and $R' = 24$ inches; it is required to determine the circumferential velocities of the two pulleys in feet *per second*. From formula (9) we have, for the circumferential velocity of the pulley R', $v' = 0.00873 \times 24 \times 100 = 20.95$ feet *per second*, and from formula (15) we have $\dfrac{v}{20.95} = \dfrac{36}{24}$, or $v = \dfrac{20.95 \times 36}{24} = 31.425$ feet *per second*.

Example 10.—In an increasing pulley-train we have the following data: Power of the driving-pulley $P = 100$ pounds, radii of the pulleys (of which there are six besides the driver, and arranged as shown in Fig. 7), $R = R' = R'' = 36''$ and $r = r' = r'' = 12''$; it is required to determine the power of the pulley-train. By substituting the above values in formula (17) we obtain $P''' = \dfrac{100 \times 36 \times 36 \times 36}{12 \times 12 \times 12} = 2700$ pounds.

Example 11.—Suppose the circumferential velocity of the driving-pulley in Example 10 is 1200 feet *per minute*; it is required to determine the circumferential velocity of the pulley r''. From formula (19) we have $\dfrac{P}{P'''} = \dfrac{v_m'''}{V_m}$ or $\dfrac{100}{2700} = \dfrac{v_m'''}{1200}$. From this, $v_m''' = \dfrac{1200 \times 100}{2700} = 44.44$ feet *per minute*.

Example 12.—Required to determine the power of a pulley which transmits 60 horse-power at a circumferential velocity of 10 feet *per second*. From formula (22) we have $P = \dfrac{550 H}{v}$ or $P = \dfrac{550 \times 60}{10} = 3300$ pounds.

Example 13.—The circumferential force or power of a pulley is 3300 pounds, and the velocity 10 feet *per second*; it is required to determine the horse-power transmitted by the pulley. Formula (23) gives $H = \dfrac{Pv}{550} = \dfrac{3300 \times 10}{550} = 60$.

§ 3. *Rules for the Proper Disposition of Pulleys.**

The axes of two pulleys which are connected by one and the same belt may bear to each other the following relations:

1. They may coincide geometrically.
2. They may be parallel.
3. They may intersect each other.
4. They may cross, without being in the same plane.

In these different cases the belt passes from the driving to the driven pulley, either directly or by means of intermediate pulleys or pulley-guides. It is, first of all, indispensable that the pulleys be placed in such a manner that the belt shall maintain its proper position upon both pulleys without running off or compelling recourse to special guides. The geometric disposition of the pulleys by which this condition may be fulfilled is called the "arrangement" of the belt.

The preceding condition will be satisfied if the pulleys are so placed with reference to each other that, for each of them, *the median line of that portion of the belt which runs toward the pulley is in the middle plane of the pulley.*

In pulleys which have rounded fellies (see § 13) slight variations from this rule (from $\frac{1}{2}°$ to $\frac{3}{4}°$) may be admissible.

---

* §§ 3, 4, and 5 from Reuleaux.

§ 4. *Transmissions by Belts without Guides.*

The simplest and most common arrangements of pulleys are those in which the belt passes directly from one pulley to the other without guides of any kind; the simplest of these dispositions, which corresponds to the case in which the axes of the pulleys are parallel, is represented in Fig. 8. In the left-hand figure the belt is open, and the pulleys rotate in the same direc-

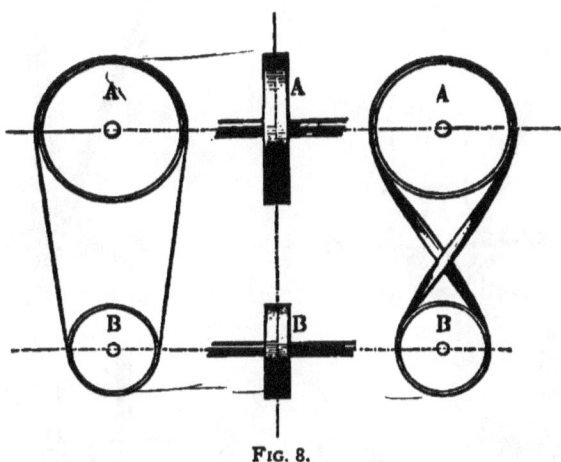

FIG. 8.

tion: in the figure on the right the belt is crossed and the pulleys rotate in opposite directions. In these two arrangements the belt may run in either direction, the condition which prevents its running off the pulleys being fulfilled for either direction of rotation.

For pulleys the axes of which coincide geometrically, as for those in which the axes intersect, it is evidently impossible to establish transmission without guides.

For the case, however, in which the axes cross without being in the same plane, belts without guides may be used with the arrangement of pulleys represented in Fig. 9, which is very frequently seen in practice.

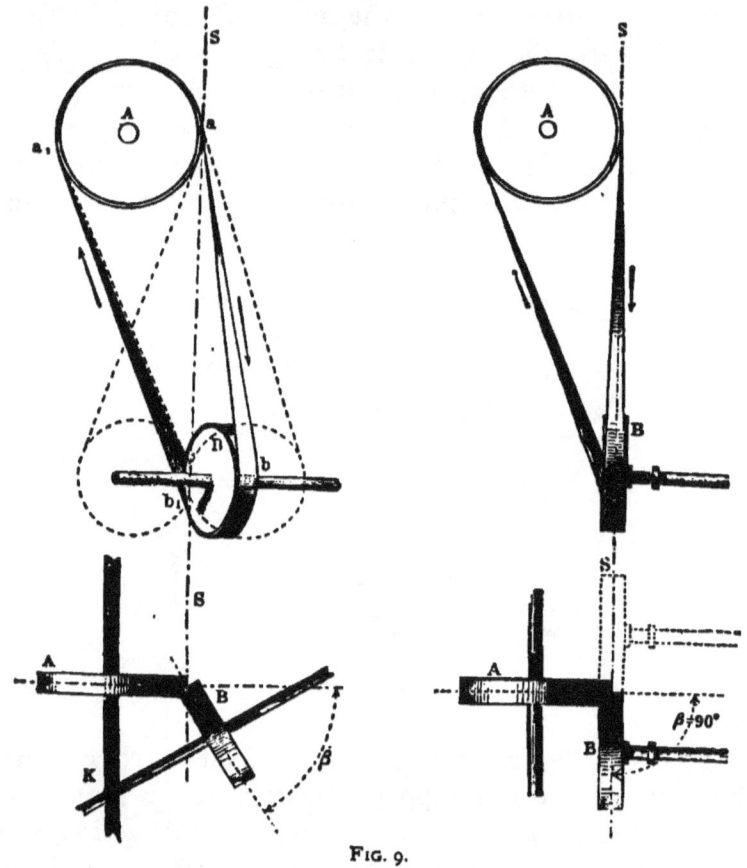

FIG. 9.

This disposition allows us to dispense with all exterior guides, if we are careful to place the pulleys in such a manner that *the line of intersection of their middle planes shall be tangent to the circles contained in these planes at the points in which the belt leaves the pulleys.* In Fig. 9, in which a and b_1 are these points, the belt must run in the direction indicated by the arrows. If we wish to run the belt in a contrary direction it is necessary to move the pulleys upon their arbors until the line of intersection of their middle-planes becomes tangent to the circles at the points a_1 and b. This condition is fulfilled when, with reference to the crossing K of the pulley-axes, the new positions occupied by the pulleys are found to be symmetrical with the positions of the pulleys before the change.

The transmission represented in Fig. 9 may be considered as the general solution of transmissions by belts without guides. It gives, in fact, the transmission by open belt, when the angle β included between the middle planes of the pulleys is equal to 0, and the transmission by crossed belt when this angle is equal to 180°. In all intermediate positions the belt is only partially crossed: for $\beta = 90°$, we have a half-crossed belt, for $\beta = 45°$ a crossing of one fourth, etc.

In short, partially crossed belts, the tendency to run off the pulleys is very great. According to Redtenbacher, in order that this accident may be avoided, the distance between the centres of the pulleys should not be less than twice the diameter of the largest pulley; that is, the angle of deviation of the belt should not exceed 25°. Moreover, in order that the wear of the belt may not be excessive, the distance between the centres of the pulleys should not be less than $10 \sqrt{bD}$, b representing the width of the belt and D the diameter of the driving-pulley. It is evident that, in each particular case, it is advantageous to take, for the separation of the pulleys, the greater of these two values.

§ 5. *Transmissions by Belts with Pulley-Guides.*

RULE.—In a transmission by belt with pulley-guides, in order that the belt may run properly upon the pulleys and pulley-guides, the point in which the belt leaves each pulley must be the point of tangency be-

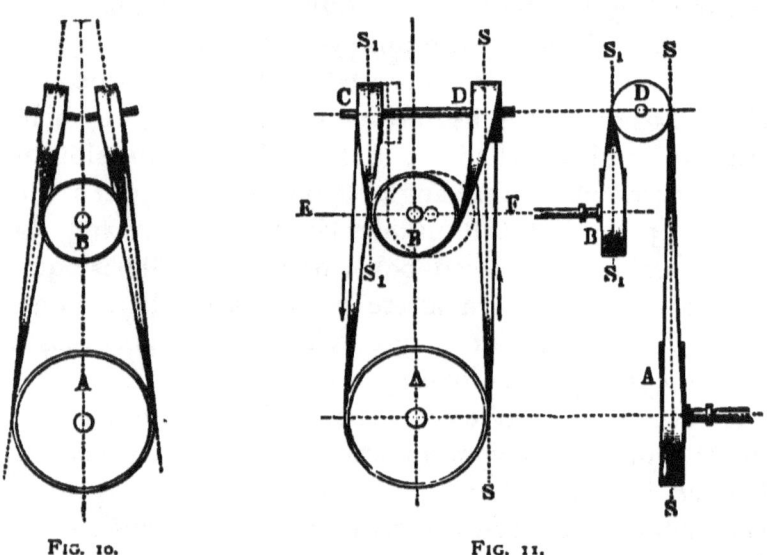

Fig. 10. Fig. 11.

tween the pulley and the line of intersection of its middle plane with that of the following pulley.

Figs. 10 and 11 represent transmissions of this kind for pulleys with parallel axes. In Fig. 10 the middle planes of the two pulley-guides are tangent to the two pulleys of transmission A and B, and their common diameter is equal to the distance between the middle planes of these pulleys. This disposition of pulleys permits of the movement of the belt in either direction. When, as is most commonly the case, a movement of the belt in one direction is sufficient, we may make use of the simpler disposition of pulleys represented in Fig. 11, in which the axes of the pulley-guides coincide geometrically. *A* and *B* are the pulleys of transmis-

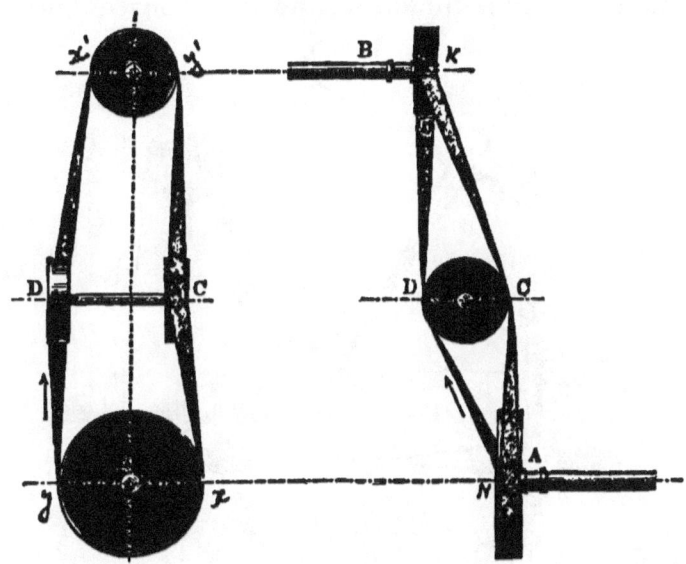

FIG. 12.

sion; the middle planes of the pulley-guides are parallel, and are tangent respectively to the pulleys *A* and *B* at the points in which the belt leaves the latter pulleys. The common diameter of the pulley-guides is equal to the distance between the middle planes of the pulleys of transmission. As indicated in the figure, the pulleys of transmission *A* and *B* rotate in opposite directions.

If we consider B as a pulley-guide (in which case it may run loose upon the arbor of A), the two pulleys C and D may be taken as pulleys of transmission, and fixed upon two separate arbors, the directions of which are the same.

If the pulley-guides C and D are placed between the arbors of A and B, as is indicated in Fig. 12, they will rotate in the same direction, and may consequently be

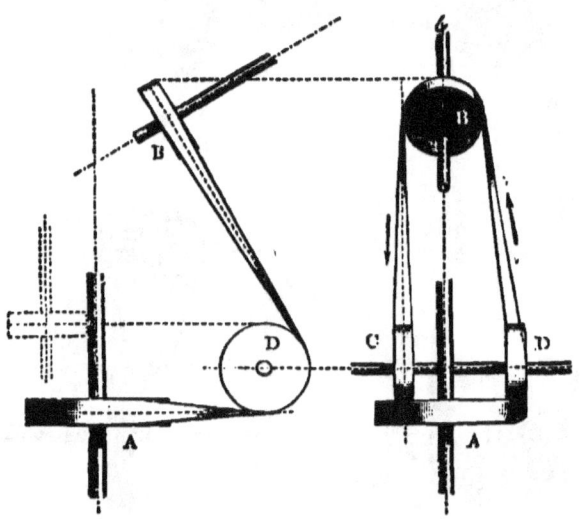

FIG. 13.

fixed upon one and the same arbor. The pulleys of transmission A and B will also rotate in the same direction. In this case the belt can move in one direction only, and remain properly upon the pulleys and guides. The two pulley-guides C and D may be replaced by a single pulley, provided it is placed obliquely so as to run on both sides of the belt without causing displace-

Fig. 13 represents a transmission by belt for two pulleys, the axes of which intersect each other. In this disposition, which differs from that of Fig. 11 only in the inclination of the axis of the pulley *B*, the movement of the belt can take place only in one direction. To obtain a movement in the other direction, it is necessary to move the pulley-guides along their

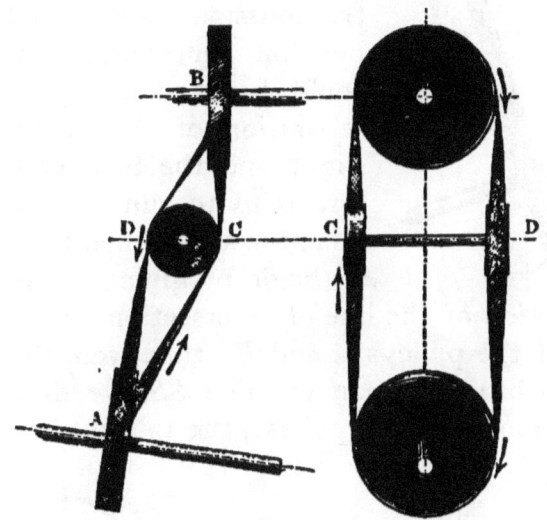

FIG. 14.

common axis until the condition necessary for maintaining the belt in position is fulfilled for this particular case. It must be remembered that the two pulley-guides rotate in contrary directions, and therefore cannot be fixed to the arbor upon which they run.

From the arrangement shown in Fig. 12, that of Fig. 14 may be devised; this disposition corresponds to the case in which there is a very slight angle between the arbors, and the pulley-guides rotate in the same

36   BELTS AND PULLEYS.

The disposition represented in Fig. 15 is still more simple, and may be used for a greater angle between the axes—as great as 25°.

FIG. 16. *Half-crossed belt with pulley-guide.*—In this case the relative positions of the pulleys of transmission are such that the disposition represented in Fig. 9 could be used, except that the separation of the pulleys is too slight, and the belt would therefore tend to run off. To determine the arrangement of the belt, we begin by giving to the part *SS* the direction of the line of intersection of the middle planes of the pulleys *A* and *B*; then from the point *c*, chosen arbitrarily upon the line *SS*, we draw, to the circumferences of the pulleys, the tangent lines *ca* and

FIG. 15.

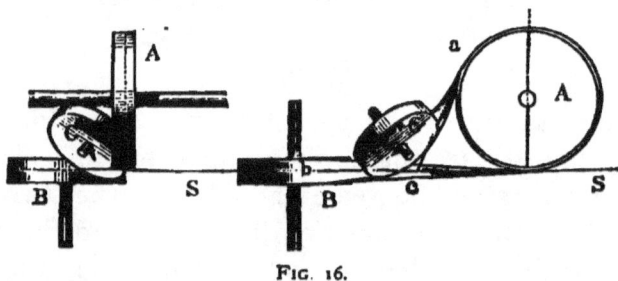

FIG. 16.

cb. The plane of these tangents determines the middle plane of the pulley-guide *C*, to which the lines are also tangents. Rotation may take place equally well in either direction. Because of the cramped position of the pulleys and the consequent difficulty in placing the arbor of the pulley-guide in proper position, this arrangement is very rarely seen in practice.

FIG. 17. *Another disposition for transmission by half-crossed belt with pulley-guide.*—In this figure the pulleys of transmission are so placed that the line of intersection SS of their middle planes is the common tangent to the circles contained in the planes, and the middle plane of the pulley-guide C coincides with that of the

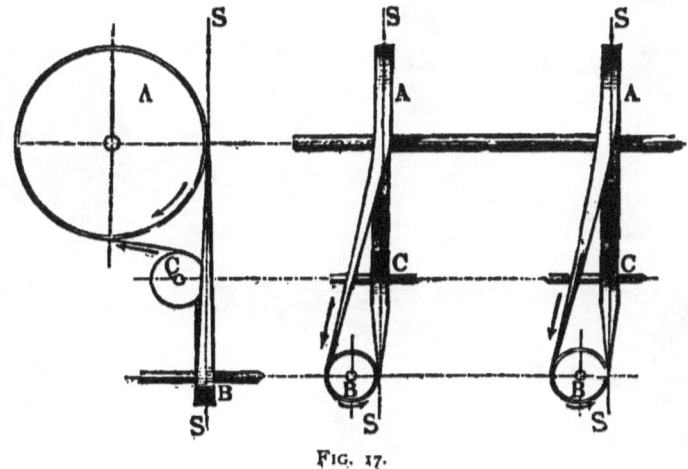

FIG. 17.

pulley of transmission A. The portion of belt which leaves the pulley A is inclined (as shown in the figure) as in the crossed belt in order that it may properly roll upon the pulley B, while the portion which leaves the pulley B is guided by the pulley-guide C. The pulley-guide is in contact with the line of intersection SS, and with a tangent to the circle A drawn from an arbitrary point upon the line SS. In this disposition the direction of rotation must be as indicated in the figure.

This mode of transmission is very convenient when we wish to drive a series of vertical arbors from one horizontal shaft; it also finds frequent employment in mills for grinding various materials, and when the separation of the pulleys of transmission is necessarily slight.

FIG. 18. *Half-crossed belt with movable pulley-guide.*—In this disposition, which is used for a greater separation of the pulleys of transmission than in that of Fig. 17, we may, by moving the pulley-guide from the posi-

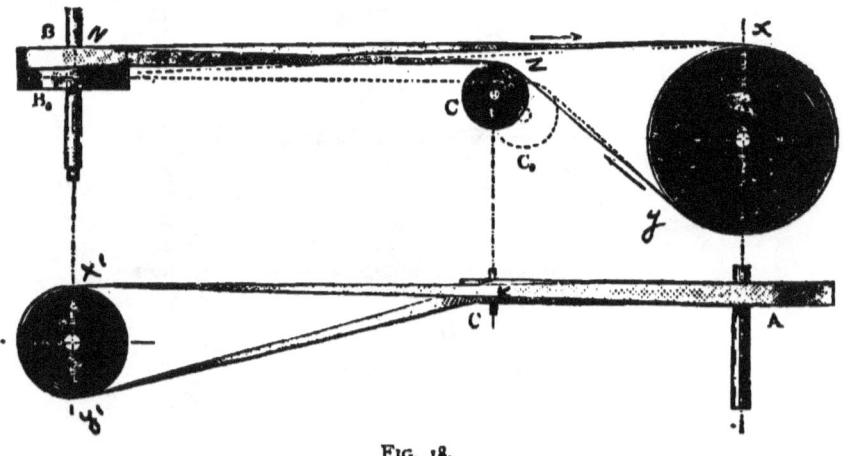

FIG. 18.

tion C to the position C_0 (shown by the dotted lines), cause the belt to pass from the fixed pulley B to the idle pulley B_0: in a similar manner, the pulley-guide may be used for running the belt off the pulleys entirely. The position C_0 should be so chosen that the tensions upon the belt for the two positions will be the same or slightly less for C_0 than for C.

General case of crossed arbors.—When the pulleys of

section of their middle planes is a common tangent to the circles contained in the planes, it becomes necessary to make use of two pulley-guides. Fig. 19 represents an arrangement which may be adopted in such cases, and which may be regarded as the general solution of the problem of transmission by belts with pulley-

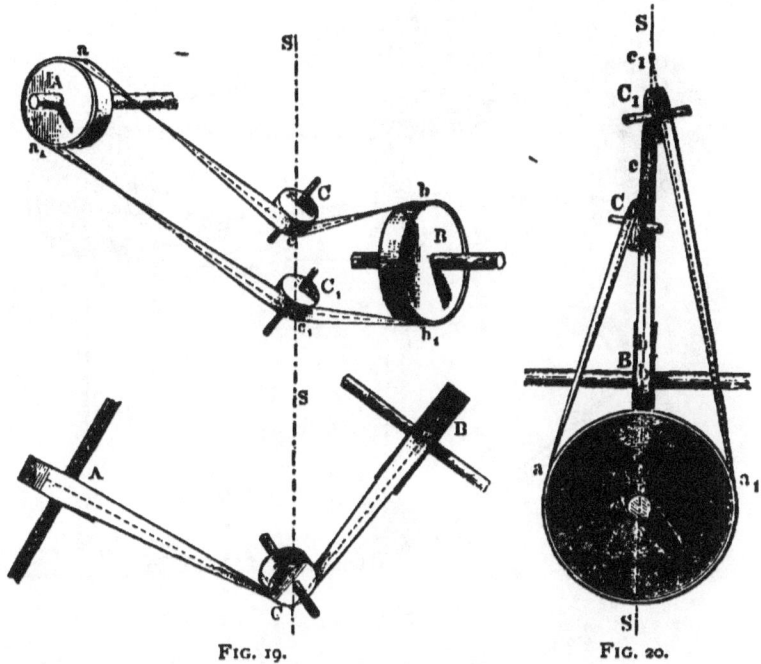

FIG. 19.   FIG. 20.

guides. Fig. 20 represents a special application for the case in which the line of intersection SS of the middle planes passes through the centre of the middle circle of one of the pulleys of transmission; in this figure the axis of the pulley B is supposed to be situated in a plane parallel to the pulley A. After having obtained the line of intersection SS, we choose upon it two arbitrary points c and c_1 through which we draw, to the middle circles of the pulleys of transmission, the tangent lines ca, cb, c_1a_1, and c_1b_1. The planes cab and $c_1a_1b_1$ which are thus determined are those of the two pulley-guides, which should be placed respectively in contact with the above-named tangent lines. With

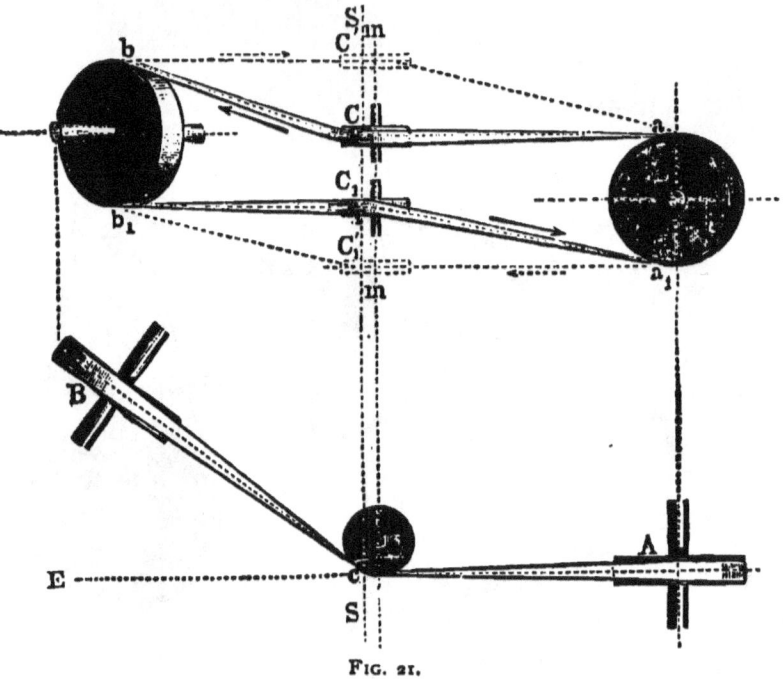

FIG. 21.

this disposition, rotation may take place equally well in either direction.

The mode of transmission represented in Fig. 19 may be simplified by giving to the axes of the two pulley-guides a common direction mm parallel to the two pulleys of transmission (Fig. 21). In this figure SS represents the intersection of the middle planes of the two pulleys of transmission, ac and b_1c_1 the intersections of planes perpendicular to SS with the middle planes of the pulleys of transmission A and B respectively. In the perpendicular planes, tangentially to the right lines ac and b_1c_1, we place the two pulley-guides C and C_1. The arrows indicate the directions of rotation; to obtain a movement of the belt in a direction contrary to the one indicated, it is necessary to give to

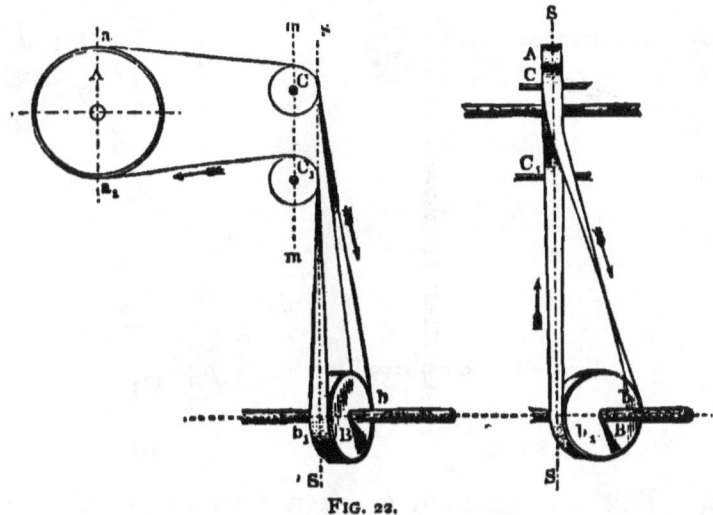

Fig. 22.

the pulley-guides C and C_1 the positions indicated at C' and C'_1 by the dotted lines.

It may be remarked here that the belt, instead of passing from c to a and from c_1 to a_1, may be made to pass from c to a_1 and from c_1 to a, which causes a change in the direction of rotation. The pulley-guides, instead of being horizontal, as in the figure, may be placed vertically—that is, respectively in the planes of the pulleys of transmission A and B; in this case, however, it becomes necessary to take account of the angle of deviation (see § 4).

When the pulleys of transmission can be so placed that the intersection SS of their middle planes is tangent to one of the pulleys, and the distance between the parallel planes containing the axes of the pulleys A and B is sufficient, we may substitute, for the disposition shown in Fig. 20, the one represented in Fig.

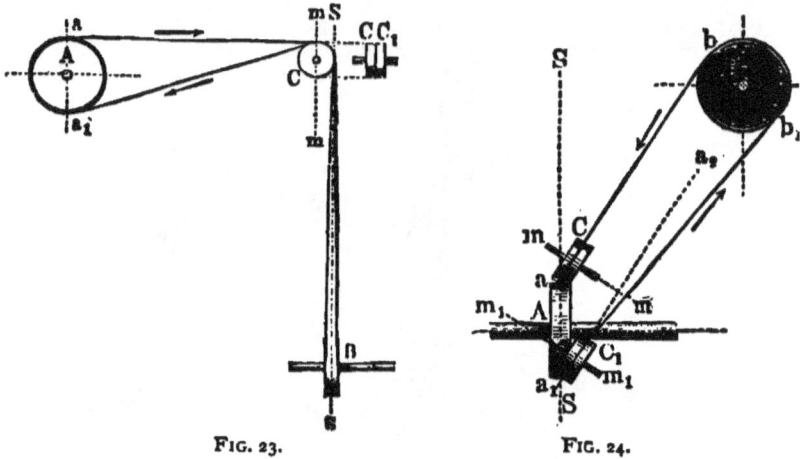

FIG. 23.   FIG. 24.

22. This arrangement is often seen in practice; the axes of the pulley-guides are parallel to that of the pulley of transmission A. The middle planes of the pulleys A and B may make any desired angle with each other.

If the distance AC is great compared with the width of the belt, the pulley-guides, instead of being the one above the other, may be placed upon the same axis, as shown in Fig. 23. If the distance between B and C is sufficiently great, the arbor B may be provided with two pulleys, one fixed and the other idle.

TRANSMISSIONS BY BELTS WITH GUIDES. 43

When, on account of lack of space, it is impossible to make use of one of the dispositions which we have described above, we ought to seek at least to place the axes of the pulley-guides in the middle plane of one of the principal pulleys and the pulley-guides themselves parallel to each other, as, for example, in Fig. 24. In this case we first draw the tangent line ab; then in a plane drawn through this line normally to the plane of

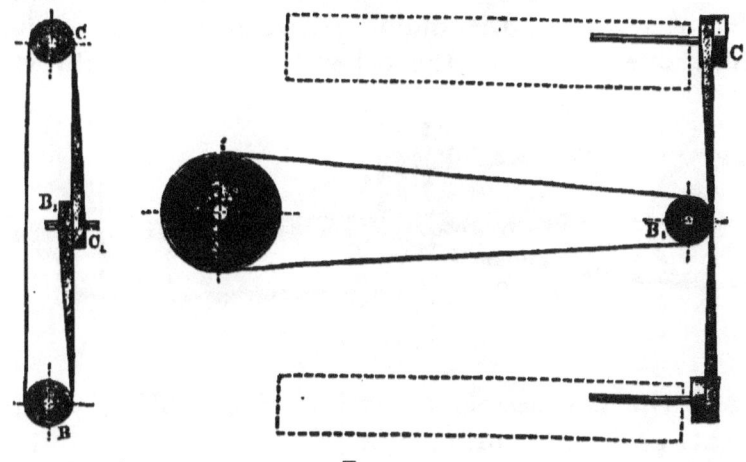

Fig. 25.

the figure we place the pulley-guide C in such a manner that it is tangent at the point a to the line of intersection of the middle planes of the pulleys A and C. Through the point a_1 we then draw the line $a_1 a_2$ parallel to ab, and in a plane drawn through this line parallel to the plane of the pulley-guide C, we place the second pulley-guide tangent to the intersection of the middle planes of the pulleys A and C, and to the middle plane of the pulley B. In this manner the axes mm and $m_1 m_1$.

of the pulley-guides are found parallel to each other, and also situated in a plane parallel to that of the pulley B.

By making the belt of Fig. 23 pass over a fourth pulley we may obtain an arrangement by which we may drive two pulleys B and C by means of a single driving-pulley A.

Fig. 25 represents a disposition of this kind much used in spinning-mills. The arbors B and C are in different stories of the building, and each bears two pulleys, one fixed and the other loose; we use, in this

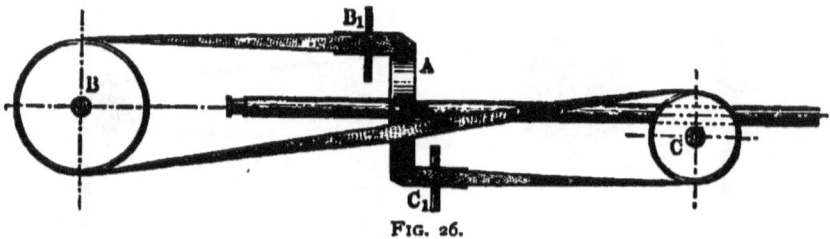

FIG. 26.

case, the permissible deviation of the belt from its exact position mentioned in § 3.

Fig. 26 represents another mode of transmission by belt, in which the two parallel arbors B and C are driven by a single pulley A. The axes of these arbors are both perpendicular to that of the arbor A; the first intersects it, while the second crosses it without intersecting. In the machinery of spinning-mills a great number of transmissions are found in which three, four, or even a greater number of pulleys are driven by means of a single driver. It may be remarked here, that in all cases of transmission by leather belt in which pulley-guides are used which are in contact with the upper surface of the belt, it is advantageous to place the belt so that the contact of the pulleys is always upon the same surface—the flesh or wrinkled side.

§ 6. Length of Belts.

It is often necessary in practice to calculate the proper length of a belt for a given separation of the axes of the pulleys upon which the belt is to run and for known pulley radii or diameters. Thus when we have two pulleys, the bearings and positions of which

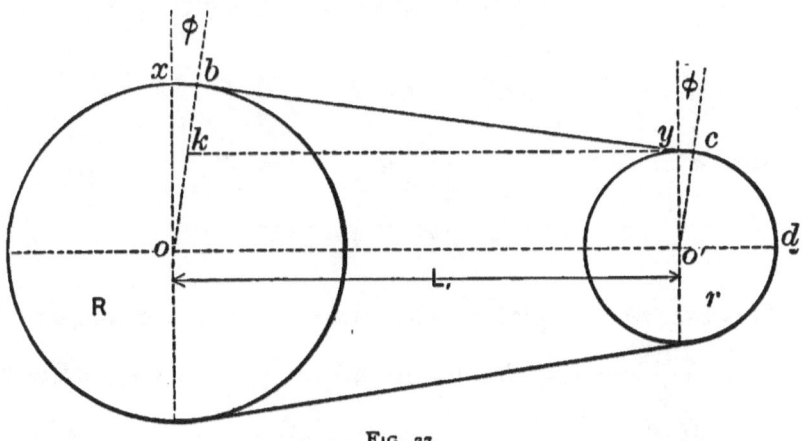

Fig. 27.

are already fixed, if we can determine the proper length for the belt, we can save time and prevent waste of belt in cutting too long or too short.

Open Belt.—Let us denote by L the total length of the required belt; by L_1 the distance between the centres of the two pulleys upon which the belt is to run; by R the radius of the larger pulley, and by r that of the smaller. Let Fig. 27 represent the pulleys connected by an open belt. In the figure the lines ob and $o'c$ are parallel, because each is perpendicular to the line bc; hence the angles xob and $yo'c$ are equal. Let us denote each of these angles by φ. It is evident from the figure that the total length of the belt must be

$$L = 2(bc + \text{arc } ab + \text{arc } cd).$$

Draw the line ck parallel to oo': we shall have $ck = L_1$, because ob and $o'c$ are parallel. In the triangle bkc, in which the angle kbc is a right angle, we shall have

$$bc = \sqrt{ck^2 - bk^2} \quad \text{or} \quad bc = \sqrt{L_1^2 - bk^2}.$$

But $ok = o'c = r$ and $bk = ob - ok = R - r$; hence

$$bc = \sqrt{L_1^2 - (R - r)^2}.$$

The arc ab is equal to the arc ax + the arc xb; arc $ax = \dfrac{2\pi R}{4} = 1.57R$, and arc $xb = \dfrac{\pi R \varphi}{180} = 0.0175 R\varphi$. Therefore

$$\text{arc } ab = 1.57R + 0.0175R\varphi = (1.57 + 0.0175\varphi)R.$$

Also the arc cd is equal to the arc dy — the arc yc; arc $dy = \dfrac{2\pi r}{4} = 1.57r$ and arc $yc = \dfrac{\pi r \varphi}{180} = 0.0175 r\varphi$. Hence we shall have

$$\text{arc } cd = 1.57r - 0.0175r\varphi = (1.57 - 0.0175\varphi)r.$$

LENGTH OF BELTS.

Add together these values of bc, arc ab, and arc cd, and we shall have for the total length of the belt

$$L = 2[\sqrt{L_1^2 - (R-r)^2} + (1.57 + 0.0175\varphi)R + (1.57 - 0.0175\varphi)r] \quad (24)$$

In the right-angled triangle kbc we have, from trigonometry, sin angle $bck = \dfrac{bk}{kc} = \dfrac{R-r}{L_1}$. But since the sides of the triangles kbc and xbo are respectively perpendicular to each other, the triangles are similar, and the angle $bck = \varphi$. Hence we shall have

$$\sin \varphi = \frac{R-r}{L_1}.* \quad \ldots \quad (25)$$

Crossed Belt.—In crossed belts the lengths differ considerably from those of open belts under the same cir-

---

* In open belts the angle φ is generally quite small, and we may without serious error take the sine of the angle equal to the angle itself expressed in circular measure. Thus we shall have, from formula (25), $\varphi_0 = \sin \varphi = \dfrac{R-r}{L_1} = 0.0175\varphi$, or $\varphi = \dfrac{R-r}{0.0175 L_1}$, φ_0 representing the angle in circular measure. This value substituted in formula (24) gives for the total length of the belt

$$L = 2\left[\sqrt{L_1^2 - (R-r)^2} + 1.57R + \frac{0.0175R}{0.0175}\frac{R-r}{L_1} + 1.57r - \frac{0.0175r}{0.0175}\frac{R-r}{L_1}\right] = 2\left[\sqrt{L_1^2 - (R-r)^2} + 1.57(R+r) + \frac{R-r}{L_1}(R-r)\right].$$

Representing $R+r$ by Σ and $R-r$ by Δ, the above expression becomes

$$L = 2\left(\sqrt{L_1^2 - \Delta^2} + 1.57\Sigma + \frac{\Delta^2}{L_1}\right). \quad \ldots \quad (25A)$$

This formula is simpler than but not so accurate as formula (24).

cumstances of separation of pulleys and pulley-radii. Let Fig. 28 represent two pulleys connected by a crossed belt. As in open belts, we shall have

$$L = 2(bc + \text{arc } ab + \text{arc } cd).$$

Draw the line ck parallel to oo' and produce bo as far as its intersection with ck. As before, we shall have $ok = o'c = r$. Hence $bk = R + r$ and $ck = L_1$.

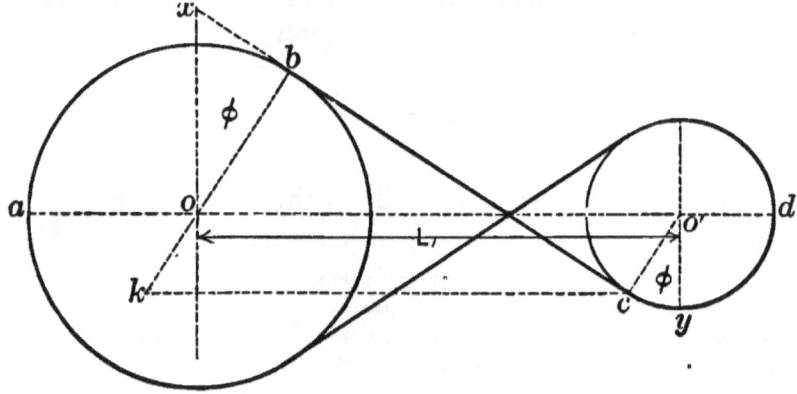

FIG. 28.

In the right-angled triangle kbc we shall have

$$bc = \sqrt{\overline{ck}^2 - \overline{bk}^2} = \sqrt{L_1^2 - (R+r)^2}.$$

The triangles obx and kbc are similar, and the angle $bck = \varphi$. We shall therefore have

$$\sin \text{ angle } bck = \frac{bk}{kc},$$

or
$$\sin \varphi = \frac{R+r}{L_1}. \quad . \quad . \quad . \quad . \quad (26)$$

LENGTH OF BELTS.

From the figure we have arc ab = arc ax + arc xb = $\frac{2\pi R}{4}$ + 0.0175$R\varphi$. Also arc cd = arc yd + arc yc = $\frac{2\pi r}{4}$ + 0.0175$r\varphi$.

Hence, by adding together these values of bc, arc ab, and arc cd, we shall obtain for the total length

$$L = 2[\sqrt{L_1^2 - (R+r)^2} + 1.57R + 0.0175R\varphi + 1.57r + 0.0175r\varphi],$$

or

$$L = 2[\sqrt{L_1^2 - (R+r)^2} + 1.57(R+r) + 0.0175\varphi(R+r)]. \quad (27)$$

Example 1.—Suppose we have two pulleys having radii of $R = 20''$ and $r = 10''$, and a distance between the axes of $L_1 = 10' = 120''$. Required the length for an open belt which will properly connect the two pulleys. From formula (25) we shall have

$$\sin \varphi = \frac{20 - 10}{120} = 0.0833, \quad \text{or} \quad \varphi = 4\frac{47°}{60}.$$

Formula (24) therefore becomes, on substituting the above data,

$$L = 2\left[\sqrt{120^2 - (20-10)^2} + \left(1.57 + 0.0175 \times 4\frac{47}{60}\right)20 \right.$$
$$\left. + \left(1.57 - 0.0175 \times 4\frac{47}{60}\right)10\right],$$

or

$$L = 2(119.58 + 33.07 + 14.86) = 335.02'' = 27' \; 11''.$$

If we wish to use formula (25A) instead of formula (24), we proceed as follows: $\Sigma = 20 + 10 = 30$, $\Delta = $

$20 - 10 = 10$. Hence, from the formula, we shall have

$$L = 2\left(\sqrt{120^2 - 10^2} + 1.57 \times 30 + \frac{10^2}{120}\right)$$
$$= 2(119.58 + 47.10 + 0.833) = 335.03''.$$

Thus the difference in the results from formulas (24) and (25A) is in this case practically 0.

Example 2.—Taking the data of Example 1, it is required to calculate the proper length for a crossed belt which runs on the above pulleys. From formula (26) we shall have

$$\sin \varphi = \frac{20 + 10}{120} = 0.25, \quad \text{or} \quad \varphi = 14\frac{29°}{60} = 14.5°.$$

Formula (27) therefore gives for the proper length of the belt

$$L = 2[\sqrt{120^2 - (20 + 10)^2} + 1.57(20 + 10) + 0.0175 \times 14.5(20 + 10)] = 2(116.19 + 47.10 + 7.61),$$

or
$$L = 341.80'' = 28\tfrac{1}{2} \text{ feet}.$$

In transmissions by belts with pulley-guides, and in all cases where the intricate arrangement of the belt renders arithmetical calculation long and tedious, the proper length of the belt may be determined more easily and with sufficient exactness graphically, by measurement with the rule. To illustrate: Suppose we have an arrangement of pulleys such as is represented in Fig. 12, which figure is a sketch (containing two projections) of the transmission, drawn to a scale of $\frac{1}{32}$.

The separation of the pulleys A and B is 5 feet $= 60''$, and the diameters respectively $21''$ and $13''$. From the figure it is evident that the total length of the belt is $L = $ arc $xy + yD + Dx' + $ arc $x'y' + y'C + Cx$. By measuring with the compasses the above arcs, we find $xy = 34\frac{1}{2}''$ and $x'y' = 20''$. The line yD in the left-hand projection is given in its true length by the line ND in the right-hand figure; hence, by measuring ND, we obtain for the true length $yD = 30''$. The distance Dx' is given in its true length in the left-hand figure, and therefore, by direct measurement, we obtain $Dx' = 34''$. In a similar manner we obtain by measuring KC the true length $y'C = 36''$, and by direct measurement, $Cx = 26''$. We have consequently $L = 34\frac{1}{2} + 30 + 34 + 20 + 36 + 26 = 180\frac{1}{2}'' = 15'\,\frac{1}{2}''$. In a similar manner in Fig. 18, by measuring the arcs xy and $x'y'$, and the length, Nx, Ky', and yz, we may obtain the length necessary for a belt which will properly run on the pulleys represented in the figure.

§ 7. *Speed-cones.*

The contrivance known to mechanics as "speed-cones" consists of two stepped pulleys arranged as shown in Fig. 29. The object of speed-cones is to obtain different speeds for the driven arbor from the constant speed of the driving-shaft. To illustrate: Suppose in Fig. 29 we assume between the radii of the pulleys the relations $R = 3r$, $R' = r'$, and $R'' = 3r''$. We have seen from formula (6) that the ratio of the revolutions of two pulleys which are connected by one and the same belt is equal to the inverse ratio of the pulley-radii. Hence, if we assume that the driving-shaft xy makes 100 revolutions per minute ($N = 100$) when the belt is on the pulleys R and r, we shall have for the revolutions of r (and consequently of the shaft $x'y'$) $n = N\dfrac{R}{r} = 100 \times 3 = 300$. When the belt is on the pulleys R' and r' we shall have for the revolutions of r' (and consequently of the shaft $x'y'$) $n' = N\dfrac{R'}{r'} = 100 \times 1 = 100$. Similarly, when the belt is on the pulleys

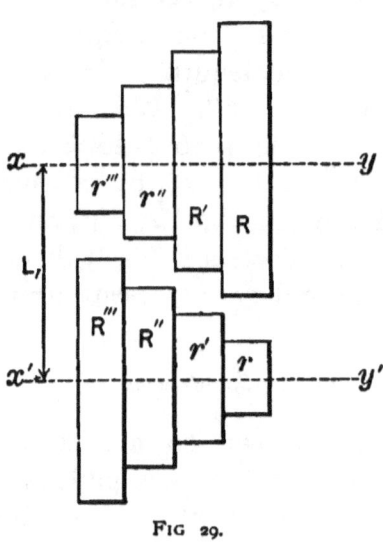

FIG 29.

R'' and r'' we have for the revolutions of R'' and the shaft $x'y'$ $N'' = N\dfrac{r''}{R''} = 100 \times \frac{1}{3} = 33\frac{1}{3}$. Such different speeds for the driven arbor are necessary in many machine-tools, as the lathe, drill, etc., because the speed of the mandrel and spindle must vary with the

Open Belt.—From formula (25A) we have for the length of the belt

$$L = 2\left(\sqrt{L_1^2 - \Delta^2} + 1.57\Sigma + \frac{\Delta^2}{L_1}\right),$$

in which $\Sigma = R + r$ and $\Delta = R - r$ (see Fig. 29). Since now the length of the belt must be the same for each pair of pulleys in the cone, we shall have

$$2\left(\sqrt{L_1^2 - \Delta^2} + 1.57\Sigma + \frac{\Delta^2}{L_1}\right) = 2\left(\sqrt{L_1^2 - \Delta'^2} + 1.57\Sigma' + \frac{\Delta'^2}{L_1}\right)$$

or

$$\sqrt{L_1^2 - \Delta^2} + 1.57\Sigma + \frac{\Delta^2}{L_1} = \sqrt{L_1^2 - \Delta'^2} + 1.57\Sigma' + \frac{\Delta'^2}{L_1},$$

in which $\Sigma' = R' + r'$ and $\Delta' = R' - r'$.

By means of the binomial formula we may extract the square roots of the quantities under the radical signs as follows:

$$\sqrt{L_1^2 - \Delta^2} = L_1 - \frac{\Delta^2}{2L_1} - \frac{\Delta^4}{8L_1^3} - \frac{\Delta^6}{16L_1^5} - \text{etc.,}$$

and

$$\sqrt{L_1^2 - \Delta'^2} = L_1 - \frac{\Delta'^2}{2L_1} - \frac{\Delta'^4}{8L_1^3} - \frac{\Delta'^6}{16L_1^5} - \text{etc.}$$

But since L_1 is usually very large compared with Δ, $\frac{\Delta^4}{8L_1^3}$ and $\frac{\Delta^6}{16L_1^5}$ are very small quantities, and may without serious error be neglected. Similarly, we may neglect the quantities $\frac{\Delta'^4}{8L_1{}^3}$ and $\frac{\Delta'^6}{16L_1{}^5}$. Hence we shall have

$$L_1 - \frac{\Delta^2}{2L_1} + 1.57\Sigma + \frac{\Delta^2}{L_1} = L_1 - \frac{\Delta'^2}{2L_1} + 1.57\Sigma' + \frac{\Delta'^2}{L_1},$$

or
$$1.57\Sigma + \frac{\Delta^2}{2L_1} = 1.57\Sigma' + \frac{\Delta'^2}{2L_1},$$

which reduces to

$$\Sigma' = \Sigma + \frac{\Delta^2 - \Delta'^2}{3.14 L_1}. \quad \ldots \quad (28)$$

If we represent by N the constant number of revolutions per minute of the driving-shaft (corresponding to R), and by n the number of revolutions per minute of the driven shaft when the belt is on the pulley r, we shall have, from formula (6),

$$\frac{R}{r} = \frac{n}{N}, \quad \text{or} \quad R = r\frac{n}{N}.$$

Also
$$\frac{R'}{r'} = \frac{n'}{N'} = \frac{n'}{N}, \quad \text{or} \quad R' = r'\frac{n'}{N},$$

in which n' represents the revolutions per minute of the driven shaft when the belt is on the pulleys R' and r', and N' the revolutions per minute of the driving-shaft, which being constant is equal to N. Hence we shall have

$$\Sigma' = R' + r' = r'\left(\frac{n'}{N} + 1\right),$$

SPEED-CONES. 55

which substituted in formula (28) gives

$$r'\left(\frac{n'}{N} + 1\right) = \Sigma + \frac{\Delta^2 - \Delta'^2}{3.14 L_1}. \quad . \quad . \quad (29)$$

We shall also have (as above for the quantity Σ')

$$\Delta' = R' - r' = r'\frac{n'}{N} - r',$$

or

$$\Delta_1 = r'\left(\frac{n'}{N} - 1\right). \quad . \quad . \quad . \quad (30)$$

Example 1.—Suppose we have two shafts, the distance between which is $L_1 = 100''$: the revolutions per minute of the driving-shaft is $N = 100$, and we wish to construct a pair of speed-cones such that the revolutions per minute of the driven shaft corresponding to the pulleys $r, r', r'',$ and R''' shall be $n = 300$, $n' = 200$, $n'' = 100$, and $N''' = 50$. From formula (6) we shall have

$$\frac{R}{r} = \frac{n}{N} = \frac{300}{100} = 3, \quad \text{or} \quad R = 3r.$$

We may choose any convenient value for r, and find from the above expression the corresponding value of R. Suppose we take $r = 4''$; hence $R = 3r = 3 \times 4 = 12''$. Then $\Sigma = 12 + 4 = 16$ and $\Delta = 12 - 4 = 8$. From formula (30) we shall have

$$\Delta' = r'\left(\frac{200}{100} - 1\right) = r',$$

and formula (29) becomes

$$r'\left(\frac{200}{100}+1\right) = 16 + \frac{64 - r'^2}{3.14 \times 100}, \text{ or } 3r' = 16 + \frac{64 - r'^2}{314}.$$

From this by reducing we shall have

$$r'^2 + 942r' = 5024 + 64.$$

Adding $\left(\frac{942}{2}\right)^2 = 471^2$ to each side of this equation gives

$$r'^2 + 942r' + 221841 = 5024 + 64 + 221841 = 226929.$$

Extracting the square root of this expression gives

$$r' + 471 = \sqrt{226929}.$$

From this $\quad r' = \sqrt{226929} - 471,$

or $\quad r' = 476.38 - 471 = 5.38''.$

Then $\quad \dfrac{R'}{r'} = \dfrac{n'}{N} = \dfrac{200}{100},\quad$ or $\quad R' = 2r' = 10.76''.$

In the same manner for the pulleys R'' and r'' we shall have from formula (30)

$$\Delta'' = r''\left(\frac{n''}{N} - 1\right) = r''\left(\frac{100}{100} - 1\right) = 0;$$

and formula (29) becomes

$$r''\left(\frac{100}{100}+1\right) = 2r'' = 16 + \frac{64}{314} = 16.204,$$

or $\quad r'' = 8.102''.$

SPEED-CONES.

For the pulleys r''' and R''' we shall have

$$\varDelta''' = r'''\left(\frac{N}{N'''} - 1\right) = r'''\left(\frac{100}{50} - 1\right) = r'''.$$

Hence formula (29) gives

$$3r''' = 16 + \frac{64 - r'''^2}{314}, \quad 942r''' = 5024 + 64 - r'''^2.$$

Hence $\qquad r'''^2 + 942r''' = 5088.$

As before, adding $\left(\frac{942}{2}\right)^2$ to each side, and extracting roots, we shall have

$$r''' = \sqrt{5088 + 221841} - 471 = 5.38''.$$

Then
$$\frac{R'''}{r'''} = \frac{N}{N'''} = \frac{100}{50} = 2, \quad \text{or} \quad R'' = 2r''' = 10.76''.$$

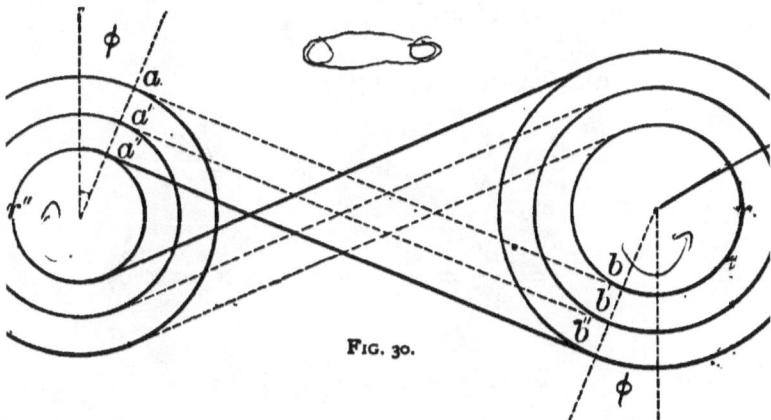

Fig. 30.

Crossed Belt.—The calculation of the radii of the speed-cone pulleys becomes very much simpler when crossed belts are used. If, in Fig. 30, we assume the relations $\Sigma = R + r = R' + r' = R'' + r''$, etc., we shall have for the corresponding angles, $\varphi, \varphi', \varphi''$, etc.; $\sin \varphi = \dfrac{R+r}{L_1} = \dfrac{\Sigma}{L_1}$, $\sin \varphi' = \dfrac{R'+r'}{L_1} = \dfrac{\Sigma}{L_1}$, $\sin \varphi'' = \dfrac{R''+r''}{L_1} = \dfrac{\Sigma}{L_1}$, and consequently $\varphi = \varphi' = \varphi''$, etc. The conditions that the length of the belt must be the same for each pair of pulleys, and that the belt must bear the same tension for each pair of pulleys, will therefore be fulfilled if we take the sums of the radii of each pair of pulleys equal to each other. Or, which is the same thing, we shall have

$$R' = \Sigma - r'. \qquad \ldots \qquad (31)$$

Letting $R' + r' = \Sigma'$, we shall have from above

$$\Sigma = \Sigma'.$$

From formula (6) we may write

$$\frac{R}{r} = \frac{n}{N} \quad \text{or} \quad R = r\frac{n}{N},$$

and
$$\frac{R'}{r'} = \frac{n'}{N'} = \frac{n'}{N} \quad \text{or} \quad R' = r'\frac{n'}{N}.$$

Hence
$$\Sigma = R + r = r\left(\frac{n}{N} + 1\right),$$

$$\Sigma' = R' + r' = r'\left(\frac{n'}{N} + 1\right),$$

SPEED-CONES.   59

and
$$r'\left(\frac{n'}{N}+1\right) = r\left(\frac{n}{N}+1\right),$$

or
$$r' = r\left(\frac{n+N}{n'+N}\right). \quad \ldots \quad (32)$$

Example 2.—Taking the data of Example 1, it is required to calculate the radii of the speed-cone pulleys for crossed belt. We obtain, as in Example 1, $R = 12''$, $r = 4''$, and $\Sigma = 16''$. From formula (32) we shall then have

$$r' = 4\left(\frac{300+100}{200+100}\right) = 4 \times \frac{4}{3} = 5.33''.$$

Formula (31) then gives

$$R' = 16 - 5.33 = 10.67''.$$

For the third pair of pulleys formula (32) gives

$$r'' = r\left(\frac{n+N}{n''+N}\right) = 4\left(\frac{300+100}{100+100}\right) = 4 \times 2 = 8'',$$

and from formula (31) we shall have

$$R'' = \Sigma - r'' = 16 - 8 = 8''.$$

For the fourth pair of pulleys from formula (32) we shall have

$$R''' = r\left(\frac{n+N}{N'''+N}\right) = 4\left(\frac{300+100}{50+100}\right) = 4 \times \frac{4}{1\frac{1}{2}} = 10.67''.$$

Formula (31) then gives

$$r''' = \Sigma - R''' = 16 - 10.67 = 5.33''.$$

Suppose now that we wish to add to the speed-cones another pair of pulleys (R^{iv} and r^{iv}) having such radii that the number of revolutions per minute of the driven shaft, when they are in use, shall be $N^{iv} = 33\tfrac{1}{3}$.

We shall have from formula (32)

$$R^{iv} = r\left(\frac{n+N}{N^{iv}+N}\right) = 4\left(\frac{300+100}{33\tfrac{1}{3}+100}\right) = 4 \times 3 = 12'',$$

and from formula (31)

$$r^{iv} = \Sigma - R^{iv} = 16 - 12 = 4''.$$

We have now two speed-cones, which are made up of pulleys as follows:

First Cone.		Second Cone.	
R	$= 1.2''$	r	$= 4''$
R'	$= 10.67''$	r'	$= 5.33''$
R''	$= 8''$	r''	$= 8''$
r'''	$= 5.33''$	R'''	$= 10.67''$
r^{iv}	$= 4''$	R^{iv}	$= 12''$

A glance at this table will show that the two cones are similar and equal, but so placed on their shafts that they taper in opposite directions. We may therefore write the following:

Rule for Speed-cones, Crossed Belt.—Use two equal and similar stepped cones tapering in opposite directions.

Mr. C. A. Smith, in the *American Machinist*, February 25, 1882, gives a very neat graphical method for determining the radii of speed-cone pulleys for open belt, as follows: Lay off (Fig. 31) AB equal to the given distance between the two shafts ($AB = L_1$), drawn to any convenient scale. Strike the circles representing the pulleys R and r (the radii of which are determined, as in Examples 1 and 2 of this section, from the given revolution-ratio $\frac{n}{N}$), and draw the portion of belt ab. Lay off (from the smaller pulley-centre) $BC = AB \times 0.496 = 0.496L_1$, and erect the perpendicular $CD = \dfrac{L_1}{3.1416}$. Then from D as a centre strike the circle x tangent to ab. Divide $AB = L_1$ into as many

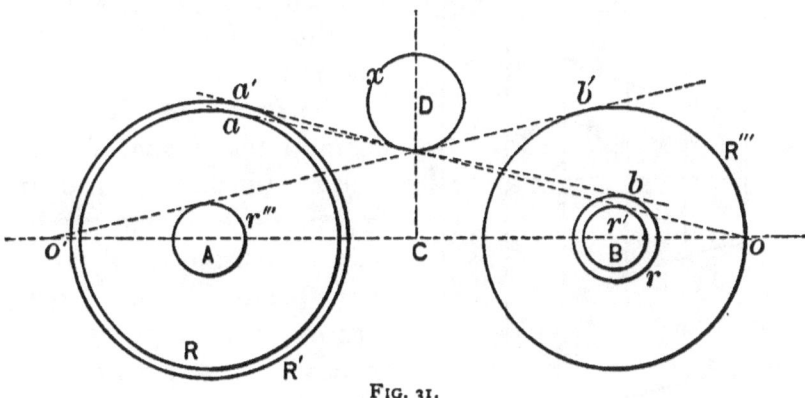

FIG. 31.

equal parts as the shaft B is to revolve, less one, while the shaft A makes one revolution, when the belt is on the required pulleys R' and r'. Lay off, from the centre of the smaller pulley, BO equal to one of these parts ($BO = L_1 \div \dfrac{n'}{N} - 1$), and from o draw the line oa' tangent to the circle x. The circles drawn from B and A as centres and tangent to oa' give the required radii r' and R'. When we wish to have the revolutions of the driven shaft B less than those of the driving-shaft A, or when the smaller pulley is to be on the shaft A, we lay off (for r''' and R''') the distance $Ao' = L_1 \div \dfrac{N}{N'''} - 1$, draw $o'b'$ tangent to the circle x, and the circles r''' and R''' give the required radii.

Crossed belts are not so often used for speed-cones as open belts, and the speed-cones for the former are so easily calculated from formula (32), that it is unnecessary to give graphical methods for determining the radii.

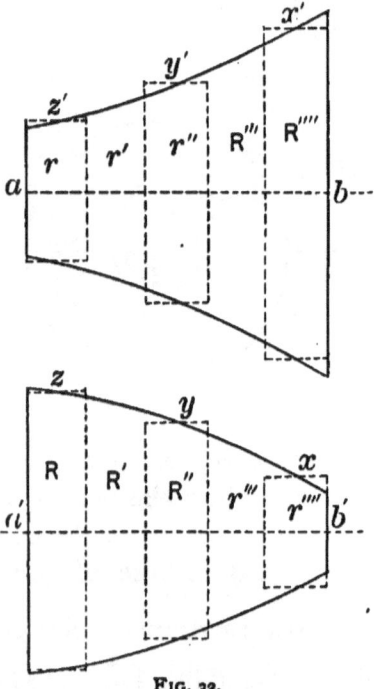

FIG. 32.

Continuous Speed-cones.—Sometimes (especially in cotton machinery and in machines requiring gradually increasing or decreasing speeds for the driven arbors) continuous speed-cones are used instead of the stepped speed-cones already described. It may, however, be remarked that in ordinary shop machinery, such as lathes, planers, drills, etc., etc., continuous speed-cones are very rarely seen.

To construct a pair of continuous speed-cones for open belt we may proceed as follows: Having given several of the different numbers of revolutions required of the driven shaft (for example, $n = 300$, $n' = -$,

$n'' = 100$, $N''' = —$, $N^{\text{iv}} = 50$, and the revolutions of the driving shaft being $N = 100$), lay off (Fig. 32) $ab = a'b' =$ the width of the belt $+$ the proper clearance $\times$ the number of changes in the speed of the driven shaft: in this case there are five changes. Then calculate, from formulas (29) and (30), the radii R, r, R'', r'', r^{iv}, and R^{iv}, corresponding to the known

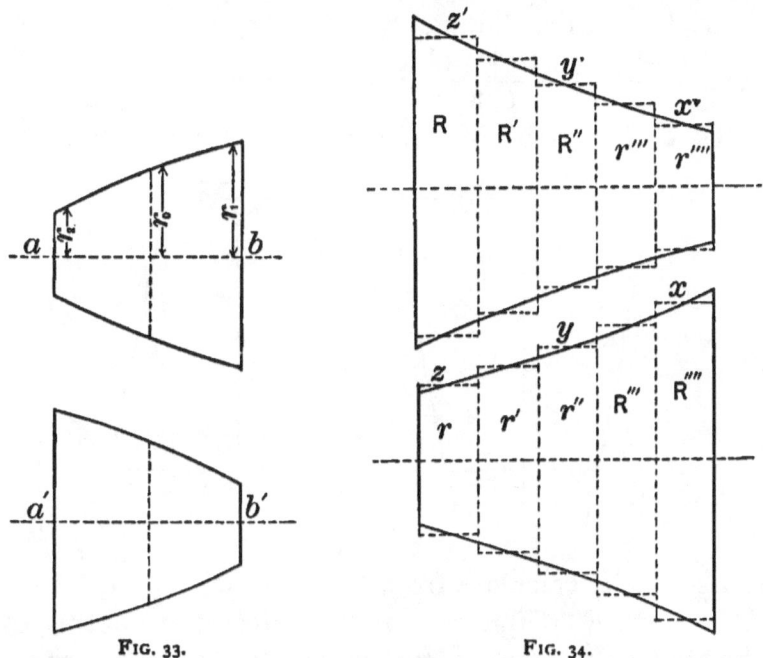

FIG. 33. FIG. 34.

numbers of revolutions, and draw the pulleys of which R, r, etc., are the radii, and which are represented by the dotted rectangles in the figure. Through the centres of the step-widths (x, y, z, x', etc.) draw the curves xyz, $x'y'z'$, and the outlines of the cones are complete.

Rankine gives for continuous speed-cones for open belt the rule, "Use two equal and similar conoids tapering in opposite ways and *bulging* in the middle, according to the formula $r_0 = \frac{r_1 + r_2}{2} + \frac{(r_1 - r_2)^2}{6.28c}$;" in which r_0 is the radius in the middle, r_1 and r_2 the radii of the larger and smaller ends respectively, and c the distance between the centres of the shafts. Fig. 33 represents a pair of continuous speed-cones, open belt, calculated from this rule, taking $r_1 = 10''$, $r_2 = 4''$, $c = 100''$, $r_0 = \frac{10+4}{2} + \frac{(10-4)^2}{628} = 7.057''$, and $ab = a'b' = 14''$.

To construct a pair of continuous speed-cones for

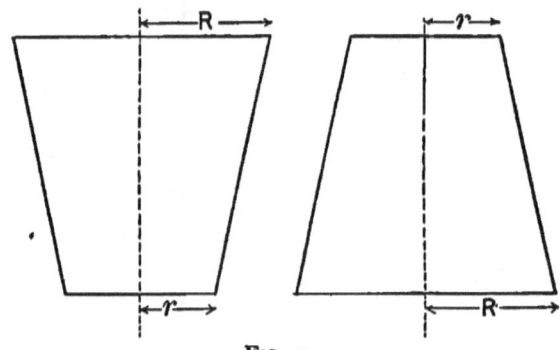

FIG. 35.

crossed belt, calculate from formula (32) the radii R, r, R'', r'', r^{iv}, R^{iv} (Fig. 34), and connect the centres of the step-widths by the curves xyz, $x'y'z'$, in the same manner as in Fig. 32. Or we may use two equal and similar cones tapering in opposite directions (Fig. 35).

An example will best explain the mode of calculation for a pair of continuous speed-cones by which we wish to obtain a given gradual change in the speed of the driven arbor. Suppose our driver makes 100 revolutions per minute, and that we wish, by slowly sliding the belt along the cones, to obtain for the driven arbor a speed varying from 100 to 10 revolutions per minute. According to the rapidity with which we wish the changes to take place we choose the number of changes—let us say in this instance 10. Of these changes, the number of revolutions per minute of the first is 100. With the 9 remaining changes we must therefore gain $100 - 10 = 90$ revolutions per minute, or 10 each. The revolutions of the changes are therefore as follows: 1st, 100; 2d, 90; 3d, 80; 4th, 70; 5th, 60; 6th, 50; 7th, 40; 8th, 30; 9th, 20; 10th, 10. We may now calculate the diameters as for stepped cones, and by drawing curves through their face-centres obtain the outlines for the required continuous cones.*

§ 8. *Materials used for Belting.*

Belts are most commonly made of leather, cut into strips of the required width, and riveted together at their ends to make up the required length. Strips taken from the back part of the hide, and oak or hemlock tanned, are generally considered the best, although some kinds of patent-tanned leather are said to have greater adhesive power. Cow's hide is almost invariably used for the leather of belts; the skins of horses, elephants, and other animals have, however, been util-

---

* In designing continuous speed-cones it is always best to make the curves as gradual in taper as possible for the given changes, in order to avoid the excessive stretching and wear of the belt which would otherwise occur.

ized for this purpose, in some cases with very good results. For very heavy work, belts made of two or more thicknesses of leather are used, in which case the strips are fastened together with cement or rivets, and the joints carefully " broken." In order to gain strength and prevent stretching, leather belts are sometimes edged on the upper side with narrow strips of leather, which are riveted, laced, or cemented fast to the belts. It has also been proposed (and to our knowledge in one case at least tried) to strengthen belts by riveting along their edges thin strips of brass, steel, or other metals.

Of late years vulcanized-rubber belts have been very successfully introduced in this country. They are usually made continuous, thus avoiding the use of rivets, and consist of one or more layers of cotton-duck placed between layers of vulcanized rubber, the rubber covering the edges in order to protect the seams from injury. Rubber belts are now made in widths about the same as leather; they weigh nearly the same, and are said to be equally strong and pliable.

The intestines of sheep, cats, and other animals have been used to a considerable extent for belts; they are exceedingly strong and tough, and can be obtained, it is said, thirty or forty feet in length. Gut belts are either round, to run in grooved pulleys, or woven into flat bands for use on ordinary flat-faced pulleys. Rawhide possesses, it is claimed, fifty per cent more strength than tanned leather; but belts of this material, unless constantly oiled, soon become stiff and ungovernable, and are not to be depended upon for general purposes of transmission. Belts of hemp, flax, canvas, sheet-iron and steel, and several combinations of leather and metallic wire, have been proposed, and in some cases used; but these at present offer no practical advantages over leather and vulcanized rubber.

For all practical purposes, then, we have two kinds of belting—leather and rubber, between which we may offer the following comparison: Those who favor leather belts claim that they are in the main stronger than rubber, and that they will wear much longer, especially when used for cross or half-cross pulleys; that leather belts cease to stretch after once or twice shortened and relaced, while those of rubber do not; and that leather will bear contact with oil and grease without harm, while rubber thus exposed will soften, and stretch out of shape. Wide leather belts can be cut up into narrow ones, while rubber belts cannot be cut without injuring the finished edges; also, leather can be more easily repaired when injured than rubber. On the other hand, rubber belts do not need to be riveted, but are made continuous; they do not slip so easily on the pulley-faces as leather, and are cheaper at first cost for the same sizes. It is also claimed that rubber belts endure exposure to cold and wet much better than leather, retain their flexibility better, and do not lose strength so rapidly from wear. Leather and vulcanized belts both are good. Thousands of each perform well their arduous duties all over the civilized world. Each has hundreds of admirers and champions. We therefore deem it best to express no preference on our own part, preferring rather to have each purchaser choose for himself, assuring him that either good leather or good vulcanized rubber will do his work as faithfully and well as any reasonable man should desire.

§ 9. *Lacing and other Modes of Fastening.*

Endless belts, of whatever material they are made, when subjected to a considerable strain for any length of time become lengthened or stretched. As a result of this lengthening, the belts hang loosely upon their pulleys, and consequently slip and slide. It is therefore necessary to have some ready means of shortening belts to their proper lengths, and thus make them again fit tight upon the pulley-faces. This is very generally done by leaving the belt with two ends (i.e., not endless), and then lacing together the free ends with leather thongs or cords. When a laced belt becomes stretched, it is unlaced, cut off to the proper length, and laced up again, new holes having been punched at the cut end.*

Lacing-thongs are commonly made of leather or good clean rawhide, softened and stretched somewhat to render it firm and even; they vary in width from one quarter to three quarters of an inch, and in thickness from one sixty-fourth to nearly one eighth of an inch, according to the width. We may say very simply, in lacing belts, punch the holes just large enough to easily admit the lacing-thong $\frac{3}{4}$ inch to 1 inch from the ends of the belt (no more material than is necessary

---

* Sometimes belts of considerable length are shortened to take up the stretch by simply running off one pulley and twisting the belts until the proper lengths are obtained. This practice is, however, a very bad one, because the twists cause the belts to become cracked and to wear out rapidly, and should never be indulged in except in cases of immediate necessity.

should be cut out, because this tends to weaken the belt); use for small belts a ¼-inch thong; for belts from 4 inches to 8 inches wide, a ⅜-inch thong; for belts from 8 inches to 15 inches wide, a ½-inch thong; and for belts over 15 inches in width, a ¾-inch thong. The first requisite in lacing together the free belt-ends is to have the ends square—that is, at right angles with the sides of the belt; if the ends are not square the belt will not lie straight on the pulleys, and will tend, consequently, to

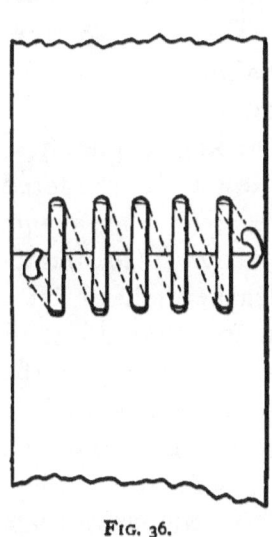

FIG. 36.

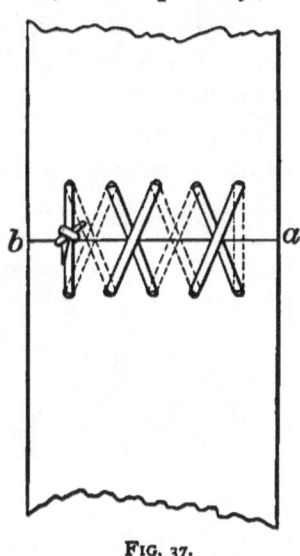

FIG. 37.

run off the pulleys, and otherwise interfere with the proper motion of the machine.

The simplest mode of lacing belts, which is represented in Fig. 36, consists in starting at one side, and lacing over and over through all the holes until the other side of the belt is reached. This does well enough for small belts not to be subjected to any factory work if laced differently; but for larger belts better and safer methods must be used.

Fig. 37 shows a style of lacing quite common among machinists, and which combines quickness of operation with strength about as well as any of the simpler methods. Begin at the side *a* in the figure, and lace with both ends of the thong, as shown, fastening the ends at *b* in a knot or other convenient manner.

A still better lacing is represented in Fig. 38. The thong is here crossed on one side of the belt only—the upper side, and care should be taken not to cross unevenly the double parts on the pulley-side.

In heavy-driving belts, and in all belts where the strain is severe, double rows of holes should be punched, and the joining thus rendered doubly secure against breakage. Messrs. J. B. Hoyt & Co., manufacturers of leather belting, New York, inform me that all their belts are laced according to the double method represented in Fig. 39, in which *a* is the side to be placed next the pulley. This lacing has the advantage that all its parts on the outside of the belt are parallel to the direction of motion, and the tendency is therefore to keep the ends of the belt at all times in their proper positions. The above-mentioned gentlemen, after many years of experience with leather belting, have come to believe this method the best in ordinary use.

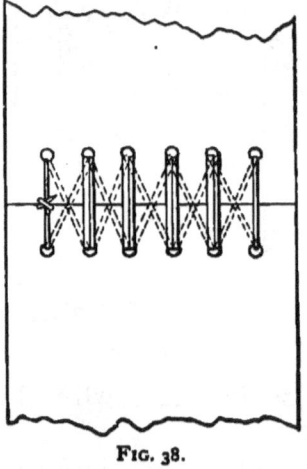

FIG. 38.

An excellent style of lacing for large belts is given by Mr. John W. Cooper in his "Use of Belting," which

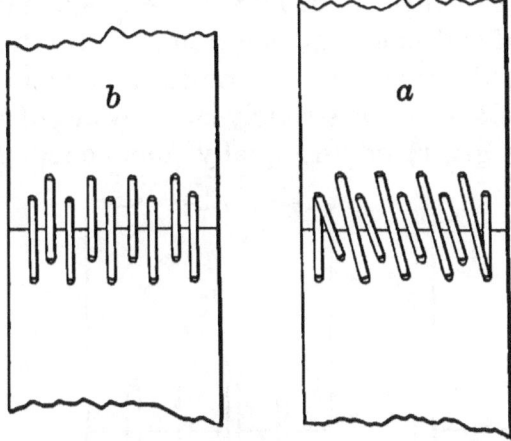

Fig. 39.

we represent in Fig. 40. Begin with one end of the lacing-thong at the point *a*, and lace successively through the holes 1, 2, 3, 4, 5, and so on, all around the rows of holes until the point *a* is again reached, where the thong is fastened off as shown in the figure. Although in this case the parts of the thong are not parallel to the direction of motion, yet they are so slanted—on the pulley-side in one direction and on the outside equally in the other—that the result is practically the same, and the lacing is, beyond doubt, one of the best in existence.

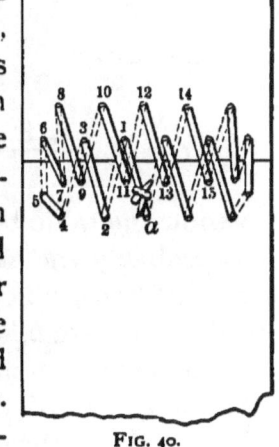

Fig. 40.

Several kinds of metallic belt-hooks or fasteners have been from time to time contrived and introduced—never, however, to our knowledge, with any great degree of success. For small belts the best of these hooks do well enough, and lessen the work of relacing and shortening; but large driving-belts, and those used to transmit large powers, must, for good results, be strongly laced by one of the methods already given, or an equally good one. Among the

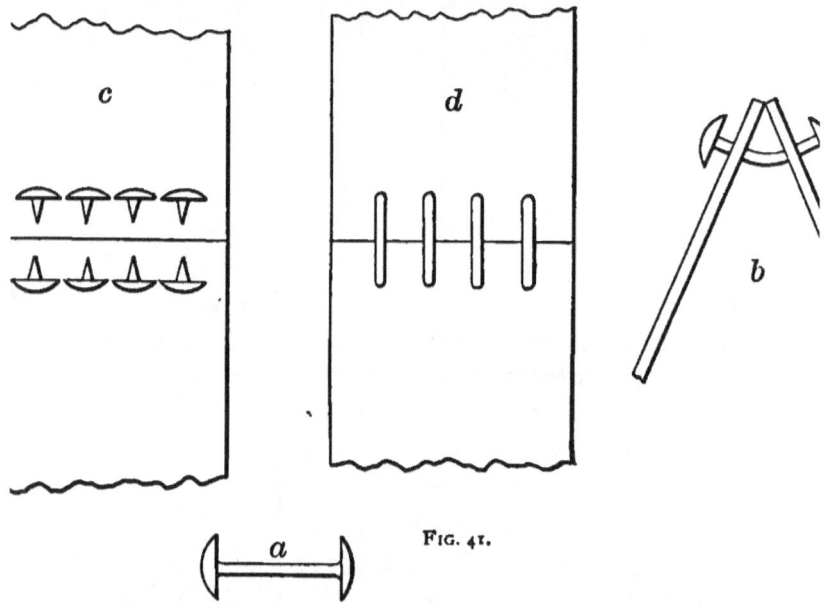

FIG. 41.

various metallic belt-hooks we may give the following as probably the best in use: Fig. 41 represents a kind of belt-hook which is quite extensively used for light belts. Figure *a* is the hook itself. To fasten, proceed as follows: Cut slits in the belt-ends parallel in length to the length of the belt; place the ends as shown in Fig. *b*; force through the slits the belt-hooks as in the figure, turn them, and flatten out the belt as in figure *c*.

Figure *d* represents the pulley-side of the belt and figure *c* the outside.

In Fig. 42 the hook (figure *a*) has a double hold on the belt through the two rows of holes, and is therefore a stronger fastener than the preceding hook. Figure *b* represents the outside of a belt fastened with

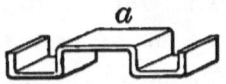

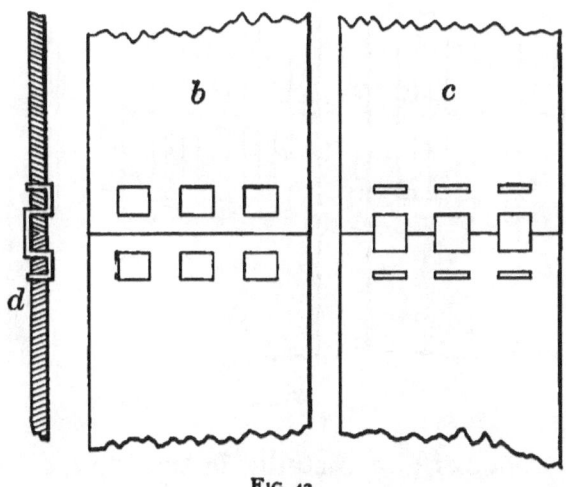

Fig. 42.

these hooks, figure *c* the pulley-side, and figure *d* a section through the two ends of the belt showing one hook.

An ingenious buckle for fastening together the belt-ends is given in Mr. Cooper's "Use of Belting," and credited to a Canadian inventor. The fastener consists of two separate parts, one containing a series of parallel metallic tongues (represented by the dotted lines in figure 43 *a*) which are inserted through holes in the belt-ends, and the other a rectangular cover which is slipped over the projecting ends of the tongues after they have been forced through the belt. Figure 43 *a* represents the outside and figure *b* the pulley-side of the belt. Figure *c* is a sectional drawing showing a pair of tongues and the cover.

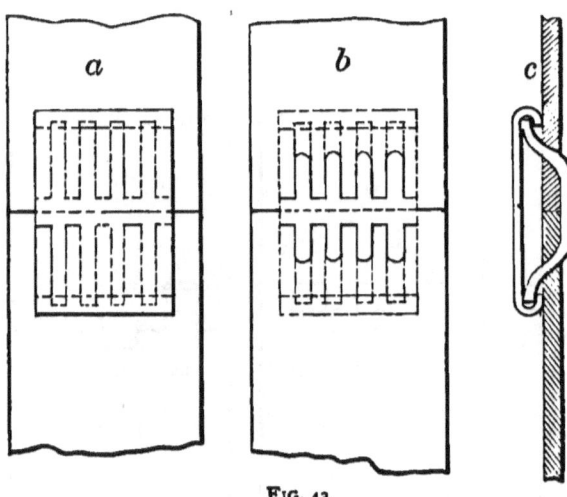

FIG. 43.

All belt-hooks and metallic fasteners used for belts to be run over pulleys should be of brass, copper, or other soft metal, in order to prevent scratching the surface of the pulley, and the consequent additional wear of the whole belt.

A very simple, if not very firm and secure, method of fastening, without the use of lacing thongs or hooks of any kind, is shown in Fig. 44. One end of the belt is cut into cleat-shaped pieces, shown in figure *b* at *y, y, y*, and the other punched with oblong slots, figure *a, x, x, x*. The cleats are forced through the slots, the belt-ends hammered out flat, and the joining is complete. Figure *c* shows a section through the ends of the belt,

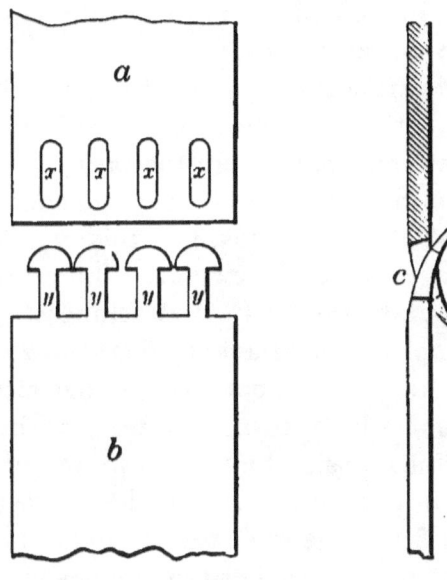

FIG. 44.

with the cleat and slot fastening. Such a fastening as this is at best weak and uncertain, and should not be used at all in practice, except for some exceptionally light work, where lacing-thongs or belt-hooks are not easily to be obtained.

§ 10. *Strength of Leather Belts—Resistance to Slipping.*

The discussion of the strength and resistance to slipping of leather belts is attended with well-nigh insurmountable difficulties, from the fact that the substance with which we have to deal is almost wanting in homogeneity. We are able by means of standard rules and formulas to calculate closely the strength of a cast-iron column or wrought girder, because within reasonable limits cast-iron and wrought-iron are homogeneous; in other words, if we know the breaking strength and safe-working strength of a certain kind of iron, we know these strengths of other iron of the same kind: they are approximately the same. Other metals also are even in texture and homogeneous in nature; many kinds of wood possess this valuable homogeneity to a remarkable extent. But this is by no means true of leather. Few substances, if any, with which mechanical men have to deal show such widely varying results under apparently similar circumstances as the leather which furnishes for us the countless number of transmission-belts seen in nearly every shop and factory in the land. In a series of tests made by a prominent firm of leather-belt manufacturers in New York City, strips of leather two inches wide were cut from one of the ordinary sides used for belting, and carefully tested in the same testing-machine and under precisely similar circumstances. These strips were broken at strains varying all the way from 1400 pounds to 3475 pounds; which result elicits the strange fact, that one strip of leather may be nearly two and a half times as strong as another strip equal in width and thickness, and taken from the same side of leather. The strips in question when in their original positions in the skin were but 15 inches apart at their nearest points. Nor is this all: in two strips which, in the side of leather, joined each other, lay immediately side by side, the difference in breaking strength was 675 pounds, or $337\frac{1}{2}$ pounds per inch of width; a variation of 32 per cent of the greater strength and of nearly 47 per cent of the smaller.

A gentleman for many years engaged in the manufacture of leather belting has informed the author that he once cut off twelve inches of solid part (i.e., without rivets or splicing) from a roll of two-inch belting; cut the piece longitudinally into two parts; tested them in a correct machine; and found that one part withstood 400 pounds greater tensional strain than the other. The gentleman also said that he had tested with a good dynamometer two eight-inch belts, made from similar leather in his own factory, running over pulleys equal in size, doing the same kind of work, and carefully stretched over their pulleys with as nearly as possible the same tensions, and found that one would transmit nearly a horse-power more work without slipping than the other. Many other similar examples from practice might be cited to show with how much of uncertainty and variation from averages the investigator of belt-transmissions is compelled to deal. Let the examples already given, however, suffice for this purpose; and let us, keeping always well on the safe side, endeavor to calculate, as simply as the complicated nature of the subject will allow, the proper strengths and sizes for the various transmission-belts in use in practice.

The strain brought to bear upon an ordinary endless belt running continuously over its pulleys, leaving out of the question considerations due to centrifugal force, etc., etc., is one of simple tension; and were it not for other complicating elements which enter into the calculations, the proper strength for a belt to withstand a certain strain could be quite easily calculated. For example, if we represent by P the actual strain on the belt in pounds, by A the cross-section of the belt in square inches, and by f the safe working tensional stress in pounds per square inch for the material of the belt, we can write the formula

$$P = Af,$$

and, by transposing, $\quad A = \dfrac{P}{f}.$

From this simple formula, were the tensional strain all which we must take into account, we could easily calculate our belt widths and thicknesses. But, unfortunately for the simplicity of our calculations, other considerations must be looked into before we can correctly obtain the necessary rules and formulas. In the first place, probably nine belts out of ten in ordinary use will slip around on their pulleys before they will break; that is, the resistance of the belt to slipping is not equal to its strength. It therefore becomes necessary to embody in our calculations

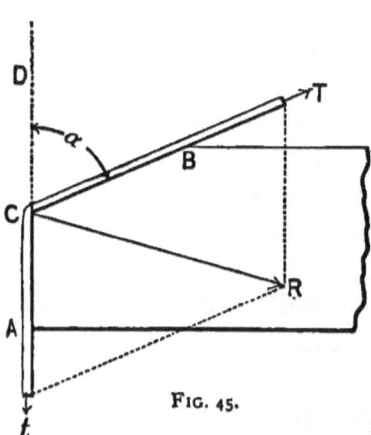

Fig. 45.

STRENGTH OF LEATHER BELTS.

for strength considerations which will prevent slipping of the belt upon its pulleys.

Let ACB (Fig. 45) represent a band or cord drawn over an angle of a solid, as shown in the figure. Let forces, represented by T and t, act at the ends of the cord in the directions shown, and let α represent the angle DCB. In drawing the cord over the angle or corner the friction between the block and cord must be overcome. By the principles of the parallelogram of forces, the resultant normal pressure R of the forces T and t is given by the expression

$$R = \sqrt{T^2 + t^2 - 2Tt \cos \alpha}; \quad \ldots \quad (33)$$

and if we represent by F the friction and by φ the coefficient of friction, we shall have

$$F = \varphi R = \varphi \sqrt{T^2 + t^2 - 2Tt \cos \alpha}.$$

In order to move the cord over the angle in the direction of the force T, this force must be able to overcome the force t acting in an opposite direction, and also the friction, that is, we must have

$$T = t + F.$$

From this, by squaring,

$$T^2 = t^2 + 2tF + F^2.$$

Substituting this value of T^2 in the above equation for the friction, and neglecting the quantity F^2, gives us the equation

$$F = \varphi \sqrt{t^2 + 2tF + t^2 - 2t^2 \cos \alpha - 2Ft \cos \alpha}$$

and by factoring we obtain

$$F = \varphi \sqrt{2(1 - \cos \alpha)(t^2 + tF)}.$$

From trigonometry we find

$$\sqrt{\tfrac{1}{2}(1 - \cos \alpha)} = \sin \tfrac{1}{2}\alpha,$$

which, multiplied by $\sqrt{4}$, becomes

$$\sqrt{\tfrac{4}{2}(1 - \cos \alpha)} = \sin \tfrac{1}{2}\alpha \sqrt{4},$$

or $\qquad \sqrt{2(1 - \cos \alpha)} = 2 \sin \tfrac{1}{2}\alpha.$

Consequently

$$F = 2\varphi \sin \frac{\alpha}{2} \sqrt{t^2 + tF}.$$

From the binomial formula, neglecting the small terms after the second, we may extract the square root of the quantity under the radical sign, and write

$$\sqrt{t^2 + tF} = t + \frac{F}{2}.$$

Hence $\qquad F = 2\varphi \sin \dfrac{\alpha}{2}\left(t + \dfrac{F}{2}\right),$

$$F = 2\varphi t \sin \frac{\alpha}{2} + \varphi F \sin \frac{\alpha}{2},$$

$$F - \varphi F \sin \frac{\alpha}{2} = 2\varphi t \sin \frac{\alpha}{2},$$

and finally
$$F = \frac{2\varphi t \sin \frac{\alpha}{2}}{1 - \varphi \sin \frac{\alpha}{2}}. \quad \ldots \quad (34)$$

The force, then, which is required to draw the cord over the angle in the direction of T is

$$T = t + F = t + \frac{2\varphi t \sin \frac{\alpha}{2}}{1 - \varphi \sin \frac{\alpha}{2}},$$

or
$$T = t\left(1 + \frac{2\varphi \sin \frac{\alpha}{2}}{1 - \varphi \sin \frac{\alpha}{2}}\right). \quad \ldots \quad (35)$$

When the angle α is very small we may say correctly enough

$$1 - \varphi \sin \frac{\alpha}{2} = 1,$$

and formula (35) becomes

$$T = t\left(1 + 2\varphi \sin \frac{\alpha}{2}\right). \quad \ldots \quad (36)$$

Suppose now instead of one angle over which to draw the cord we have several, as shown in Fig. 46, the angles being equal each to each. Let t be the tension at one end of the cord, t_1 that at the first angle, t_2 that at the second angle, etc., to the tension $T = t_n$ at the other end. From what precedes, we shall have for the force necessary to draw the cord over the first angle

$$t_1 = t\left(1 + 2\varphi \sin \frac{\alpha}{2}\right).$$

For the force necessary to draw the cord over the second angle we shall have

$$t_2 = t_1\left(1 + 2\varphi \sin \frac{\alpha}{2}\right).$$

Hence

$$t_2 = t\left(1 + 2\varphi \sin \frac{\alpha}{2}\right)\left(1 + 2\varphi \sin \frac{\alpha}{2}\right),$$

or

$$t_2 = t\left(1 + 2\varphi \sin \frac{\alpha}{2}\right)^2.$$

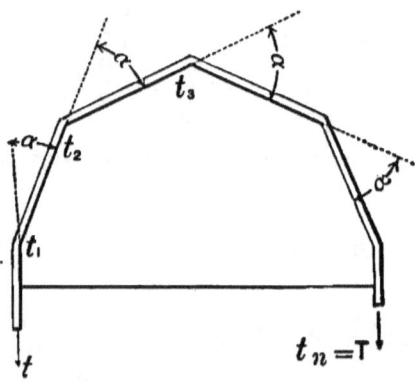

Fig. 46.

In a similar manner

$$t_3 = t_2\left(1 + 2\varphi \sin \frac{\alpha}{2}\right),$$

$$t_3 = t\left(1 + 2\varphi \sin \frac{\alpha}{2}\right)^2\left(1 + 2\varphi \sin \frac{\alpha}{2}\right) = t\left(1 + 2\varphi \sin \frac{\alpha}{2}\right)^3.$$

STRENGTH OF LEATHER BELTS.

And finally

$$t_n = T = t\left(1 + 2\varphi \sin \frac{\alpha}{2}\right)^n \quad . \quad . \quad . \quad (37)$$

By means of this formula we are able to calculate the forces which tend to cause an endless belt to slip upon its pulley, the tensions in the belt necessary to prevent slipping, and consequently the strength and width of the belt itself.

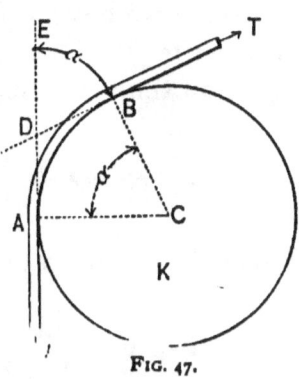

FIG. 47.

Let K, Fig. 47, be a pulley, over which, embracing a centre angle $BCA = EDB = \alpha$, a belt $tABT$ passes as shown in the figure. We can assume the arc AB to be composed of an infinite number (n) of infinitely small sides; each will then be expressed by $\frac{\alpha}{n}$.

From formula (37) we have for the force T the expression

$$T = t\left(1 + 2\varphi \sin \frac{\alpha}{2n}\right)^n,$$

and since for the infinitely small arcs their sines are equal to the arcs themselves, we may write, $\sin \frac{\alpha}{2n} = \frac{\alpha}{2n}$, and therefore

$$T = t\left(1 + \frac{\varphi\alpha}{n}\right)^n.$$

This expression we may develop by means of the binomial theorem into

$$T = t\left(1 + n\frac{\varphi\alpha}{n} + \frac{n(n-1)(\varphi\alpha)^2}{1\times 2n^2} + \frac{n(n-1)(n-2)(\varphi\alpha)^3}{1\times 2\times 3n^3} + \ldots \text{etc.}\right);$$

and since we have assumed n to be infinitely great, we may write $n-1 = n-2 = n-3 = n$. Our last equation therefore becomes

$$T = t\left(1 + \varphi\alpha + \frac{(\varphi\alpha)^2}{1\times 2} + \frac{(\varphi\alpha)^3}{1\times 2\times 3} + \ldots \text{etc.}\right).$$

This is in the form of the series

$$1 + x + \frac{x^2}{1\times 2} + \frac{x^3}{1\times 2\times 3} + \ldots \text{etc.} = e^x,$$

in which e represents the base of the Naperian or hyperbolic system of logarithms ($e = 2.71828$), and the above equation reduces to

$$T = te^{\varphi\alpha}. \quad\ldots\ldots\quad (38)$$

From this we have

$$\text{hyp. log } T - \text{hyp. log } t = \varphi\alpha,$$

and $\qquad$ * $\text{hyp. log } \dfrac{T}{t} = \varphi\alpha. \quad\ldots\quad (39)$

---

* This may be very neatly demonstrated by means of the integral calculus as follows: Let α represent the entire arc embraced by the belt, and $d.\alpha$ one of the small portions which we represented above by $\dfrac{\alpha}{n}$.

Common logarithms are better known and more easily handled than the hyperbolic. To reduce formula (39) to common logarithms it is necessary only to multiply by 0.434. Thus

$$\log \frac{T}{t} = 0.434 \varphi \alpha, \quad \ldots \quad (40)$$

where α is expressed in circular measure, i.e., parts of π.

If α is taken in degrees, substitute $\alpha = \dfrac{\alpha \pi}{180}$, and we obtain

$$\log \frac{T}{t} = 0.007578 \varphi \alpha. \quad \ldots \quad (41)$$

If α is taken in fraction of the circumference, substitute $\alpha = 2\pi\alpha$. We obtain thus

$$\log \frac{T}{t} = 2.729 \varphi \alpha. \quad \ldots \quad (42)$$

---

the increase is $d.t$, and this is due to the friction in the unit of arc. This friction is $d.F = 2\varphi t \sin \dfrac{d.\alpha}{2}$; or, since $d.\alpha$ is very small, $d.F = 2\varphi t \dfrac{d.\alpha}{2} = \varphi t d.\alpha$.

Hence we have $d.t = \varphi t d.\alpha$ or $\dfrac{d.t}{t} = \varphi d.\alpha$.

Integrating between the limits T and t, α and 0, gives us

$$\int_t^T \frac{d.t}{t} = \varphi \int_0^\alpha d.\alpha, \quad \text{or} \quad \text{hyp. log } \frac{T}{t} = \varphi \alpha.$$

The best and most recent experiments made use of for determining the coefficient of friction permit us to use, for ordinary belt-leather over cast-iron pulleys, the value

$$* \varphi = 0.4 \quad \ldots \quad (43)$$

This value substituted in formula (40) gives

$$\log \frac{T}{t} = 0.434 \times 0.4\alpha,$$

or, when α is in circular measure,

$$\log \frac{T}{t} = 0.1736\alpha. \quad \ldots \quad (44)$$

Substituting $\varphi = 0.4$ in formula (41) gives

$$\log \frac{T}{t} = 0.007578 \times 0.4\alpha,$$

or, when α is in degrees,

$$\log \frac{T}{t} = 0.00303\alpha. \quad \ldots \quad (45)$$

---

* See Appendix I.

STRENGTH OF LEATHER BELTS.

Similarly, by substituting in formula (42),

$$\log \frac{T}{t} = 2.729 \times 0.4\alpha,$$

or, where α is a fraction of the circumference,

$$\log \frac{T}{t} = 1.0916\alpha. \quad \ldots \quad (46)$$

The following table, calculated from formulas (44), (45), and (46), gives values of $\frac{T}{t}$ for different values of the arc α from 30° to 300° corresponding to from 0.524 to 5.236 in circular measure, and from $\frac{1}{12} = 0.083$ to $\frac{5}{6} = 0.833$ in fractions of the circumference.

To illustrate the application of the table, suppose we have a pair of cast-iron pulleys over which we propose to run a leather belt. Suppose the arc embraced by the belt, upon the pulley over which it is most likely to slip (the pulley having the smaller amount of contact with the belt, or the smaller pulley), is 75° = 1.309 in circular measure = $\frac{5}{24}$ = 0.208 in fraction of the circumference.

We look along the column of degrees until we find the value 75°, along the column of circular measures until we find 1.309, or along the column of fractions of the circumference until we find $\frac{5}{24} = 0.208$, and, opposite to these values we find the required value for the ratio of the tensions, $\frac{T}{t} = 1.689$.

TABLE OF TENSIONS FOR LEATHER BELTS OVER CAST-IRON PULLEYS.

In degrees.	$a =$ In circular measure.	$a =$ In fractions of the circumference.	$\dfrac{T}{t} =$
30	0.524	$\frac{1}{12} = 0.083$	1.233
45	0.785	$\frac{1}{8} = 0.125$	1.369
60	1.047	$\frac{1}{6} = 0.167$	1.521
75	1.309	$\frac{5}{24} = 0.208$	1.689
90	1.571	$\frac{1}{4} = 0.250$	1.874
105	1.833	$\frac{7}{24} = 0.292$	2.082
120	2.094	$\frac{1}{3} = 0.333$	2.312
135	2.356	$\frac{3}{8} = 0.375$	2.565
150	2.618	$\frac{5}{12} = 0.417$	2.849
165	2.880	$\frac{11}{24} = 0.458$	3.163
180	3.142	$\frac{1}{2} = 0.500$	3.514
195	3.403	$\frac{13}{24} = 0.541$	3.901
210	3.665	$\frac{7}{12} = 0.583$	4.333
240	4.189	$\frac{2}{3} = 0.667$	5.340
270	4.712	$\frac{3}{4} = 0.750$	6.589
300	5.236	$\frac{5}{6} = 0.833$	8.117

The greatest strain brought to bear upon an endless belt, or the strain tending in the greatest degree to cause breakage, is the tension in the driving part of the belt, that is T. This tension acts in one direction and the lesser tension t in a contrary direction. Consequently it is the excess of the greater over the lesser tension which overcomes the resistance of the pulley and causes rotation. If we represent the force of resistance in pounds at the circumference of the pulley (which is the force transmitted by the pulley) by P, we shall have the expression

Hence
$$T = P + t,$$

which may be put in the form

$$T = P\left(1 + \frac{t}{P}\right).$$

By substituting for P within the parenthesis its value from formula (47), we obtain

$$T = P\left(1 + \frac{t}{T-t}\right).$$

But
$$\frac{t}{T-t} = \frac{1}{\frac{T}{t} - 1};$$

Hence
$$T = P\left(1 + \frac{1}{\frac{T}{t} - 1}\right);$$

$$T = P\left(\frac{\frac{T}{t} - 1 + 1}{\frac{T}{t} - 1}\right),$$

or
$$T = P\left(\frac{\frac{T}{t}}{\frac{T}{t} - 1}\right), \quad \ldots \ldots (48)$$

by means of which and the preceding table the tension T for different values of α may be determined.

The following table, calculated from formula (48), gives values of $\dfrac{\frac{T}{t}}{\frac{T}{t}-1}$ for different values of the arc α.

TABLE OF GREATEST TENSION FOR LEATHER BELTS OVER CAST-IRON PULLEYS.

In degrees.	$\alpha =$ In circular measure.	In fractions of the circumference.	$T = P \times$
30	0.524	$\frac{1}{12} = 0.083$	5.29
45	0.785	$\frac{1}{8} = 0.125$	3.71
60	1.047	$\frac{1}{6} = 0.167$	2.92
75	1.309	$\frac{5}{24} = 0.208$	2.45
90	1.571	$\frac{1}{4} = 0.250$	2.14
105	1.833	$\frac{7}{24} = 0.292$	1.93
120	2.094	$\frac{1}{3} = 0.333$	1.77
135	2.356	$\frac{3}{8} = 0.375$	1.64
150	2.618	$\frac{5}{12} = 0.417$	1.54
165	2.880	$\frac{11}{24} = 0.458$	1.47
180	3.142	$\frac{1}{2} = 0.500$	1.40
195	3.403	$\frac{13}{24} = 0.541$	1.35
210	3.665	$\frac{7}{12} = 0.583$	1.30
240	4.189	$\frac{2}{3} = 0.667$	1.23
270	4.712	$\frac{3}{4} = 0.750$	1.18
300	5.236	$\frac{5}{6} = 0.833$	1.14

To illustrate the use of the table: Suppose the force transmitted by a pulley is $P = 500$ pounds and the angle embraced by the belt $\alpha = 105°$. In the table opposite to the value $\alpha = 105°$ we find the value 1.93. Hence $T = P \times 1.93 = 500 \times 1.93$ or $T = 965$ pounds.

We have now developed rules by which the actual strain upon the belt may be determined: we have still to determine the strength of the belt, or, in other words, the amount of material necessary in the belt to safely sustain the given strain. We have said that the strain T upon an endless belt is a tensional strain. If, therefore, we represent by b the breadth of the belt in inches, by δ its thickness, also in inches, and by f the greatest safe-working stress in pounds per square inch, we shall have, for the relation between the strain and the strength, the expression

$$T = b\delta f, \quad \ldots \ldots \quad (49)$$

and consequently $\quad b\delta = \dfrac{T}{f}. \quad \ldots \ldots \quad (50)$

Because of the great variations in the strength of leather the quantity f can be only approximately determined. Experiments and tests upon the strength of leather, be they ever so numerous and carefully made, serve only to impress more strongly upon the mind of the experimenter this unfortunate lack of homogeneity in the substance with which he is dealing. In this predicament he who would investigate the subject of leather belts must be satisfied with an average value taken from a great many widely differing values for his coefficient of strength; and until our manufacturers are able to produce leather which shall be to a reasonable extent uniform, the subject of strength of belting must remain as it is now—the most uncertain and indefinite one with which mechanical men have to deal.

The weakest part of an endless belt is obviously at the joint: the value of the safe-working stress f must therefore be taken for this part. The author has during the last three years tried a great many experiments with the view of obtaining the average strength of laced and riveted joints. These average breaking strengths he has found to be about as follows:

For ordinary single leather-lacing,
        950 pounds per square inch;
For ordinary single rawhide-lacing,
        1000 pounds per square inch;
For good double leather-lacing,
        1200 pounds per square inch;
For good double rawhide-lacing,
        1400 pounds per square inch;
For ordinary riveted joints,
        1750 pounds per square inch.

We may therefore take for our safe-working stress in pounds per square inch the following values:

    Single leather-lacing, $f = 325$;
    Single rawhide-lacing, $f = 350$;
    Double leather-lacing, $f = 375$;
    Double rawhide-lacing, $f = 400$;
    Riveted joints, $f = 575$.

By substituting these values successively in formula (50), we obtain the following formulas:

For single leather-lacing, $\quad b\delta = \dfrac{T}{325}$; . . . . (51)

For single rawhide-lacing, $\quad b\delta = \dfrac{T}{350}$; . . . . (52)

For double leather-lacing, $\quad b\delta = \dfrac{T}{375}$; . . . . (53)

For double rawhide-lacing, $\quad b\delta = \dfrac{T}{400}$; . . . . (54)

For a riveted joints, $\quad b\delta = \dfrac{T}{575}$. . . . . (55)

Example.—Required the width of a leather belt $\frac{1}{4}$ inch thick, which will safely transmit a force of $P = 600$ pounds when laced according to each of the above-mentioned methods, the pulleys over which the belt is to run being of the same diameter—that is, the angle embraced by the belt being $\alpha = 180°$.

From the table on page 90 we have, $T = P \times 1.40 = 600 \times 1.40 = 840$ pounds. From formula (51), therefore, we have

$$b \times \frac{1}{4} = \frac{840}{325}, \quad b = \frac{4 \times 840}{325},$$

or, for single leather-lacing,

From formula (52),

$$b \times \frac{1}{4} = \frac{840}{350}, \quad b = \frac{4 \times 840}{350},$$

or, for single rawhide-lacing,

$$b = 9.6'' = 9\tfrac{38}{64}''.$$

From formula (53),

$$b \times \frac{1}{4} = \frac{840}{375}, \quad b = \frac{4 \times 840}{375},$$

or, for double leather-lacing,

$$b = 8.96'' = 8\tfrac{31}{32}''.$$

From formula (54),

$$b \times \frac{1}{4} = \frac{840}{400}, \quad b = \frac{4 \times 840}{400}$$

or, for double rawhide-lacing,

$$b = 8.40'' = 8\tfrac{13}{32}''.$$

From formula (55),

$$b \times \frac{1}{4} = \frac{840}{575}, \quad b = \frac{4 \times 840}{575}$$

or, for a riveted joint,

$$b = 5.84'' = 5\tfrac{27}{32}''.$$

STRENGTH OF LEATHER BELTS. 95

The following tables of formulas have been calculated from the table on page 90 and formulas (51), (52), (53), (54), and (55), respectively. The above example may be calculated from these tables as follows: We have for our data, $P = 600$ pounds, $\alpha = 180°$, and $\delta = \frac{1}{4}''$. From formula (66), for single leather-lacing,

$$b\delta = 0.00431 \times 600;$$
$$b = 0.00431 \times 600 \times 4 = 10.34''.$$

From formula (82), for single rawhide-lacing,

$$b\delta = 0.004 \times 600;$$
$$b = 0.004 \times 600 \times 4 = 9.60''.$$

From formula (98), for double leather-lacing,

$$b\delta = 0.00373 \times 600;$$
$$b = 0.00373 \times 600 \times 4 = 8.952''.$$

From formula (114), for double rawhide-lacing,

$$b\delta = 0.0035 \times 600;$$
$$b = 0.0035 \times 600 \times 4 = 8.40''.$$

From formula (130), for a riveted joint,

$$b\delta = 0.00243 \times 600;$$
$$b = 0.00243 \times 600 \times 4 = 5.832''.$$

Table of Formulas for Leather Belts over Cast-Iron Pulleys.
Single Leather Lacing.

α in degrees.	α in circular measure.	α in fractions of circumference.	Formula.	No.
30	0.524	$\frac{1}{12}$ = 0.083	$b\delta = 0.01628P$	56
45	0.785	$\frac{1}{8}$ = 0.125	$b\delta = 0.01142P$	57
60	1.047	$\frac{1}{6}$ = 0.167	$b\delta = 0.00898P$	58
75	1.309	$\frac{5}{24}$ = 0.208	$b\delta = 0.00754P$	59
90	1.571	$\frac{1}{4}$ = 0.250	$b\delta = 0.00658P$	60
105	1.833	$\frac{7}{24}$ = 0.292	$b\delta = 0.00594P$	61
120	2.094	$\frac{1}{3}$ = 0.333	$b\delta = 0.00545P$	62
135	2.356	$\frac{3}{8}$ = 0.375	$b\delta = 0.00505P$	63
150	2.618	$\frac{5}{12}$ = 0.417	$b\delta = 0.00474P$	64
165	2.880	$\frac{11}{24}$ = 0.458	$b\delta = 0.00452P$	65
180	3.142	$\frac{1}{2}$ = 0.500	$b\delta = 0.00431P$	66
195	3.403	$\frac{13}{24}$ = 0.541	$b\delta = 0.00415P$	67
210	3.665	$\frac{7}{12}$ = 0.583	$b\delta = 0.00400P$	68
240	4.189	$\frac{2}{3}$ = 0.667	$b\delta = 0.00378P$	69
270	4.712	$\frac{3}{4}$ = 0.750	$b\delta = 0.00363P$	70
300	5.236	$\frac{5}{6}$ = 0.833	$b\delta = 0.00351P$	71

Table of Formulas for Leather Belts over Cast-Iron Pulleys.
Single Rawhide Lacing.

α in degrees.	α in circular measure.	α in fractions of circumference.	Formula.	No.
30	0.524	$\frac{1}{12}$ = 0.083	$b\delta = 0.01511P$	72
45	0.785	$\frac{1}{8}$ = 0.125	$b\delta = 0.01060P$	73
60	1.047	$\frac{1}{6}$ = 0.167	$b\delta = 0.00834P$	74
75	1.309	$\frac{5}{24}$ = 0.208	$b\delta = 0.00700P$	75
90	1.571	$\frac{1}{4}$ = 0.250	$b\delta = 0.00611P$	76
105	1.833	$\frac{7}{24}$ = 0.292	$b\delta = 0.00551P$	77
120	2.094	$\frac{1}{3}$ = 0.333	$b\delta = 0.00506P$	78
135	2.356	$\frac{3}{8}$ = 0.375	$b\delta = 0.00469P$	79
150	2.618	$\frac{5}{12}$ = 0.417	$b\delta = 0.00440P$	80
165	2.880	$\frac{11}{24}$ = 0.458	$b\delta = 0.00420P$	81
180	3.142	$\frac{1}{2}$ = 0.500	$b\delta = 0.00400P$	82
195	3.403	$\frac{13}{24}$ = 0.541	$b\delta = 0.00386P$	83
210	3.665	$\frac{7}{12}$ = 0.583	$b\delta = 0.00371P$	84
240	4.189	$\frac{2}{3}$ = 0.667	$b\delta = 0.00351P$	85
270	4.712	$\frac{3}{4}$ = 0.750	$b\delta = 0.00337P$	86
300	5.236	$\frac{5}{6}$ = 0.833	$b\delta = 0.00326P$	87

STRENGTH OF LEATHER BELTS.

TABLE OF FORMULAS FOR LEATHER BELTS OVER CAST-IRON PULLEYS.
Double Leather-Lacing.

a in degrees.	a in circular measure.	a in fractions of circumference.	Formula.	No.
30	0.524	$\frac{1}{12} = 0.083$	$b\delta = 0.01411 P$	88
45	0.785	$\frac{1}{8} = 0.125$	$b\delta = 0.00989 P$	89
60	1.047	$\frac{1}{6} = 0.167$	$b\delta = 0.00779 P$	90
75	1.309	$\frac{5}{24} = 0.208$	$b\delta = 0.00653 P$	91
90	1.571	$\frac{1}{4} = 0.250$	$b\delta = 0.00571 P$	92
105	1.833	$\frac{7}{24} = 0.292$	$b\delta = 0.00514 P$	93
120	2.094	$\frac{1}{3} = 0.333$	$b\delta = 0.00472 P$	94
135	2.356	$\frac{3}{8} = 0.375$	$b\delta = 0.00437 P$	95
150	2.618	$\frac{5}{12} = 0.417$	$d\delta = 0.00411 P$	96
165	2.880	$\frac{11}{24} = 0.458$	$b\delta = 0.00392 P$	97
180	3.142	$\frac{1}{2} = 0.500$	$b\delta = 0.00373 P$	98
195	3.403	$\frac{13}{24} = 0.541$	$b\delta = 0.00360 P$	99
210	3.665	$\frac{7}{12} = 0.583$	$b\delta = 0.00347 P$	100
240	4.189	$\frac{2}{3} = 0.667$	$b\delta = 0.00328 P$	101
270	4.712	$\frac{3}{4} = 0.750$	$b\delta = 0.00315 P$	102
300	5.236	$\frac{5}{6} = 0.833$	$b\delta = 0.00304 P$	103

TABLE OF FORMULAS FOR LEATHER BELTS OVER CAST-IRON PULLEYS.
Double Rawhide-Lacing.

a in degrees.	a in circular measure.	a in fractions of circumference.	Formula.	No.
30	0.524	$\frac{1}{12} = 0.083$	$b\delta = 0.01323 P$	104
45	0.785	$\frac{1}{8} = 0.125$	$b\delta = 0.00928 P$	105
60	1.047	$\frac{1}{6} = 0.167$	$b\delta = 0.00730 P$	106
75	1.309	$\frac{5}{24} = 0.208$	$b\delta = 0.00613 P$	107
90	1.571	$\frac{1}{4} = 0.250$	$b\delta = 0.00535 P$	108
105	1.833	$\frac{7}{24} = 0.292$	$b\delta = 0.00483 P$	109
120	2.094	$\frac{1}{3} = 0.333$	$b\delta = 0.00443 P$	110
135	2.356	$\frac{3}{8} = 0.375$	$b\delta = 0.00410 P$	111
150	2.618	$\frac{5}{12} = 0.417$	$b\delta = 0.00385 P$	112
165	2.880	$\frac{11}{24} = 0.458$	$b\delta = 0.00368 P$	113
180	3.142	$\frac{1}{2} = 0.500$	$b\delta = 0.00350 P$	114
195	3.403	$\frac{13}{24} = 0.541$	$b\delta = 0.00338 P$	115
210	3.665	$\frac{7}{12} = 0.583$	$b\delta = 0.00325 P$	116
240	4.189	$\frac{2}{3} = 0.667$	$b\delta = 0.00308 P$	117
270	4.712	$\frac{3}{4} = 0.750$	$b\delta = 0.00295 P$	118
300	5.236	$\frac{5}{6} = 0.833$	$b\delta = 0.00285 P$	119

TABLE OF FORMULAS FOR LEATHER BELTS OVER CAST-IRON PULLEYS.
Riveted Joint.

a in degrees.	a in circular measure.	a in fractions of circumference.	Formula.	No.
30	0.524	$\frac{1}{12} = 0.083$	$b\delta = 0.00920 P$	120
45	0.785	$\frac{1}{8} = 0.125$	$b\delta = 0.00645 P$	121
60	1.047	$\frac{1}{6} = 0.167$	$b\delta = 0.00508 P$	122
75	1.309	$\frac{5}{24} = 0.208$	$b\delta = 0.00426 P$	123
90	1.571	$\frac{1}{4} = 0.250$	$b\delta = 0.00372 P$	124
105	1.833	$\frac{7}{24} = 0.292$	$b\delta = 0.00336 P$	125
120	2.094	$\frac{1}{3} = 0.333$	$b\delta = 0.00308 P$	126
135	2.356	$\frac{3}{8} = 0.375$	$b\delta = 0.00285 P$	127
150	2.618	$\frac{5}{12} = 0.417$	$b\delta = 0.00268 P$	128
165	2.880	$\frac{11}{24} = 0.458$	$b\delta = 0.00256 P$	129
180	3.142	$\frac{1}{2} = 0.500$	$b\delta = 0.00243 P$	130
195	3.403	$\frac{13}{24} = 0.541$	$b\delta = 0.00235 P$	131
210	3.665	$\frac{7}{12} = 0.583$	$b\delta = 0.00226 P$	132
240	4.189	$\frac{2}{3} = 0.667$	$b\delta = 0.00214 P$	133
270	4.712	$\frac{3}{4} = 0.750$	$b\delta = 0.00205 P$	134
300	5.236	$\frac{5}{6} = 0.833$	$b\delta = 0.00198 P$	135

STRENGTH OF LEATHER BELTS.

Often, when we know the horse-power to be transmitted, it is convenient to calculate belt-widths from this, without finding the circumferential force. From formula (20) we have, when v_m represents the velocity in feet *per minute*, and H the horse-power,

$$P = \frac{33000H}{v_m}; \quad \ldots \ldots \quad (136)$$

and from formula (22), when v represents the velocity in feet *per second*,

$$P = \frac{550H}{v}. \quad \ldots \ldots \quad (137)$$

By substituting this last value of P in formulas (56) to (135), and reducing, we may obtain the following tables of formulas for calculating belt-widths from the horse-power transmitted and the velocity in feet per second:*

---

* By substituting the value of P given in formula (136) in formulas (56) to (135), we may obtain formulas for belt-widths in terms of the horse-power and velocity in feet *per minute*. For example, formula (68) gives $b\delta = 0.004 \frac{33000H}{v_m} = 132 \frac{H}{v_m}$. Such formulas are, however, seldom needed in practice, the velocity being almost always taken in feet per second.

TABLE OF FORMULAS FOR LEATHER-BELTS OVER CAST-IRON PULLEYS.

Single Leather-Lacing.

a in degrees.	a in circular measure.	a in fractions of circumference.	Formula.	No.
30	0.524	$\frac{1}{12} = 0.083$	$b\delta = 8.954\frac{H}{v}$	138
45	0.785	$\frac{1}{8} = 0.125$	$b\delta = 6.281\frac{H}{v}$	139
60	1.047	$\frac{1}{6} = 0.167$	$b\delta = 4.939\frac{H}{v}$	140
75	1.309	$\frac{5}{24} = 0.208$	$b\delta = 4.147\frac{H}{v}$	141
90	1.571	$\frac{1}{4} = 0.250$	$b\delta = 3.619\frac{H}{v}$	142
105	1.833	$\frac{7}{24} = 0.292$	$b\delta = 3.267\frac{H}{v}$	143
120	2.094	$\frac{1}{3} = 0.333$	$b\delta = 2.998\frac{H}{v}$	144
135	2.356	$\frac{3}{8} = 0.375$	$b\delta = 2.778\frac{H}{v}$	145
150	2.618	$\frac{5}{12} = 0.417$	$b\delta = 2.607\frac{H}{v}$	146
165	2.880	$\frac{11}{24} = 0.458$	$b\delta = 2.486\frac{H}{v}$	147
180	3.142	$\frac{1}{2} = 0.500$	$b\delta = 2.371\frac{H}{v}$	148
195	3.403	$\frac{13}{24} = 0.541$	$b\delta = 2.283\frac{H}{v}$	149
210	3.665	$\frac{7}{12} = 0.583$	$b\delta = 2.200\frac{H}{v}$	150
240	4.189	$\frac{2}{3} = 0.667$	$b\delta = 2.079\frac{H}{v}$	151
270	4.712	$\frac{3}{4} = 0.750$	$b\delta = 1.997\frac{H}{v}$	152
300	5.236	$\frac{5}{6} = 0.833$	$b\delta = 1.931\frac{H}{v}$	153

Table of Formulas for Leather-Belts over Cast-Iron Pulleys.

Single Rawhide-Lacing.

a in degrees.	a in circular measure.	a in fractions of circumference.	Formula.	No.
30	0.524	$\frac{1}{12} = 0.083$	$b\delta = 8.311\frac{H}{v}$	154
45	0.785	$\frac{1}{8} = 0.125$	$b\delta = 5.830\frac{H}{v}$	155
60	1.047	$\frac{1}{6} = 0.167$	$b\delta = 4.587\frac{H}{v}$	156
75	1.309	$\frac{5}{24} = 0.208$	$b\delta = 3.850\frac{H}{v}$	157
90	1.571	$\frac{1}{4} = 0.250$	$b\delta = 3.361\frac{H}{v}$	158
105	1.833	$\frac{7}{24} = 0.292$	$b\delta = 3.031\frac{H}{v}$	159
120	2.094	$\frac{1}{3} = 0.333$	$b\delta = 2.783\frac{H}{v}$	160
135	2.356	$\frac{3}{8} = 0.375$	$b\delta = 2.580\frac{H}{v}$	161
150	2.618	$\frac{5}{12} = 0.417$	$b\delta = 2.420\frac{H}{v}$	162
165	2.880	$\frac{11}{24} = 0.458$	$b\delta = 2.310\frac{H}{v}$	163
180	3.142	$\frac{1}{2} = 0.500$	$b\delta = 2.200\frac{H}{v}$	164
195	3.403	$\frac{13}{24} = 0.541$	$b\delta = 2.123\frac{H}{v}$	165
210	3.665	$\frac{7}{12} = 0.583$	$b\delta = 2.041\frac{H}{v}$	166
240	4.187	$\frac{2}{3} = 0.667$	$b\delta = 1.931\frac{H}{v}$	167
270	4.712	$\frac{3}{4} = 0.750$	$b\delta = 1.854\frac{H}{v}$	168
300	5.236	$\frac{5}{6} = 0.833$	$b\delta = 1.793\frac{H}{v}$	169

TABLE OF FORMULAS FOR LEATHER BELTS OVER CAST-IRON PULLEYS.

Double Leather-Lacing.

a in degrees.	a in circular measure.	a in fractions of circumference.	Formula.	No.
30	0.524	$\frac{1}{12} = 0.083$	$b\delta = 7.761\frac{H}{v}$	170
45	0.785	$\frac{1}{8} = 0.125$	$b\delta = 5.440\frac{H}{v}$	171
60	1.047	$\frac{1}{6} = 0.167$	$b\delta = 4.285\frac{H}{v}$	172
75	1.309	$\frac{5}{24} = 0.208$	$b\delta = 3.592\frac{H}{v}$	173
90	1.571	$\frac{1}{4} = 0.250$	$b\delta = 3.141\frac{H}{v}$	174
105	1.833	$\frac{7}{24} = 0.292$	$b\delta = 2.827\frac{H}{v}$	175
120	2.094	$\frac{1}{3} = 0.333$	$b\delta = 2.596\frac{H}{v}$	176
135	2.356	$\frac{3}{8} = 0.375$	$b\delta = 2.404\frac{H}{v}$	177
150	2.618	$\frac{5}{12} = 0.417$	$b\delta = 2.261\frac{H}{v}$	178
165	2.880	$\frac{11}{24} = 0.458$	$b\delta = 2.156\frac{H}{v}$	179
180	3.142	$\frac{1}{2} = 0.500$	$b\delta = 2.052\frac{H}{v}$	180
195	3.403	$\frac{13}{24} = 0.541$	$b\delta = 1.980\frac{H}{v}$	181
210	3.665	$\frac{7}{12} = 0.583$	$b\delta = 1.909\frac{H}{v}$	182
240	4.189	$\frac{2}{3} = 0.667$	$b\delta = 1.804\frac{H}{v}$	183
270	4.712	$\frac{3}{4} = 0.750$	$b\delta = 1.733\frac{H}{v}$	184
300	5.236	$\frac{5}{6} = 0.833$	$b\delta = 1.672\frac{H}{v}$	185

Table of Formulas for Leather Belts over Cast-iron Pulleys.

Double Rawhide-Lacing.

α in degrees.	α in circular measure.	α in fractions of circumference.	Formula.	No.
30	0.524	$\frac{1}{12} = 0.083$	$b\delta = 7.277\frac{H}{v}$	186
45	0.785	$\frac{1}{8} = 0.125$	$b\delta = 5.104\frac{H}{v}$	187
60	1.047	$\frac{1}{6} = 0.167$	$b\delta = 4.015\frac{H}{v}$	188
75	1.309	$\frac{5}{24} = 0.208$	$b\delta = 3.372\frac{H}{v}$	189
90	1.571	$\frac{1}{4} = 0.250$	$b\delta = 2.943\frac{H}{v}$	190
105	1.833	$\frac{7}{24} = 0.292$	$b\delta = 2.657\frac{H}{v}$	191
120	2.094	$\frac{1}{3} = 0.333$	$b\delta = 2.437\frac{H}{v}$	192
135	2.356	$\frac{3}{8} = 0.375$	$b\delta = 2.225\frac{H}{v}$	193
150	2.618	$\frac{5}{12} = 0.417$	$b\delta = 2.118\frac{H}{v}$	194
165	2.880	$\frac{11}{24} = 0.458$	$b\delta = 2.024\frac{H}{v}$	195
180	3.142	$\frac{1}{2} = 0.500$	$b\delta = 1.925\frac{H}{v}$	196
195	3.403	$\frac{13}{24} = 0.541$	$b\delta = 1.859\frac{H}{v}$	197
210	3.665	$\frac{7}{12} = 0.583$	$b\delta = 1.788\frac{H}{v}$	198
240	4.189	$\frac{2}{3} = 0.667$	$b\delta = 1.694\frac{H}{v}$	199
270	4.712	$\frac{3}{4} = 0.750$	$b\delta = 1.623\frac{H}{v}$	200
300	5.236	$\frac{5}{6} = 0.833$	$b\delta = 1.568\frac{H}{v}$	201

TABLE OF FORMULAS FOR LEATHER BELTS OVER CAST-IRON PULLEYS.

Riveted Joint.

a in degrees.	a in circular measure.	a in fractions of circumference.	Formula.	No.
30	0.524	$\frac{1}{12} = 0.083$	$b\delta = 5.060\frac{H}{v}$	202
45	0.785	$\frac{1}{8} = 0.125$	$b\delta = 3.548\frac{H}{v}$	203
60	1.047	$\frac{1}{6} = 0.167$	$b\delta = 2.794\frac{H}{v}$	204
75	1.309	$\frac{5}{24} = 0.208$	$b\delta = 2.343\frac{H}{v}$	205
90	1.571	$\frac{1}{4} = 0.250$	$b\delta = 2.046\frac{H}{v}$	206
105	1.833	$\frac{7}{24} = 0.292$	$b\delta = 1.848\frac{H}{v}$	207
120	2.094	$\frac{1}{3} = 0.333$	$b\delta = 1.694\frac{H}{v}$	208
135	2.356	$\frac{3}{8} = 0.375$	$b\delta = 1.568\frac{H}{v}$	209
150	2.618	$\frac{5}{12} = 0.417$	$b\delta = 1.474\frac{H}{v}$	210
165	2.880	$\frac{11}{24} = 0.458$	$b\delta = 1.408\frac{H}{v}$	211
180	3.142	$\frac{1}{2} = 0.500$	$b\delta = 1.337\frac{H}{v}$	212
195	3.403	$\frac{13}{24} = 0.541$	$b\delta = 1.293\frac{H}{v}$	213
210	3.665	$\frac{7}{12} = 0.583$	$b\delta = 1.243\frac{H}{v}$	214
240	4.189	$\frac{2}{3} = 0.667$	$b\delta = 1.177\frac{H}{v}$	215
270	4.712	$\frac{3}{4} = 0.750$	$b\delta = 1.128\frac{H}{v}$	216
300	5.236	$\frac{5}{6} = 0.833$	$b\delta = 1.089\frac{H}{v}$	217

STRENGTH OF LEATHER BELTS.

Example.—Required the width for a leather belt $\frac{5}{16}$ inch thick which will transmit a force of 15 horse-power at a velocity of 10 feet per second, the angle α being 105°. In this case $\frac{H}{v} = \frac{15}{10} = 1.5$ and $\delta = \frac{5}{16}$. Hence from formula (143) we have

$$b \times \frac{5}{16} = 3.267 \frac{15}{10} = 3.267 \times 1.5.$$

Therefore $\quad b = 3.267 \times 1.5 \times \frac{16}{5},$

or, for single leather-lacing,

$$b = 15.682'' = 15\tfrac{11}{16}'' \text{ nearly.}$$

From formula (159),

$$b \times \frac{5}{16} = 3.031 \times 1.5,$$

$$b = 3.031 \times 1.5 \times \frac{16}{5},$$

or, for single rawhide-lacing,

$$b = 14.549'' = 14\tfrac{35}{64}''.$$

From formula (175),

$$b \times \frac{5}{16} = 2.827 \times 1.5,$$

$$b = 2.827 \times 1.5 \times \frac{16}{5},$$

or, for double leather-lacing,

$$b = 13.570'' = 13\tfrac{37}{64}''.$$

From formula (191),

$$b \times \tfrac{5}{16} = 2.657 \times 1.5,$$

$$b = 2.657 \times 1.5 \times \tfrac{16}{5},$$

or, for double rawhide-lacing,

$$b = 12.754'' = 12\tfrac{3}{4}''.$$

From formula (207),

$$b \times \tfrac{5}{16} = 1.848 \times 1.5,$$

$$b = 1.848 \times 1.5 \times \tfrac{16}{5},$$

or, for a riveted joint,

$$b = 8.870'' = 8\tfrac{7}{8}''.$$

In the majority of cases leather belts (single) are approximately $\tfrac{7}{32}$ inch thick. Very often the arc embraced by the belt is 180°—that is, the pulleys are equal; and, perhaps, more often the arc α is about $135° = \tfrac{3}{8}$ the circumference. For these cases, then, we may obtain formulas which will prove very useful in practice.

STRENGTH OF LEATHER BELTS.

By substituting $\delta = \frac{7}{32}$ inch in formulas (66), (82), (98), (114), (130), (148), (164), (180), (196), and (212), successively, and reducing, we obtain the following formulas:

When $\alpha = 180°$ and $\delta = \frac{7}{32}$ inch,

Single leather-lacing,	$b = 0.0197P$;	(218)
Single rawhide-lacing,	$b = 0.0183P$;	(219)
Double leather-lacing,	$b = 0.0171P$;	(220)
Double rawhide-lacing,	$b = 0.0160P$;	(221)
Riveted joint,	$b = 0.0111P$.	(222)

Single leather-lacing,	$b = 10.839\dfrac{H}{v}$;	. . . (223)
Single rawhide-lacing,	$b = 10.057\dfrac{H}{v}$;	. . . (224)
Double leather-lacing,	$b = 9.381\dfrac{H}{v}$;	. . . (225)
Double rawhide-lacing,	$b = 8.800\dfrac{H}{v}$;	. . . (226)
Riveted joint	$b = 6.112\dfrac{H}{v}$.	. . . (227)

By substituting $\delta = \frac{7}{32}$ inch in formulas (63), (79), (95), (111), (127), (145), (161), (177), (193), and (209), successively, we obtain the following formulas:

When $\alpha = 135°$ and $\delta = \frac{7}{32}$ inch,

Single leather-lacing,	$b = 0.0231P$;	(228)
Single rawhide-lacing,	$b = 0.0214P$;	(229)
Double leather-lacing,	$b = 0.0200P$;	(230)
Double rawhide-lacing,	$b = 0.0187P$;	(231)
Riveted joint,	$b = 0.0130P$.	(232)

Single leather-lacing, $b = 12.699 \dfrac{H}{v}$; . . . (233)

Single rawhide-lacing, $b = 11.794 \dfrac{H}{v}$; . . . (234)

Double leather-lacing, $b = 10.990 \dfrac{H}{v}$; . . . (235)

Double rawhide-lacing, $b = 10.171 \dfrac{H}{v}$; . . . (236)

Riveted joint, $b = 7.168 \dfrac{H}{v}$. . . . (237)

Example.—Required the width of a $\tfrac{7}{32}$-inch leather belt, single leather-lacing, to transmit a force of 600 pounds, the pulleys being equal.

From formula (218) we have

$$b = 0.0197 \times 600,$$

$$b = 11.82'' = 11\tfrac{53}{64}''.$$

Example.—Required the width of a $\tfrac{7}{32}$-inch leather belt, single rawhide-lacing, to transmit a force of 15 horse-power at a velocity of 10 feet per second, the pulleys being equal.

From formula (224) we have

$$b = 10.057 \times \dfrac{15}{10},$$

$$b = 15.085'' = 15\tfrac{3}{32}''.$$

Example.—Required the width of a $\tfrac{7}{32}$-inch leather belt, double rawhide-lacing, to transmit a force of 600 pounds, the arc embraced by the belt being about 135°.

From formula (231) we have

$$b = 0.0187 \times 600,$$

$$b = 11.22'' = 11\tfrac{7}{32}''.$$

Example.—Required the width of a $\tfrac{7}{32}$-inch leather belt, riveted joint, to transmit a force of 15 horse-power at a velocity of 10 feet per second, the arc embraced by the belt being about 135°.

From formula (237) we have

$$b = 7.168 \times \frac{15}{10},$$

$$b = 10.75'' = 10\tfrac{3}{4}''.$$

The following tables give the forces in pounds (P), and the values of the horse-power divided by the velocity in feet per second $\left(\dfrac{H}{v}\right)$, corresponding to different widths of $\tfrac{7}{32}$-inch leather belts from 1 inch to 30 inches for $\alpha = 180°$ and $\alpha = 135°$ for each of the five methods of joint-fastening given above. For a great many cases which arise in practice the tables will prove convenient and labor-saving.

TABLE OF WIDTHS OF LEATHER BELTS OVER CAST-IRON PULLEYS, WHEN $\alpha = 180°$ AND $\delta = \frac{7}{32}''$. From Formulas (218)–(222).

Width in inches.	P, single leather-lacing.	P, single rawhide-lacing.	P, double leather-lacing.	P, double rawhide-lacing.	P, riveted joints.	No.
1	50.76	54.64	58.48	62.50	90.09	1
1½	76.14	81.97	87.72	93.75	135.14	2
2	101.52	109.29	116.96	125.00	180.18	3
2½	126.90	136.61	146.20	156.25	225.23	4
3	152.28	163.93	175.44	187.50	270.27	5
3½	177.66	191.26	204.68	218.75	315.32	6
4	203.05	218.58	233.92	250.00	360.36	7
4½	228.43	245.90	263.16	281.25	405.41	8
5	252.71	273.22	292.40	312.50	450.45	9
5¼	279.19	300.46	321.64	343.75	495.50	10
6	304.57	327.87	350.88	375.00	540.54	11
7	355.33	382.51	409.36	437.50	630.63	12
8	406.09	437.16	467.84	500.00	720.72	13
9	456.85	491.80	526.32	562.50	810.81	14
10	507.61	546.45	584.80	625.00	900.90	15
11	558.38	601.09	643.27	687.50	990.99	16
12	608.57	655.74	701.75	750.00	1081.08	17
14	710.00	765.03	818.71	875.00	1261.26	18
16	812.18	874.32	935.67	1000.00	1441.44	19
18	913.71	983.61	1052.63	1125.00	1621.62	20
20	1015.22	1092.90	1169.59	1250.00	1801.80	21
22	1116.75	1202.19	1286.55	1375.00	1981.98	22
24	1218.27	1311.48	1403.51	1500.00	2162.16	23
26	1319.79	1400.77	1520.47	1625.00	2342.34	24
28	1421.31	1530.05	1637.43	1750.00	2522.52	25
30	1522.84	1639.34	1754.44	1875.00	2702.70	26

TABLE OF WIDTHS OF LEATHER BELTS OVER CAST-IRON PULLEYS, WHEN $\alpha = 180°$ AND $\delta = \frac{7}{88}''$. From Formulas (223)–(227).

Width in inches.	$\frac{H}{v}$, single leather-lacing.	$\frac{H}{v}$, single rawhide-lacing.	$\frac{H}{v}$, double leather-lacing.	$\frac{H}{v}$, double rawhide-lacing.	$\frac{H}{v}$, riveted joints.	No.
1	0.0923	0.0994	0.1066	0.1136	0.1636	1
1½	0.1384	0.1491	0.1599	0.1705	0.2454	2
2	0.1845	0.1989	0.2132	0.2273	0.3272	3
2½	0.2307	0.2486	0.2665	0.2841	0.4090	4
3	0.2768	0.2983	0.3198	0.3409	0.4908	5
3½	0.3229	0.3480	0.3731	0.3977	0.5726	6
4	0.3690	0.3977	0.4264	0.4546	0.6544	7
4½	0.4152	0.4474	0.4797	0.5114	0.7362	8
5	0.4613	0.4972	0.5330	0.5682	0.8181	9
5½	0.5074	0.5469	0.5863	0.6250	0.8999	10
6	0.5536	0.5966	0.6396	0.6818	0.9817	11
7	0.6458	0.6960	0.7462	0.7955	1.1453	12
8	0.7381	0.7954	0.8528	0.9091	1.3089	13
9	0.8303	0.8949	0.9594	1.0228	1.4725	14
10	0.9226	0.9943	1.0659	1.1364	1.6361	15
11	1.0149	1.0937	1.1726	1.2500	1.7997	16
12	1.1071	1.1932	1.2792	1.3637	1.9633	17
14	1.2916	1.3920	1.4924	1.5910	2.2905	18
16	1.4762	1.5909	1.7056	1.8182	2.6178	19
18	1.6607	1.7897	1.9188	2.0455	2.9450	20
20	1.8452	1.9886	2.1318	2.2728	3.2722	21
22	2.0297	2.1875	2.3452	2.5001	3.5994	22
24	2.2142	2.3863	2.5584	2.7274	3.9266	23
26	2.3988	2.5852	2.7716	2.9546	4.2539	24
28	2.5833	2.7840	2.9848	3.1819	4.5811	25
30	2.7678	2.9829	3.1977	3.4092	4.9083	26

TABLE OF WIDTHS OF LEATHER BELTS OVER CAST-IRON PULLEYS, WHEN $\alpha = 135°$ AND $\delta = \frac{7}{88}''$. From Formulas (228)–(232).

Width in inches.	P, single leather-lacing.	P, single rawhide-lacing.	P, double leather-lacing.	P, double rawhide-lacing.	P, riveted joints.	No.
1	43.29	46.73	50.00	53.48	76.92	1
1½	64.94	70.09	75.00	80.21	115.38	2
2	86.58	93.46	100.00	106.95	153.85	3
2½	108.23	116.82	125.00	133.69	192.31	4
3	129.87	140.19	150.00	160.43	230.77	5
3½	151.51	163.55	175.00	187.17	269.23	6
4	173.16	186.92	200.00	213.90	307.69	7
4½	194.81	210.28	225.00	240.64	346.15	8
5	216.45	233.65	250.00	267.38	384.62	9
5½	238.10	257.01	275.00	294.12	423.08	10
6	259.74	280.37	300.00	320.86	461.54	11
7	303.03	327.10	350.00	374.33	538.46	12
8	346.32	373.83	400.00	427.81	615.38	13
9	389.61	420.56	450.00	481.28	692.31	14
10	432.90	467.29	500.00	534.76	769.23	15
11	476.19	514.02	550.00	588.24	846.15	16
12	519.48	560.75	600.00	641.71	923.08	17
14	606.06	654.21	700.00	748.66	1076.92	18
16	692.64	747.66	800.00	845.62	1230.77	19
18	779.22	841.12	900.00	962.57	1384.61	20
20	865.80	934.58	1000.00	1069.52	1538.46	21
22	952.38	1028.04	1100.00	1176.47	1692.31	22
24	1038.96	1121.50	1200.00	1283.42	1846.15	23
26	1125.54	1214.95	1300.00	1380.38	2000.00	24
28	1212.12	1308.41	1400.00	1497.33	2153.84	25
30	1298.70	1401.87	1500.00	1604.28	2307.69	26

STRENGTH OF LEATHER BELTS.

TABLE OF WIDTHS OF LEATHER BELTS OVER CAST-IRON PULLEYS, WHEN $\alpha = 135°$ AND $\delta = \frac{7}{32}''$. From Formulas (233)–(237).

Width in inches.	$\frac{H}{v}$, single leather-lacing.	$\frac{H}{v}$, single rawhide-lacing.	$\frac{H}{v}$, double leather-lacing.	$\frac{H}{v}$, double rawhide-lacing.	$\frac{H}{v}$, riveted joints.	No.
1	0.0787	0.0879	0.0910	0.0983	0.1395	1
1½	0.1181	0.1272	0.1365	0.1475	0.2093	2
2	0.1575	0.1696	0.1820	0.1966	0.2790	3
2½	0.1969	0.2120	0.2275	0.2458	0.3488	4
3	0.2362	0.2544	0.2730	0.2950	0.4185	5
3½	0.2756	0.2968	0.3185	0.3441	0.4883	6
4	0.3150	0.3392	0.3640	0.3933	0.5580	7
4½	0.3544	0.3816	0.4095	0.4424	0.6278	8
5	0.3937	0.4239	0.4550	0.4916	0.6976	9
5½	0.4331	0.4663	0.5004	0.5108	0.7673	10
6	0.4725	0.5087	0.5459	0.5899	0.8371	11
7	0.5512	0.5935	0.6396	0.6882	0.9766	12
8	0.6300	0.6783	0.7279	0.7866	1.1161	13
9	0.7087	0.7631	0.8189	0.8849	1.2556	14
10	0.7875	0.8479	0.9099	0.9832	1.3951	15
11	0.8662	0.9327	1.0009	1.0815	1.5346	16
12	0.9450	1.0175	1.0919	1.1799	1.6741	17
14	1.1024	1.1870	1.2739	1.3765	1.9532	18
16	1.2600	1.3566	1.4558	1.5731	2.2322	19
18	1.4174	1.5262	1.6378	1.7698	2.5112	20
20	1.5749	1.6958	1.8198	1.9664	2.7902	21
22	1.7324	1.8654	2.0018	2.1630	3.0692	22
24	1.8900	2.0349	2.1838	2.3597	3.3482	23
26	2.0475	2.2045	2.3657	2.5563	3.6273	24
28	2.2048	2.3741	2.5477	2.7530	3.9063	25
30	2.3623	2.5676	2.7297	2.9496	4.1853	26

Example.—Required the force in pounds which can be safely transmitted by a leather belt 20 inches wide and $\frac{7}{32}$ inch thick, running over two pulleys of equal diameters ($\alpha = 180°$), the joint being fastened by a double rawhide-lacing.

In the table on page 110, column of belt-widths, line 21, we find our width of 20 inches, and corresponding to this, in the column for double rawhide-lacing, we find the required force $P = 1250$ pounds.

Example.—Required the width of a leather belt $\frac{7}{32}$ inch thick, which will safely transmit a force of 1000 pounds running over two pulleys of equal diameters, the fastening being a riveted joint.

In the table on page 110, column for riveted joints, line 17, we find $P = 1081.08$ pounds;—the nearest value, not less than 1000 pounds,—and, in the column for belt-widths, we find the value corresponding to $P = 1081.08$, $b = 12$ inches.

Example.—Required the horse-power which can be safely transmitted by a leather belt 12 inches wide and $\frac{7}{32}$ inch thick, running over two pulleys of equal diameters at a velocity of 15 feet per second, the fastening being a single rawhide-lacing.

In the table on page 111, column of belt-widths, line 17, we have $b = 12$ inches, and, in the column for single rawhide-lacing, the corresponding value

$$\frac{H}{v} = 1.1932.$$

Hence $\quad \dfrac{H}{15} = 1.1932, \quad H = 15 \times 1.1932,$

or $\quad H = 17.90.$

Example.—Required the velocity at which a leather belt 12 inches wide and $\frac{7}{32}$ inch thick can be driven over two pulleys of equal diameters, in order to transmit a force of 17.90 horse-power, the fastening being a single rawhide-lacing.

In the table on page 111, column for single rawhide-lacing, we find, corresponding to a belt-width of 12 inches,

$$\frac{H}{v} = 1.1932.$$

Consequently $\frac{17.90}{v} = 1.1932$, $v = \frac{17.90}{1.1932}$,

or $\qquad v = 15$ feet per second.

Example.—Given the data $\alpha = 135°$, $\delta = \frac{7}{32}$ inch, $H = 30$, $v = 15$, double leather-lacing, required the belt-width. In this case

$$\frac{H}{v} = \frac{30}{15} = 2.$$

The table on page 113, column for double leather-lacing, line 22, gives

$$\frac{H}{v} = 2.0018,$$

and a corresponding belt-width of $b = 22$ inches.

§ 11. *Leather Belts over Leather-covered Pulleys.*

As we have demonstrated in the foregoing pages, the average leather belt will not transmit a force equal to its strength, for the reason that it will slip upon its pulley before it will break. If we can conveniently increase the adhesion between the belt and pulley,—i.e.,

vent slipping, the belt can be made to do more work without increasing its size. Various methods have been from time to time proposed for obtaining a greater coefficient of friction, such as coating the pulley-faces with gum, rosin, etc.; but these methods have more often than otherwise proved useless, from the fact that the belt is soon rendered stiff and clumsy by the substance placed upon the face of the pulley. Probably the best of all contrivances in use for this purpose is the pulley with a leather-covered face. The leather is easily fastened securely upon the pulley, and we have then practically a leather belt running over a leather pulley. A series of carefully tried experiments has given the coefficient of friction for leather belts over leather-covered pulleys equal to 0.45—0.05 greater than that for leather belts over cast-iron pulleys.*

If we substitute $\varphi = 0.45$ successively in formulas (40), (41), and (42), and reduce, we shall obtain for leather belts over leather-covered pulleys the following expressions:

$$\log \frac{T}{t} = 0.1953\alpha; \quad \ldots \quad (238)$$

when α is expressed in circular measure,

$$\log \frac{T}{t} = 0.00341\alpha; \quad \ldots \quad (239)$$

---

* Reuleaux says: "For a covering entirely new the value of $\frac{T}{t}$ is between 6 and 7; after some service this value decreases, but still does not become less than 4 to 5; the arc embraced by the belt being equal to π. The smaller value, i.e., $\frac{T}{t} = 4$, corresponds to 0.44 for the coefficient of friction." See also Appendix I.

when α is expressed in degrees,

$$\log \frac{T}{t} = 1.228\alpha; \quad \ldots \ldots \quad (240)$$

when α is expressed in fractions of the circumference.

The following table, calculated from the above formulas, gives values of $\frac{T}{t}$ for different values of α from 30° to 300°. The arrangement is similar to that of the table on page 88.

TABLE OF TENSIONS FOR LEATHER BELTS OVER LEATHER-COVERED PULLEYS.

	$\alpha =$		$\frac{T}{t} =$
In degrees.	In circular measure.	In fractions of circumference.	
30	0.524	$\frac{1}{12} = 0.083$	1.266
45	0.785	$\frac{1}{8} = 0.125$	1.424
60	1.047	$\frac{1}{6} = 0.167$	1.601
75	1.309	$\frac{5}{24} = 0.208$	1.802
90	1.571	$\frac{1}{4} = 0.250$	2.027
105	1.833	$\frac{7}{24} = 0.292$	2.281
120	2.094	$\frac{1}{3} = 0.333$	2.566
135	2.356	$\frac{3}{8} = 0.375$	2.886
150	2.618	$\frac{5}{12} = 0.417$	3.247
165	2.880	$\frac{11}{24} = 0.458$	3.653
180	3.142	$\frac{1}{2} = 0.500$	4.110
195	3.403	$\frac{13}{24} = 0.541$	4.623
210	3.665	$\frac{7}{12} = 0.583$	5.201
240	4.189	$\frac{2}{3} = 0.667$	6.583
270	4.712	$\frac{3}{4} = 0.750$	8.331
300	5.236	$\frac{5}{6} = 0.833$	12.655

By substituting the successive values of $\frac{T}{t}$ from the above table in formula (48), we obtain the following table, similar to the one on page 90:

TABLE OF GREATEST TENSION FOR LEATHER BELTS OVER LEATHER-COVERED PULLEYS.

In degrees.	$\alpha =$ In circular measure.	$\alpha =$ In fractions of circumference.	$T = P \times$
30	0.524	$\frac{1}{12} = 0.083$	4.76
45	0.785	$\frac{1}{8} = 0.125$	3.36
60	1.047	$\frac{1}{6} = 0.167$	2.66
75	1.309	$\frac{5}{24} = 0.208$	2.25
90	1.571	$\frac{1}{4} = 0.250$	1.97
105	1.833	$\frac{7}{24} = 0.292$	1.79
120	2.094	$\frac{1}{3} = 0.333$	1.64
135	2.356	$\frac{3}{8} = 0.375$	1.53
150	2.618	$\frac{5}{12} = 0.417$	1.44
165	2.880	$\frac{11}{24} = 0.458$	1.38
180	3.142	$\frac{1}{2} = 0.500$	1.32
195	3.403	$\frac{13}{24} = 0.541$	1.28
210	3.665	$\frac{7}{12} = 0.583$	1.24
240	4.189	$\frac{2}{3} = 0.667$	1.18
270	4.712	$\frac{3}{4} = 0.750$	1.14
300	5.236	$\frac{5}{6} = 0.833$	1.09

Example.—A leather belt running over a leather-covered pulley transmits a force of 500 pounds. It is required to determine the greatest tension on the belt, assuming that the belt embraces $\frac{2}{3}$ the circumference of the pulley. From the table we find, corresponding to $\alpha = \frac{2}{3}$ the circumference,

$$T = P \times 1.18 = 500 \times 1.18,$$

or $\quad T = 590$ pounds.

Example.—The greatest tension on a leather belt, running over a leather-covered pulley and embracing $\frac{1}{2}$ the circumference, is $T = 792$ pounds. Required the force in pounds which it can transmit. The table gives as the greatest tension corresponding to $\alpha = \frac{1}{2}$ the circumference. Hence

$$792 = P \times 1.32, \qquad P = \frac{792}{1.32};$$

or $\qquad P = 600$ pounds.

By substituting the values of T from the above table successively in formulas (51), (52), (53), (54), and (55), the following tables of formulas have been obtained.

The application of these formulas will be easily understood from the explanation of the similar tables on pages 96–98.

TABLE OF FORMULAS FOR LEATHER BELTS OVER LEATHER-COVERED PULLEYS.

Single Leather-Lacing.

α in degrees.	α in circular measure.	α in fractions of circumference.	Formula.	No.
30	0.524	$\frac{1}{12}$ = 0.083	$b\delta = 0.01464P$	241
45	0.785	$\frac{1}{8}$ = 0.125	$b\delta = 0.01034P$	242
60	1.047	$\frac{1}{6}$ = 0.167	$b\delta = 0.00818P$	243
75	1.309	$\frac{5}{24}$ = 0.208	$b\delta = 0.00692P$	244
90	1.571	$\frac{1}{4}$ = 0.250	$b\delta = 0.00606P$	245
105	1.833	$\frac{7}{24}$ = 0.292	$b\delta = 0.00551P$	246
120	2.094	$\frac{1}{3}$ = 0.333	$b\delta = 0.00503P$	247
135	2.356	$\frac{3}{8}$ = 0.375	$b\delta = 0.00471P$	248
150	2.618	$\frac{5}{12}$ = 0.417	$b\delta = 0.00443P$	249
165	2.880	$\frac{11}{24}$ = 0.458	$b\delta = 0.00424P$	250
180	3.142	$\frac{1}{2}$ = 0.500	$b\delta = 0.00406P$	251
195	3.403	$\frac{13}{24}$ = 0.541	$b\delta = 0.00394P$	252
210	3.665	$\frac{7}{12}$ = 0.583	$b\delta = 0.00382P$	253
240	4.189	$\frac{2}{3}$ = 0.667	$b\delta = 0.00363P$	254
270	4.712	$\frac{3}{4}$ = 0.750	$b\delta = 0.00351P$	255
300	5.236	$\frac{5}{6}$ = 0.833	$b\delta = 0.00335P$	256

TABLE OF FORMULAS FOR LEATHER BELTS OVER LEATHER-COVERED PULLEYS.
Single Rawhide-Lacing.

a in degrees.	a in circular measure.	a in fractions of circumference.	Formula.	No.
30	0.524	$\frac{1}{12} = 0.083$	$b\delta = 0.01360P$	257
45	0.785	$\frac{1}{8} = 0.125$	$b\delta = 0.00960P$	258
60	1.047	$\frac{1}{6} = 0.167$	$b\delta = 0.00760P$	259
75	1.309	$\frac{5}{24} = 0.208$	$b\delta = 0.00643P$	260
90	1.571	$\frac{1}{4} = 0.250$	$b\delta = 0.00563P$	261
105	1.833	$\frac{7}{24} = 0.292$	$b\delta = 0.00311P$	262
120	2.094	$\frac{1}{3} = 0.333$	$b\delta = 0.00469P$	263
135	2.356	$\frac{3}{8} = 0.375$	$b\delta = 0.00437P$	264
150	2.618	$\frac{5}{12} = 0.417$	$b\delta = 0.00411P$	265
165	2.880	$\frac{11}{24} = 0.458$	$b\delta = 0.00394P$	266
180	3.142	$\frac{1}{2} = 0.500$	$b\delta = 0.00377P$	267
195	3.403	$\frac{13}{24} = 0.541$	$b\delta = 0.00366P$	268
210	3.665	$\frac{7}{12} = 0.583$	$b\delta = 0.00354P$	269
240	4.189	$\frac{2}{3} = 0.667$	$b\delta = 0.00337P$	270
270	4.712	$\frac{3}{4} = 0.750$	$b\delta = 0.00326P$	271
300	5.236	$\frac{5}{6} = 0.833$	$b\delta = 0.00311P$	272

TABLE OF FORMULAS FOR LEATHER BELTS OVER LEATHER-COVERED PULLEYS.
Double Leather-Lacing.

a in degrees.	a in circular measure.	a in fractions of circumference.	Formula.	No.
30	0.524	$\frac{1}{12} = 0.083$	$b\delta = 0.01269P$	273
45	0.785	$\frac{1}{8} = 0.125$	$b\delta = 0.00896P$	274
60	1.047	$\frac{1}{6} = 0.167$	$b\delta = 0.00709P$	275
75	1.309	$\frac{5}{24} = 0.208$	$b\delta = 0.00600P$	276
90	1.571	$\frac{1}{4} = 0.250$	$b\delta = 0.00525P$	277
105	1.833	$\frac{7}{24} = 0.292$	$b\delta = 0.00477P$	278
120	2.094	$\frac{1}{3} = 0.333$	$b\delta = 0.00437P$	279
135	2.356	$\frac{3}{8} = 0.375$	$b\delta = 0.00408P$	280
150	2.618	$\frac{5}{12} = 0.417$	$b\delta = 0.00384P$	281
165	2.880	$\frac{11}{24} = 0.458$	$b\delta = 0.00368P$	282
180	3.142	$\frac{1}{2} = 0.500$	$b\delta = 0.00352P$	283
195	3.403	$\frac{13}{24} = 0.541$	$b\delta = 0.00341P$	284
210	3.665	$\frac{7}{12} = 0.583$	$b\delta = 0.00331P$	285
240	4.189	$\frac{2}{3} = 0.667$	$b\delta = 0.00315P$	286
270	4.712	$\frac{3}{4} = 0.750$	$b\delta = 0.00304P$	287
300	5.236	$\frac{5}{6} = 0.833$	$b\delta = 0.00291P$	288

LEATHER-COVERED PULLEYS.

TABLE OF FORMULAS FOR LEATHER BELTS OVER LEATHER-COVERED PULLEYS.
Double Rawhide-Lacing.

a in degrees.	a in circular measure.	a in fractions of circumference.	Formula.	No.
30	0.524	$\frac{1}{12} = 0.083$	$b\delta = 0.01190 P$	289
45	0.785	$\frac{1}{8} = 0.125$	$b\delta = 0.00840 P$	290
60	1.047	$\frac{1}{6} = 0.167$	$b\delta = 0.00665 P$	291
75	1.309	$\frac{5}{24} = 0.208$	$b\delta = 0.00563 P$	292
90	1.571	$\frac{1}{4} = 0.250$	$b\delta = 0.00493 P$	293
105	1.833	$\frac{7}{24} = 0.292$	$b\delta = 0.00448 P$	294
120	2.094	$\frac{1}{3} = 0.333$	$b\delta = 0.00410 P$	295
135	2.356	$\frac{3}{8} = 0.375$	$b\delta = 0.00383 P$	296
150	2.618	$\frac{5}{12} = 0.417$	$b\delta = 0.00360 P$	297
165	2.880	$\frac{11}{24} = 0.458$	$b\delta = 0.00345 P$	298
180	3.142	$\frac{1}{2} = 0.500$	$b\delta = 0.00330 P$	299
195	3.403	$\frac{13}{24} = 0.541$	$b\delta = 0.00320 P$	300
210	3.665	$\frac{7}{12} = 0.583$	$b\delta = 0.00310 P$	301
240	4.189	$\frac{2}{3} = 0.667$	$b\delta = 0.00295 P$	302
270	4.712	$\frac{3}{4} = 0.750$	$b\delta = 0.09285 P$	303
300	5.236	$\frac{5}{6} = 0.833$	$b\delta = 0.00273 P$	304

TABLE OF FORMULAS FOR LEATHER BELTS OVER LEATHER-COVERED PULLEYS.
Riveted Joint.

a in degrees.	a in circular measure.	a in fractions of circumference.	Formula.	No.
30	0.524	$\frac{1}{12} = 0.083$	$b\delta = 0.00828 P$	305
45	0.785	$\frac{1}{8} = 0.125$	$b\delta = 0.00584 P$	306
60	1.047	$\frac{1}{6} = 0.167$	$b\delta = 0.00463 P$	307
75	1.309	$\frac{5}{24} = 0.208$	$b\delta = 0.00391 P$	308
90	1.571	$\frac{1}{4} = 0.250$	$b\delta = 0.00343 P$	309
105	1.833	$\frac{7}{24} = 0.291$	$b\delta = 0.00311 P$	310
120	2.094	$\frac{1}{3} = 0.333$	$b\delta = 0.00285 P$	311
135	2.356	$\frac{3}{8} = 0.375$	$b\delta = 0.00266 P$	312
150	2.618	$\frac{5}{12} = 0.417$	$b\delta = 0.00250 P$	313
165	2.880	$\frac{11}{24} = 0.458$	$b\delta = 0.00240 P$	314
180	3.142	$\frac{1}{2} = 0.500$	$b\delta = 0.00229 P$	315
195	3.403	$\frac{13}{24} = 0.541$	$b\delta = 0.00222 P$	316
210	3.665	$\frac{7}{12} = 0.583$	$b\delta = 0.00216 P$	317
240	4.189	$\frac{2}{3} = 0.667$	$b\delta = 0.00205 P$	318
270	4.712	$\frac{3}{4} = 0.750$	$b\delta = 0.00198 P$	319
300	5.236	$\frac{5}{6} = 0.833$	$b\delta = 0.00190 P$	320

Example.—A leather belt $\frac{1}{4}$ inch thick, running over a leather-covered pulley, transmits a force of 500 pounds. Required the width of the belt for single leather-lacing and single rawhide-lacing, taking $\alpha = 45°$. From formula (242) we have

$$b \times \tfrac{1}{4} = 0.01034 \times 500, \quad b = 0.01034 \times 500 \times 4,$$

or, for single leather-lacing,

$$b = 20.68'' = 20\tfrac{11}{16}'' \text{ nearly.}$$

From formula (258) we have

$$b \times \tfrac{1}{4} = 0.00960 \times 500, \quad b = 0.00960 \times 500 \times 4,$$

or, for single rawhide-lacing,

$$b = 19.20'' = 19\tfrac{13}{64}''.*$$

Example.—With the data $\alpha = 1.833$, circular measure, $\delta = \frac{1}{4}$ inch, and $b = 20$ inches, required the forces in pounds which the belt can transmit for each of the

---

* If we take the above data, $P = 500$, $\alpha = 45°$, $\delta = \frac{1}{4}$ inch, and calculate the width of a leather belt running over a cast-iron pulley, we shall have, from formula (57), for single leather-lacing, $b = 0.01142 \times 500 \times 4 = 22.84$ inches. The difference between the widths of the belt necessary for transmission over cast-iron and leather-covered pulleys is therefore $22.84 - 20.68 = 2.16$ inches, which shows a gain for the leather-covered pulley of nearly 10 per cent over the cast-iron pulley.

above methods of joint-fastening, supposing the belt to run over a leather covered pulley.

From formula (246) we have

$$20 \times \tfrac{1}{4} = 0.00551 P, \qquad P = \frac{20 \times 0.25}{0.00551};$$

or, for single leather-lacing,

$$P = 907.44 \text{ pounds.}$$

From formula (262),

$$20 \times \tfrac{1}{4} = 0.00511 P, \qquad P = \frac{20 \times 0.25}{0.00511};$$

or, for single rawhide-lacing,

$$P = 978.47 \text{ pounds.}$$

From formula (278),

$$20 \times \tfrac{1}{4} = 0.00477 P, \qquad P = \frac{20 \times 0.25}{0.00477};$$

or, for double leather-lacing,

From formula (294),

$$20 \times \tfrac{1}{4} = 0.00448 P, \qquad P = \frac{20 \times 0.25}{0.00448};$$

or, for double rawhide-lacing,

$$P = 1116.07 \text{ pounds.}$$

From formula (310),

$$20 \times \tfrac{1}{4} = 0.00311 P, \qquad P = \frac{20 \times 0.25}{0.00311};$$

or, for a riveted joint,

$$P = 1607.71 \text{ pounds.}$$

The formulas of the following tables, obtained by substituting $P = 550\dfrac{H}{v}$ in formulas (241) to (320), and similar to the formulas on pages 100–104, will prove convenient in calculating widths of leather belts over leather-covered pulleys from the horse-power transmitted and the velocity in feet per second:

TABLE OF FORMULAS FOR LEATHER BELTS OVER LEATHER COVERED PULLEYS.

Single Leather-Lacing.

a in degrees.	a in circular measure.	a in fractions of circumference.	Formula.	No.
30	0.524	$\frac{1}{12} = 0.083$	$b\delta = 8.052\frac{H}{v}$	321
45	0.785	$\frac{1}{8} = 0.125$	$b\delta = 5.687\frac{H}{v}$	322
60	1.047	$\frac{1}{6} = 0.167$	$b\delta = 4.499\frac{H}{v}$	323
75	1.309	$\frac{5}{24} = 0.208$	$b\delta = 3.806\frac{H}{v}$	324
90	1.571	$\frac{1}{4} = 0.250$	$b\delta = 3.333\frac{H}{v}$	325
105	1.833	$\frac{7}{24} = 0.292$	$b\delta = 3.031\frac{H}{v}$	326
120	2.094	$\frac{1}{3} = 0.333$	$b\delta = 2.767\frac{H}{v}$	327
135	2.356	$\frac{3}{8} = 0.375$	$b\delta = 2.591\frac{H}{v}$	328
150	2.618	$\frac{5}{12} = 0.417$	$b\delta = 2.437\frac{H}{v}$	329
165	2.880	$\frac{11}{24} = 0.458$	$b\delta = 2.332\frac{H}{v}$	330
180	3.142	$\frac{1}{2} = 0.500$	$b\delta = 2.233\frac{H}{v}$	331
195	3.403	$\frac{13}{24} = 0.541$	$b\delta = 2.167\frac{H}{v}$	332
210	3.665	$\frac{7}{12} = 0.583$	$b\delta = 2.101\frac{H}{v}$	333
240	4.189	$\frac{2}{3} = 0.667$	$b\delta = 1.997\frac{H}{v}$	334
270	4.712	$\frac{3}{4} = 0.750$	$b\delta = 1.931\frac{H}{v}$	335
300	5.236	$\frac{5}{6} = 0.833$	$b\delta = 1.843\frac{H}{v}$	336

Table of Formulas for Leather Belts over Leather-covered Pulleys.

Single Rawhide-Lacing.

a in degrees.	a in circular measure.	a in fractions of circumference.	Formula.	No.
30	0.524	$\frac{1}{12} = 0.083$	$b\delta = 7.480\frac{H}{v}$	337
45	0.785	$\frac{1}{8} = 0.125$	$b\delta = 5.280\frac{H}{v}$	338
60	1.047	$\frac{1}{6} = 0.167$	$b\delta = 4.180\frac{H}{v}$	339
75	1.309	$\frac{5}{24} = 0.208$	$b\delta = 3.537\frac{H}{v}$	340
90	1.571	$\frac{1}{4} = 0.250$	$b\delta = 3.097\frac{H}{v}$	341
105	1.833	$\frac{7}{24} = 0.292$	$b\delta = 2.811\frac{H}{v}$	342
120	2.094	$\frac{1}{3} = 0.333$	$b\delta = 2.580\frac{H}{v}$	343
135	2.356	$\frac{3}{8} = 0.375$	$b\delta = 2.404\frac{H}{v}$	344
150	2.618	$\frac{5}{12} = 0.417$	$b\delta = 2.261\frac{H}{v}$	345
165	2.880	$\frac{11}{24} = 0.458$	$b\delta = 2.167\frac{H}{v}$	346
180	3.142	$\frac{1}{2} = 0.500$	$b\delta = 2.074\frac{H}{v}$	347
195	3.403	$\frac{13}{24} = 0.541$	$b\delta = 2.013\frac{H}{v}$	348
210	3.665	$\frac{7}{12} = 0.583$	$b\delta = 1.947\frac{H}{v}$	349
240	4.189	$\frac{2}{3} = 0.667$	$b\delta = 1.854\frac{H}{v}$	350
270	4.712	$\frac{3}{4} = 0.750$	$b\delta = 1.793\frac{H}{v}$	351
300	5.236	$\frac{5}{6} = 0.833$	$b\delta = 1.701\frac{H}{v}$	352

TABLE OF FORMULAS FOR LEATHER BELTS OVER LEATHER-COVERED PULLEYS.

Double Leather-Lacing.

a in degrees.	a in circular measure.	a in fractions of circumference.	Formula.	No.
30	0.524	$\frac{1}{12} = 0.083$	$b\delta = 6.980\frac{H}{v}$	353
45	0.785	$\frac{1}{8} = 0.125$	$b\delta = 4.928\frac{H}{v}$	354
60	1.047	$\frac{1}{6} = 0.167$	$b\delta = 3.900\frac{H}{v}$	355
75	1.309	$\frac{5}{24} = 0.208$	$b\delta = 3.300\frac{H}{v}$	356
90	1.571	$\frac{1}{4} = 0.250$	$b\delta = 2.888\frac{H}{v}$	357
105	1.833	$\frac{7}{24} = 0.292$	$b\delta = 2.624\frac{H}{v}$	358
120	2.094	$\frac{1}{3} = 0.333$	$b\delta = 2.404\frac{H}{v}$	359
135	2.356	$\frac{3}{8} = 0.375$	$b\delta = 2.244\frac{H}{v}$	360
150	2.618	$\frac{5}{12} = 0.417$	$b\delta = 2.112\frac{H}{v}$	361
165	2.880	$\frac{11}{24} = 0.458$	$b\delta = 2.024\frac{H}{v}$	362
180	3.142	$\frac{1}{2} = 0.500$	$b\delta = 1.936\frac{H}{v}$	363
195	3.403	$\frac{13}{24} = 0.541$	$b\delta = 1.876\frac{H}{v}$	364
210	3.665	$\frac{7}{12} = 0.583$	$b\delta = 1.821\frac{H}{v}$	365
240	4.189	$\frac{2}{3} = 0.667$	$b\delta = 1.733\frac{H}{v}$	366
270	4.712	$\frac{3}{4} = 0.750$	$b\delta = 1.672\frac{H}{v}$	367
300	5.236	$\frac{5}{6} = 0.833$	$b\delta = 1.601\frac{H}{v}$	368

Table of Formulas for Leather-Belts over Leather-covered Pulleys.

Double Rawhide-Lacing.

α in degrees.	α in circular measure.	α in fractions of circumference.	Formula.	No.
30	0.524	$\frac{1}{12} = 0.083$	$b\delta = 6.545\frac{H}{v}$	369
45	0.785	$\frac{1}{8} = 0.125$	$b\delta = 4.620\frac{H}{v}$	370
60	1.047	$\frac{1}{6} = 0.167$	$b\delta = 3.658\frac{H}{v}$	371
75	1.309	$\frac{5}{24} = 0.208$	$b\delta = 3.097\frac{H}{v}$	372
90	1.571	$\frac{1}{4} = 0.250$	$b\delta = 2.712\frac{H}{v}$	373
105	1.833	$\frac{7}{24} = 0.292$	$b\delta = 2.464\frac{H}{v}$	374
120	2.094	$\frac{1}{3} = 0.333$	$b\delta = 2.255\frac{H}{v}$	375
135	2.356	$\frac{3}{8} = 0.375$	$b\delta = 2.107\frac{H}{v}$	376
150	2.618	$\frac{5}{12} = 0.417$	$b\delta = 1.980\frac{H}{v}$	377
165	2.880	$\frac{11}{24} = 0.458$	$b\delta = 1.898\frac{H}{v}$	378
180	3.142	$\frac{1}{2} = 0.500$	$b\delta = 1.815\frac{H}{v}$	379
195	3.403	$\frac{13}{24} = 0.541$	$b\delta = 1.760\frac{H}{v}$	380
210	3.665	$\frac{7}{12} = 0.583$	$b\delta = 1.705\frac{H}{v}$	381
240	4.189	$\frac{2}{3} = 0.667$	$b\delta = 1.623\frac{H}{v}$	382
270	4.712	$\frac{3}{4} = 0.750$	$b\delta = 1.568\frac{H}{v}$	383
300	5.236	$\frac{5}{6} = 0.833$	$b\delta = 1.502\frac{H}{v}$	384

LEATHER-COVERED PULLEYS.

Table of Formulas for Leather Belts over Leather-covered Pulleys.

Riveted Joints.

a in degrees.	a in circular measure.	a in fractions of circumference.	Formula.	No.
30	0.524	$\frac{1}{12} = 0.083$	$b\delta = 4.554\frac{H}{v}$	385
45	0.785	$\frac{1}{8} = 0.125$	$b\delta = 3.212\frac{H}{v}$	386
60	1.047	$\frac{1}{6} = 0.167$	$b\delta = 2.547\frac{H}{v}$	387
75	1.309	$\frac{5}{24} = 0.208$	$b\delta = 2.151\frac{H}{v}$	388
90	1.571	$\frac{1}{4} = 0.250$	$b\delta = 1.887\frac{H}{v}$	389
105	1.833	$\frac{7}{24} = 0.292$	$b\delta = 1.711\frac{H}{v}$	390
120	2.094	$\frac{1}{3} = 0.333$	$b\delta = 1.568\frac{H}{v}$	391
135	2.356	$\frac{3}{8} = 0.375$	$b\delta = 1.463\frac{H}{v}$	392
150	2.618	$\frac{5}{12} = 0.417$	$b\delta = 1.375\frac{H}{v}$	393
165	2.880	$\frac{11}{24} = 0.458$	$b\delta = 1.320\frac{H}{v}$	394
180	3.142	$\frac{1}{2} = 0.500$	$b\delta = 1.260\frac{H}{v}$	395
195	3.403	$\frac{13}{24} = 0.541$	$b\delta = 1.221\frac{H}{v}$	396
210	3.665	$\frac{7}{12} = 0.583$	$b\delta = 1.188\frac{H}{v}$	397
240	4.189	$\frac{2}{3} = 0.667$	$b\delta = 1.128\frac{H}{v}$	398
270	4.712	$\frac{3}{4} = 0.750$	$b\delta = 1.089\frac{H}{v}$	399
300	5.236	$\frac{5}{6} = 0.833$	$b\delta = 1.045\frac{H}{v}$	400

Example.—A leather belt ¼ inch thick, running over a leather-covered pulley, transmits a force of 20 horse-power at a velocity of 15 feet per second. Required the width of the belt for single and double rawhide-lacing, assuming that the belt embraces an arc of the pulley equal to 2.880 circular measure. From formula (346) we have

$$b \times \tfrac{1}{4} = 2.167 \times \frac{20}{15}, \qquad b = 2.167 \times \frac{20}{15} \times 4,$$

or, for single rawhide-lacing,

$$b = 11.557'' = 11\tfrac{9}{16}''.$$

Formula (378) gives

$$b \times \tfrac{1}{4} = 1.898 \times \frac{20}{15}, \qquad b = 1.898 \times \frac{20}{15} \times 4,$$

or, for double rawhide-lacing,

$$b = 10.123'' = 10\tfrac{1}{8}''.$$

Example.—A leather belt running over leather-covered pulleys is $\tfrac{7}{32}$ inch thick and 12 inches wide. Required the velocity at which the belt can transmit a force of 10 horse-power, assuming $\alpha = 45°$, and that the belt has a double leather-lacing. We have from formula (354)

$$12 \times \tfrac{7}{32} = 4.928 \times \frac{10}{v}, \qquad v = \frac{4.928 \times 10}{12 \times \tfrac{7}{32}},$$

LEATHER-COVERED PULLEYS.

Example.—A leather belt (with a riveted joint) running over leather-covered pulleys is 16 inches wide and $\frac{3}{16}$ inch thick; the arc embraced by the belt on the smaller pulley is 150°, and the velocity of the belt 10 feet per second. It is required to determine the horse-power which can be transmitted by the belt. From formula (393) we have

$$16 \times \tfrac{3}{16} = 1.375 \times \frac{H}{10}, \qquad H = \frac{16 \times \tfrac{3}{16} \times 10}{1.375},$$

or $\qquad H = 21.82.$

By substituting $\delta = \tfrac{7}{32}$ in formulas (251), (267), (283), (299), (315), (331), (347), (363), (379), and (395), successively, we obtain the following formulas:

When $\alpha = 180°$ and $\delta = \tfrac{7}{32}''$,

Single leather-lacing, $\quad b = 0.0186P.$ . . . . (401)

Single rawhide-lacing, $\quad b = 0.0172P.$ . . . . (402)

Double leather-lacing, $\quad b = 0.0161P.$ . . . . (403)

Double rawhide-lacing, $b = 0.0151P.$ . . . . (404)

Riveted joint, $\qquad b = 0.0105P.$ . . . . (405)

Single leather-lacing, $\quad b = 10.208\dfrac{H}{v}.$ . . . . (406)

Single rawhide-lacing, $\quad b = 9.481\dfrac{H}{v}.$ . . . . (407)

Double leather-lacing, $b = 8.850\dfrac{H}{v}$. . . . . (408)

Double rawhide-lacing, $b = 8.297\dfrac{H}{v}$. . . . . (409)

Riveted joint, $b = 5.760\dfrac{H}{v}$. . . . . (410)

By substituting $\delta = \tfrac{7}{32}$ in formulas (248), (264), (280), (296), (312), (328), (344), (360), (376), and (392), successively, the following formulas may be obtained·

When $\alpha = 135°$ and $\delta = \tfrac{7}{32}''$,

Single leather-lacing, $b = 0.0215P$. . . . . (411)

Single rawhide-lacing, $b = 0.0200P$. . . . . (412)

Double leather-lacing, $b = 0.0187P$. . . . . (413)

Double rawhide-lacing, $b = 0.0175P$. . . . . (414)

Riveted joint, $b = 0.0122P$. . . . . (415)

Single leather-lacing, $b = 11.845\dfrac{H}{v}$. . . . . (416)

Single rawhide-lacing, $b = 10.990\dfrac{H}{v}$. . . . . (417)

Double leather-lacing, $b = 10.258\dfrac{H}{v}$. . . . . (418)

Double rawhide-lacing, $b = 9.632\dfrac{H}{v}$. . . . (419)

Riveted joint, $b = 6.688\dfrac{H}{v}$. . . . (420)

Example.—A leather belt, running over leather-covered pulleys, transmits a force of 600 pounds. The pulleys are of equal diameters ($\alpha = 180°$) and the thickness of the belt is $\frac{7}{32}$ inch. Required the width of the belt for double leather-lacing. We have from formula (403)

$$b = 0.0161 \times 600,$$
$$b = 9.66'' = 9\tfrac{21}{32}''.$$

Example.—A $\frac{7}{32}$-inch leather belt, running over two equal leather-covered pulleys, transmits a force of 15 horse-power at a velocity of 10 feet per second. Required the width of the belt for a riveted joint.

Formula (410) gives

$$b = 5.760 \times \tfrac{15}{10},$$
$$b = 8.64'' = 8\tfrac{41}{64}''.$$

Example.—A $\frac{7}{32}$-inch leather belt (double rawhide-lacing), running over leather-covered pulleys, transmits a force of 600 pounds. The arc embraced by the belt on the smaller pulley is 135°. Required the width of the belt. From formula (414) we have

$$b = 0.0175 \times 600,$$
$$b = 10.50'' = 10\tfrac{1}{2}''.$$

Example.—A leather belt $\frac{7}{32}$ inch thick, running over leather-covered pulleys, transmits a force of 15 horse-power at a velocity of 10 feet per second. It is required to determine the width of the belt, for single leather-lacing, taking $\alpha = 135°$. Formula (416) gives

$$b = 11.845 \times \frac{15}{10},$$
$$b = 17.77'' = 17\tfrac{49}{64}''.$$

Example.—A leather belt $\frac{7}{32}$ inch thick and 20 inches wide, running over leather-covered pulleys, transmits a force of 20 horse-power. The arc embraced by the belt on the smaller pulley is 135°. It is required to determine the velocity at which the belt can be driven for double rawhide-lacing. We have from formula (419)

$$20 = 9.632 \times \frac{20}{v}, \qquad v = \frac{9.632 \times 20}{20},$$

or $\quad v = 9.632 = 9\tfrac{5}{16}$ feet per second.

The following tables, calculated from formulas (401) to (420), give the forces in pounds (P) and the values of the horse-power divided by the velocity in feet per second $\left(\dfrac{H}{v}\right)$ corresponding to different widths (from 1 inch to 30 inches) of $\frac{7}{32}$-inch leather belts running over leather-covered pulleys for $\alpha = 180°$ and $\alpha = 135°$ for each of the five methods of joint-fastening given above:

TABLE OF WIDTHS OF LEATHER BELTS OVER LEATHER-COVERED PULLEYS, WHEN $\alpha = 180°$ AND $\delta = \frac{7}{88}''$. From Formulas (401)–(405).

Width in inches.	P, single leather-lacing.	P, single rawhide-lacing.	P, double leather-lacing.	P, double rawhide-lacing.	P, riveted joint.	No.
1	53.88	58.04	62.15	66.27	95.51	1
1½	80.82	87.06	93.23	99.40	143.27	2
2	107.76	116.08	124.30	132.54	191.02	3
2½	134.70	145.10	155.38	165.67	238.78	4
3	161.64	174.11	186.45	198.81	286.53	5
3½	188.58	203.13	217.53	231.94	334.29	6
4	215.52	232.15	248.60	265.08	382.04	7
4½	242.46	261.17	279.68	298.21	429.80	8
5	269.40	290.19	310.75	331.35	477.56	9
5½	296.34	319.21	341.83	364.48	525.31	10
6	323.28	348.23	372.90	397.61	573.07	11
7	377.16	406.27	435.05	463.88	668.58	12
8	431.03	464.31	497.20	530.15	764.09	13
9	484.91	522.34	559.35	596.42	859.60	14
10	538.79	580.38	621.50	662.69	955.11	15
11	592.67	638.42	683.65	728.96	1050.62	16
12	646.55	696.46	745.80	795.23	1146.13	17
14	754.31	812.54	870.10	927.77	1337.15	18
16	862.07	928.61	994.40	1060.31	1528.18	19
18	969.83	1044.69	1118.71	1192.84	1719.20	20
20	1077.59	1160.77	1243.01	1325.38	1910.22	21
22	1185.34	1276.84	1367.31	1457.92	2101.24	22
24	1293.10	1392.92	1491.61	1590.46	2292.26	23
26	1400.86	1509.00	1615.91	1723.00	2483.29	24
28	1508.62	1625.07	1740.21	1825.53	2674.31	25
30	1616.38	1741.15	1864.51	1988.07	2865.33	26

TABLE OF WIDTHS OF LEATHER BELTS OVER LEATHER-COVERED PULLEYS, WHEN $\alpha = 180°$ and $\delta = \frac{7}{32}''$. From Formulas (406)–(410).

Width in inches.	$\frac{H}{v}$, single leather-lacing.	$\frac{H}{v}$, single rawhide-lacing.	$\frac{H}{v}$, double leather-lacing.	$\frac{H}{v}$, double rawhide-lacing.	$\frac{H}{v}$, riveted joint.	No.
1	0.0980	0.1055	0.1130	0.1205	0.1736	1
1½	0.1469	0.1582	0.1695	0.1808	0.2604	2
2	0.1959	0.2109	0.2260	0.2410	0.3472	3
2½	0.2449	0.2637	0.2825	0.3013	0.4340	4
3	0.2939	0.3164	0.3390	0.3616	0.5208	5
3½	0.3429	0.3692	0.3955	0.4218	0.6076	6
4	0.3918	0.4219	0.4520	0.4821	0.6944	7
4½	0.4408	0.4746	0.5085	0.5424	0.7812	8
5	0.4898	0.5274	0.5650	0.6026	0.8681	9
5½	0.5388	0.5801	0.6214	0.6629	0.9549	10
6	0.5878	0.6328	0.6779	0.7231	1.0417	11
7	0.6857	0.7383	0.7909	0.8437	1.2153	12
8	0.7837	0.8438	0.9039	0.9642	1.3889	13
9	0.8817	0.9493	1.0169	1.0847	1.5625	14
10	0.9796	1.0547	1.1299	1.2052	1.7361	15
11	1.0776	1.1602	1.2429	1.3258	1.9097	16
12	1.1755	1.2657	1.3559	1.4463	2.0833	17
14	1.3715	1.4766	1.5819	1.6873	2.4306	18
16	1.5674	1.6876	1.8078	1.9284	2.7778	19
18	1.7633	1.8985	2.0338	2.1694	3.1250	20
20	1.9592	2.1095	2.2598	2.4105	3.4722	21
22	2.1552	2.3204	2.4858	2.6515	3.8194	22
24	2.3511	2.5314	2.7118	2.8926	4.1667	23
26	2.5470	2.7423	2.9377	3.1336	4.5139	24
28	2.7429	2.9532	3.1637	3.3747	4.8611	25
30	2.9389	3.1642	3.3897	3.6157	5.2083	26

TABLE OF WIDTHS OF LEATHER BELTS OVER LEATHER-COVERED PULLEYS, WHEN $\alpha = 135°$ AND $\delta = \frac{7}{32}''$. From Formulas (411)–(415).

Width in inches.	P, single leather-lacing.	P, single rawhide-lacing.	P, double leather-lacing.	P, double rawhide-lacing.	P, riveted joint.	No.
1	46.45	50.05	53.62	57.11	82.24	1
1½	69.67	75.08	80.43	85.67	123.36	2
2	92.89	100.10	107.24	114.22	164.47	3
2½	116.12	125.13	134.05	142.78	205.59	4
3	139.34	150.15	160.86	171.33	246.71	5
3½	162.56	175.18	187.67	199.89	287.83	6
4	185.79	200.20	214.48	228.44	328.95	7
4½	209.01	225.23	241.29	257.00	370.07	8
5	232.23	250.25	268.10	285.55	411.18	9
5½	255.46	275.28	294.91	314.11	452.30	10
6	278.68	300.30	321.72	342.66	493.42	11
7	325.13	350.35	375.34	399.77	575.66	12
8	371.57	400.40	428.95	456.88	657.89	13
9	418.02	450.45	482.57	513.99	740.13	14
10	464.47	500.50	536.19	571.10	822.37	15
11	510.91	550.55	589.81	628.21	904.60	16
12	557.36	600.60	643.43	685.32	986.84	17
14	650.26	700.70	750.67	799.54	1151.32	18
16	743.15	800.80	857.91	913.76	1315.79	19
18	836.04	900.90	965.15	1027.98	1480.26	20
20	928.94	1001.00	1072.39	1142.20	1644.74	21
22	1021.83	1101.10	1179.62	1256.42	1809.21	22
24	1114.72	1201.20	1286.86	1370.64	1973.68	23
26	1207.62	1301.30	1394.10	1484.87	2138.16	24
28	1300.51	1401.40	1501.34	1599.09	2302.63	25
30	1393.40	1501.50	1608.58	1713.31	2467.10	26

TABLE OF WIDTHS OF LEATHER BELTS OVER LEATHER COVERED PULLEYS, WHEN $\alpha = 135°$ AND $\delta = \frac{7}{32}''$. From Formulas (416)–(420).

Width in inches.	$\frac{H}{v}$, single leather-lacing.	$\frac{H}{v}$, single rawhide-lacing.	$\frac{H}{v}$, double leather-lacing.	$\frac{H}{v}$, double rawhide-lacing.	$\frac{H}{v}$, riveted joint.	No.
1	0.0844	0.0910	0.0975	0.1038	0.1495	1
1½	0.1266	0.1365	0.1462	0.1557	0.2243	2
2	0.1689	0.1820	0.1950	0.2076	0.2990	3
2½	0.2111	0.2275	0.2437	0.2596	0.3738	4
3	0.2533	0.2730	0.2924	0.3115	0.4486	5
3½	0.2955	0.3185	0.3412	0.3634	0.5233	6
4	0.3377	0.3640	0.3899	0.4153	0.5981	7
4½	0.3799	0.4095	0.4387	0.4672	0.6728	8
5	0.4221	0.4550	0.4874	0.5191	0.7476	9
5½	0.4643	0.5005	0.5362	0.5710	0.8224	10
6	0.5066	0.5460	0.5849	0.6229	0.8971	11
7	0.5910	0.6370	0.6824	0.7267	1.0466	12
8	0.6754	0.7280	0.7799	0.8306	1.1962	13
9	0.7598	0.8189	0.8773	0.9344	1.3457	14
10	0.8443	0.9099	0.9748	1.0382	1.4952	15
11	0.9287	1.0009	1.0723	1.1420	1.6447	16
12	1.0131	1.0919	1.1698	1.2458	1.7942	17
14	1.1820	1.2739	1.3647	1.4535	2.0933	18
16	1.3508	1.4559	1.5597	1.6611	2.3923	19
18	1.5197	1.6380	1.7547	1.8688	2.6914	20
20	1.6885	1.8199	1.9496	2.0764	2.9904	21
22	1.8574	2.0019	2.1446	2.2840	3.2894	22
24	2.0262	2.1839	2.3396	2.4917	3.5885	23
26	2.1951	2.3658	2.5345	2.6993	3.8875	24
28	2.3640	2.5478	2.7295	2.9070	4.1866	25
30	2.5328	2.7298	2.9245	3.1146	4.4856	26

Example.—Required the force in pounds which can be transmitted by a $\frac{7}{32}$-inch leather belt, 20 inches wide, running over two equal leather-covered pulleys, the belt-joint being riveted. From the table on page 135, column for riveted joint, line 21, we have

$$P = 1910.22 \text{ pounds}.$$

Example.—A $\frac{7}{32}$-inch leather belt running over leather-covered pulleys, and embracing an arc of 135° on the smaller pulley, transmits a force of 1000 pounds. It is required to determine the proper width for the belt for single rawhide-lacing. The table on page 137, column for single rawhide-lacing, line 21, gives, corresponding to $P = $ 1001.10 pounds, a width of

$$b = 20''.$$

Example.—A $\frac{7}{32}$-inch leather belt, running over two equal leather-covered pulleys at a velocity of 10 feet per second, transmits a force of 22 horse-power. Required the width for the belt for a double leather-lacing. We have in this case $\frac{H}{v} = \frac{22}{10} = 2.2$, and the table on page 136, column for double leather-lacing, line 21, gives for $\frac{H}{v} = 2.2598$ a belt-width of

$$b = 20''$$

Example.—A leather belt $\frac{7}{32}$ inch thick and 28 inches wide, running over leather-covered pulleys and embracing an arc of 135° on the smaller pulley, transmits a force of 25 horse-power. It is required to determine the velocity at which the belt can be driven for a double rawhide-lacing. From the table on page 138, column for double rawhide-lacing, line 25, we have

or $v = 8.60$ feet per second.

Example.—A leather belt $\frac{7}{32}$ inch thick and 28 inches wide, running over leather-covered pulleys and embracing an arc of 135° on the smaller pulley, is driven at a velocity of 8.60 feet per second. It is required to determine the horse-power which can be transmitted by the belt, the joint-fastening being a double rawhide-lacing. From the table on page 138, column for double rawhide-lacing, line 25, we have

$$\frac{H}{v} = \frac{H}{8.60} = 2.9070, \quad H = 8.60 \times 2.9070,$$

or $H = 25$.

§ 12. Vulcanized-rubber Belts.

Vulcanized-rubber belts are usually made, as explained in § 8, by placing one or more layers of cotton duck between layers of vulcanized rubber. The number of these layers is indicated by the term *ply:* thus a one-ply belt contains one layer of duck, a three-ply belt contains three layers, etc. The thickness of each layer of duck varies more or less according to the amount of material and the force with which the layers are pressed together in the manufacture. We may, however, with sufficient correctness for ordinary purposes, take for the average thickness of a ply $\frac{1}{12}$ inch. A three-ply belt is therefore approximately $\frac{1}{4}$ inch thick, a four-ply belt $\frac{1}{3}$ inch thick, etc.

The strength of vulcanized-rubber belting seems to be about that of leather of the same thickness. A series of tests made for the author by Messrs. Fairbanks & Co., on their standard testing-machine, gave for superior new vulcanized-rubber belting an average strength of nearly 4000 pounds per square inch of section. A great number of other tests made by the author on ordinary vulcanized-rubber belts which had been in practical use for a short time gave results essentially the same as for leather.

We shall therefore use for the safe-working stress in pounds per square inch for vulcanized-rubber belting the following values, given in § 10:

$$\begin{aligned}
&\text{Single leather-lacing,} & f &= 325; \\
&\text{Single rawhide-lacing,} & f &= 350; \\
&\text{Double leather-lacing,} & f &= 375; \\
&\text{Double rawhide-lacing,} & f &= 400; \\
&\text{Riveted joint,} & f &= 575.
\end{aligned}$$

The coefficient of friction for vulcanized rubber over cast-iron seems to be slightly greater than for leather over leather-covered pulleys.* Since, however, rubber belts are very seriously injured by slipping about their pulleys, and for this reason greater care should be taken to prevent slipping, we propose to neglect the apparently small difference and take the coefficient equal

---

* See Appendix I.

to that for leather over leather-covered pulleys. We have then

$$\varphi = 0.45.$$

The formulas for widths of vulcanized-rubber belts over cast-iron pulleys may be copied directly from those for leather belts over leather-covered pulleys without the trouble of copying the preliminary tables and formulas.

TABLE OF FORMULAS FOR VULCANIZED-RUBBER BELTS OVER CAST-IRON PULLEYS.

Single Leather-Lacing.

a in degrees.	a in circular measure.	a in fractions of circumference.	Formula.	No.
30	0.524	$\frac{1}{12} = 0.083$	$b\delta = 0.01464P$	421
45	0.785	$\frac{1}{8} = 0.125$	$b\delta = 0.01034P$	422
60	1.047	$\frac{1}{6} = 0.167$	$b\delta = 0.00818P$	423
75	1.309	$\frac{5}{24} = 0.208$	$b\delta = 0.00692P$	424
90	1.571	$\frac{1}{4} = 0.250$	$b\delta = 0.00606P$	425
105	1.833	$\frac{7}{24} = 0.292$	$b\delta = 0.00551P$	426
120	2.094	$\frac{1}{3} = 0.333$	$b\delta = 0.00503P$	427
135	2.356	$\frac{3}{8} = 0.375$	$b\delta = 0.00471P$	428
150	2.618	$\frac{5}{12} = 0.417$	$b\delta = 0.00443P$	429
165	2.880	$\frac{11}{24} = 0.458$	$b\delta = 0.00424P$	430
180	3.142	$\frac{1}{2} = 0.500$	$b\delta = 0.00406P$	431
195	3.403	$\frac{13}{24} = 0.541$	$b\delta = 0.00394P$	432
210	3.665	$\frac{7}{12} = 0.583$	$b\delta = 0.00382P$	433
240	4.189	$\frac{2}{3} = 0.667$	$b\delta = 0.00363P$	434
270	4.712	$\frac{3}{4} = 0.750$	$b\delta = 0.00351P$	435
300	5.236	$\frac{5}{6} = 0.833$	$b\delta = 0.00335P$	436

VULCANIZED-RUBBER BELTS.   143

TABLE OF FORMULAS FOR VULCANIZED-RUBBER BELTS OVER CAST-IRON PULLEYS.
Single Rawhide Lacing.

α in degrees.	α in circular measure.	α in fractions of circumference.	Formula.	No.
30	0.524	$\frac{1}{12} = 0.083$	$b\delta = 0.01360P$	437
45	0.785	$\frac{1}{8} = 0.125$	$b\delta = 0.00960P$	438
60	1.047	$\frac{1}{6} = 0.167$	$b\delta = 0.00760P$	439
75	1.309	$\frac{5}{24} = 0.208$	$b\delta = 0.00643P$	440
90	1.571	$\frac{1}{4} = 0.250$	$b\delta = 0.00563P$	441
105	1.833	$\frac{7}{24} = 0.292$	$b\delta = 0.00511P$	442
120	2.094	$\frac{1}{3} = 0.333$	$b\delta = 0.00469P$	443
135	2.356	$\frac{3}{8} = 0.375$	$b\delta = 0.00437P$	444
150	2.618	$\frac{5}{12} = 0.417$	$b\delta = 0.00411P$	445
165	2.880	$\frac{11}{24} = 0.458$	$b\delta = 0.00394P$	446
180	3.142	$\frac{1}{2} = 0.500$	$b\delta = 0.00377P$	447
195	3.403	$\frac{13}{24} = 0.541$	$b\delta = 0.00366P$	448
210	3.665	$\frac{7}{12} = 0.583$	$b\delta = 0.00354P$	449
240	4.189	$\frac{2}{3} = 0.667$	$b\delta = 0.00337P$	450
270	4.712	$\frac{3}{4} = 0.750$	$b\delta = 0.00326P$	451
300	5.236	$\frac{5}{6} = 0.833$	$b\delta = 0.00311P$	452

TABLE OF FORMULAS FOR VULCANIZED-RUBBER BELTS OVER CAST-IRON PULLEYS.
Double Leather-Lacing.

α in degrees.	α in circular measure.	α in fractions of circumference.	Formula.	No.
30	0.524	$\frac{1}{12} = 0.083$	$b\delta = 0.01269P$	453
45	0.785	$\frac{1}{8} = 0.125$	$b\delta = 0.00896P$	454
60	1.047	$\frac{1}{6} = 0.167$	$b\delta = 0.00709P$	455
75	1.309	$\frac{5}{24} = 0.208$	$b\delta = 0.00600P$	456
90	1.571	$\frac{1}{4} = 0.250$	$b\delta = 0.00525P$	457
105	1.833	$\frac{7}{24} = 0.292$	$b\delta = 0.00477P$	458
120	2.094	$\frac{1}{3} = 0.333$	$b\delta = 0.00437P$	459
135	2.356	$\frac{3}{8} = 0.375$	$b\delta = 0.00408P$	460
150	2.618	$\frac{5}{12} = 0.417$	$b\delta = 0.00384P$	461
165	2.880	$\frac{11}{24} = 0.458$	$b\delta = 0.00368P$	462
180	3.142	$\frac{1}{2} = 0.500$	$b\delta = 0.00352P$	463
195	3.403	$\frac{13}{24} = 0.541$	$b\delta = 0.00341P$	464
210	3.665	$\frac{7}{12} = 0.583$	$b\delta = 0.00331P$	465
240	4.189	$\frac{2}{3} = 0.667$	$b\delta = 0.00315P$	466
270	4.712	$\frac{3}{4} = 0.750$	$b\delta = 0.00304P$	467
300	5.236	$\frac{5}{6} = 0.833$	$b\delta = 0.00291P$	468

TABLE OF FORMULAS FOR VULCANIZED-RUBBER BELTS OVER CAST-IRON PULLEYS.
Double Rawhide-Lacing.

a in degrees.	a in circular measure.	a in fractions of circumference.	Formula.	No.
30	0.524	$\frac{1}{12}$ = 0.083	$b\delta = 0.01190P$	469
45	0.785	$\frac{1}{8}$ = 0.125	$b\delta = 0.00840P$	470
60	1.047	$\frac{1}{6}$ = 0.167	$b\delta = 0.00665P$	471
75	1.309	$\frac{5}{24}$ = 0.208	$b\delta = 0.00563P$	472
90	1.571	$\frac{1}{4}$ = 0.250	$b\delta = 0.00493P$	473
105	1.833	$\frac{7}{24}$ = 0.292	$b\delta = 0.00448P$	474
120	2.094	$\frac{1}{3}$ = 0.333	$b\delta = 0.00410P$	475
135	2.356	$\frac{3}{8}$ = 0.375	$b\delta = 0.00383P$	476
150	2.618	$\frac{5}{12}$ = 0.417	$b\delta = 0.00360P$	477
165	2.880	$\frac{11}{24}$ = 0.458	$b\delta = 0.00345P$	478
180	3.142	$\frac{1}{2}$ = 0.500	$b\delta = 0.00330P$	479
195	3.403	$\frac{13}{24}$ = 0.541	$b\delta = 0.00320P$	480
210	3.665	$\frac{7}{12}$ = 0.583	$b\delta = 0.00310P$	481
240	4.189	$\frac{2}{3}$ = 0.667	$b\delta = 0.00295P$	482
270	4.712	$\frac{3}{4}$ = 0.750	$b\delta = 0.00285P$	483
300	5.236	$\frac{5}{6}$ = 0.833	$b\delta = 0.00273P$	484

TABLE OF FORMULAS FOR VULCANIZED-RUBBER BELTS OVER CAST-IRON PULLEYS.
Riveted Joints.

a in degrees.	a in circular measure.	a in fractions of circumference.	Formula.	No.
30	0.524	$\frac{1}{12}$ = 0.083	$b\delta = 0.00828P$	485
45	0.785	$\frac{1}{8}$ = 0.125	$b\delta = 0.00584P$	486
60	1.047	$\frac{1}{6}$ = 0.167	$b\delta = 0.00463P$	487
75	1.309	$\frac{5}{24}$ = 0.208	$b\delta = 0.00391P$	488
90	1.571	$\frac{1}{4}$ = 0.250	$b\delta = 0.00343P$	489
105	1.833	$\frac{7}{24}$ = 0.291	$b\delta = 0.00311P$	490
120	2.094	$\frac{1}{3}$ = 0.333	$b\delta = 0.00285P$	491
135	2.356	$\frac{3}{8}$ = 0.375	$b\delta = 0.00266P$	492
150	2.618	$\frac{5}{12}$ = 0.417	$b\delta = 0.00250P$	493
165	2.880	$\frac{11}{24}$ = 0.458	$b\delta = 0.00240P$	494
180	3.142	$\frac{1}{2}$ = 0.500	$b\delta = 0.00229P$	495
195	3.403	$\frac{13}{24}$ = 0.541	$b\delta = 0.00222P$	496
210	3.665	$\frac{7}{12}$ = 0.583	$b\delta = 0.00216P$	497
240	4.189	$\frac{2}{3}$ = 0.667	$b\delta = 0.00205P$	498
270	4.712	$\frac{3}{4}$ = 0.750	$b\delta = 0.00198P$	499
300	5.236	$\frac{5}{6}$ = 0.833	$b\delta = 0.00190P$	500

Table of Formulas for Vulcanized-rubber Belts over Cast-Iron Pulleys.

Single Leather-Lacing.

a in degrees.	a in circular measure.	a in fractions of circumference.	Formula.	No.
30	0.524	$\frac{1}{12} = 0.083$	$b\delta = 8.052\frac{H}{v}$	501
45	0.785	$\frac{1}{8} = 0.125$	$b\delta = 5.687\frac{H}{v}$	502
60	1.047	$\frac{1}{6} = 0.167$	$b\delta = 4.499\frac{H}{v}$	503
75	1.309	$\frac{5}{24} = 0.208$	$b\delta = 3.806\frac{H}{v}$	504
90	1.571	$\frac{1}{4} = 0.250$	$b\delta = 3.333\frac{H}{v}$	505
105	1.833	$\frac{7}{24} = 0.292$	$b\delta = 3.031\frac{H}{v}$	506
120	2.094	$\frac{1}{3} = 0.333$	$b\delta = 2.767\frac{H}{v}$	507
135	2.356	$\frac{3}{8} = 0.375$	$b\delta = 2.591\frac{H}{v}$	508
150	2.618	$\frac{5}{12} = 0.417$	$b\delta = 2.437\frac{H}{v}$	509
165	2.880	$\frac{11}{24} = 0.458$	$b\delta = 2.332\frac{H}{v}$	510
180	3.142	$\frac{1}{2} = 0.500$	$b\delta = 2.233\frac{H}{v}$	511
195	3.403	$\frac{13}{24} = 0.541$	$b\delta = 2.167\frac{H}{v}$	512
210	3.665	$\frac{7}{12} = 0.583$	$b\delta = 2.101\frac{H}{v}$	513
240	4.189	$\frac{2}{3} = 0.667$	$b\delta = 1.997\frac{H}{v}$	514
270	4.712	$\frac{3}{4} = 0.750$	$b\delta = 1.931\frac{H}{v}$	515
300	5.236	$\frac{5}{6} = 0.833$	$b\delta = 1.843\frac{H}{v}$	516

TABLE OF FORMULAS FOR VULCANIZED-RUBBER BELTS OVER CAST-IRON PULLEYS.

Single Rawhide-Lacing.

a in degrees.	a in circular measure.	a in fractions of circumference.	Formula.	No.
30	0.524	$\frac{1}{12} = 0.083$	$b\delta = 7.480\frac{H}{v}$	517
45	0.785	$\frac{1}{8} = 0.125$	$b\delta = 5.280\frac{H}{v}$	518
60	1.047	$\frac{1}{6} = 0.167$	$b\delta = 4.180\frac{H}{v}$	519
75	1.309	$\frac{5}{24} = 0.208$	$b\delta = 3.537\frac{H}{v}$	520
90	1.571	$\frac{1}{4} = 0.250$	$b\delta = 3.097\frac{H}{v}$	521
105	1.833	$\frac{7}{24} = 0.292$	$b\delta = 2.811\frac{H}{v}$	522
120	2.094	$\frac{1}{3} = 0.333$	$b\delta = 2.580\frac{H}{v}$	523
135	2.356	$\frac{3}{8} = 0.375$	$b\delta = 2.404\frac{H}{v}$	524
150	2.618	$\frac{5}{12} = 0.417$	$b\delta = 2.261\frac{H}{v}$	525
165	2.880	$\frac{11}{24} = 0.458$	$b\delta = 2.167\frac{H}{v}$	526
180	3.142	$\frac{1}{2} = 0.500$	$b\delta = 2.074\frac{H}{v}$	527
195	3.403	$\frac{13}{24} = 0.541$	$b\delta = 2.013\frac{H}{v}$	528
210	3.665	$\frac{7}{12} = 0.583$	$b\delta = 1.947\frac{H}{v}$	529
240	4.189	$\frac{2}{3} = 0.667$	$b\delta = 1.854\frac{H}{v}$	530
270	4.712	$\frac{3}{4} = 0.750$	$b\delta = 1.793\frac{H}{v}$	531
300	5.236	$\frac{5}{6} = 0.833$	$b\delta = 1.701\frac{H}{v}$	532

Table of Formulas for Vulcanized-rubber Belts over Cast-iron Pulleys.

Double Leather-Lacing.

a in degrees.	a in circular measure.	a in fractions of circumference.	Formula.	No.
30	0.524	$\frac{1}{12} = 0.083$	$b\delta = 6.980\frac{H}{v}$	533
45	0.785	$\frac{1}{8} = 0.125$	$b\delta = 4.928\frac{H}{v}$	534
60	1.047	$\frac{1}{6} = 0.167$	$b\delta = 3.900\frac{H}{v}$	535
75	1.309	$\frac{5}{24} = 0.208$	$b\delta = 3.300\frac{H}{v}$	536
90	1.571	$\frac{1}{4} = 0.250$	$b\delta = 2.888\frac{H}{v}$	537
105	1.833	$\frac{7}{24} = 0.292$	$b\delta = 2.624\frac{H}{v}$	538
120	2.094	$\frac{1}{3} = 0.333$	$b\delta = 2.404\frac{H}{v}$	539
135	2.356	$\frac{3}{8} = 0.375$	$b\delta = 2.244\frac{H}{v}$	540
150	2.618	$\frac{5}{12} = 0.417$	$b\delta = 2.112\frac{H}{v}$	541
165	2.880	$\frac{11}{24} = 0.458$	$b\delta = 2.024\frac{H}{v}$	542
180	3.142	$\frac{1}{2} = 0.500$	$b\delta = 1.936\frac{H}{v}$	543
195	3.403	$\frac{13}{24} = 0.541$	$b\delta = 1.876\frac{H}{v}$	544
210	3.665	$\frac{7}{12} = 0.583$	$b\delta = 1.821\frac{H}{v}$	545
240	4.189	$\frac{2}{3} = 0.667$	$b\delta = 1.733\frac{H}{v}$	546
270	4.712	$\frac{3}{4} = 0.750$	$b\delta = 1.672\frac{H}{v}$	547
300	5.236	$\frac{5}{6} = 0.833$	$b\delta = 1.601\frac{H}{v}$	548

148   BELTS AND PULLEYS.

TABLE OF FORMULAS FOR VULCANIZED-RUBBER BELTS OVER CAST-IRON PULLEYS.

Double Rawhide-Lacing.

a in degrees.	a in circular measure.	a in fractions of circumference.	Formula.	No.
30	0.524	$\frac{1}{12} = 0.083$	$b\delta = 6.545\frac{H}{v}$	549
45	0.785	$\frac{1}{8} = 0.125$	$b\delta = 4.620\frac{H}{v}$	550
60	1.047	$\frac{1}{6} = 0.167$	$b\delta = 3.658\frac{H}{v}$	551
75	1.309	$\frac{5}{24} = 0.208$	$b\delta = 3.057\frac{H}{v}$	552
90	1.571	$\frac{1}{4} = 0.250$	$b\delta = 2.712\frac{H}{v}$	553
105	1.833	$\frac{7}{24} = 0.292$	$b\delta = 2.464\frac{H}{v}$	554
120	2.094	$\frac{1}{3} = 0.333$	$b\delta = 2.225\frac{H}{v}$	555
135	2.356	$\frac{3}{8} = 0.375$	$b\delta = 2.107\frac{H}{v}$	556
150	2.618	$\frac{5}{12} = 0.417$	$b\delta = 1.980\frac{H}{v}$	557
165	2.880	$\frac{11}{24} = 0.458$	$b\delta = 1.898\frac{H}{v}$	558
180	3.142	$\frac{1}{2} = 0.500$	$b\delta = 1.815\frac{H}{v}$	559
195	3.403	$\frac{13}{24} = 0.541$	$b\delta = 1.760\frac{H}{v}$	560
210	3.665	$\frac{7}{12} = 0.583$	$b\delta = 1.705\frac{H}{v}$	561
240	4.189	$\frac{2}{3} = 0.667$	$b\delta = 1.623\frac{H}{v}$	562
270	4.712	$\frac{3}{4} = 0.750$	$b\delta = 1.568\frac{H}{v}$	563
300	5.236	$\frac{5}{6} = 0.833$	$b\delta = 1.502\frac{H}{v}$	564

Table of Formulas for Vulcanized-rubber Belts over Cast-iron Pulleys.

Riveted Joints.

a in degrees.	a in circular measure.	a in fractions of circumference.	Formula.	No.
30	0.524	$\frac{1}{12} = 0.083$	$b\delta = 4.554\frac{H}{v}$	565
45	0.785	$\frac{1}{8} = 0.125$	$b\delta = 3.212\frac{H}{v}$	566
60	1.047	$\frac{1}{6} = 0.167$	$b\delta = 2.547\frac{H}{v}$	567
75	1.309	$\frac{5}{24} = 0.208$	$b\delta = 2.151\frac{H}{v}$	568
90	1.571	$\frac{1}{4} = 0.250$	$b\delta = 1.887\frac{H}{v}$	569
105	1.833	$\frac{7}{24} = 0.292$	$b\delta = 1.711\frac{H}{v}$	570
120	2.094	$\frac{1}{3} = 0.333$	$b\delta = 1.568\frac{H}{v}$	571
135	2.356	$\frac{3}{8} = 0.375$	$b\delta = 1.463\frac{H}{v}$	572
150	2.618	$\frac{5}{12} = 0.417$	$b\delta = 1.375\frac{H}{v}$	573
165	2.880	$\frac{11}{24} = 0.458$	$b\delta = 1.320\frac{H}{v}$	574
180	3.142	$\frac{1}{2} = 0.500$	$b\delta = 1.260\frac{H}{v}$	575
195	3.403	$\frac{13}{24} = 0.541$	$b\delta = 1.221\frac{H}{v}$	576
210	3.665	$\frac{7}{12} = 0.583$	$b\delta = 1.188\frac{H}{v}$	577
240	4.189	$\frac{2}{3} = 0.667$	$b\delta = 1.128\frac{H}{v}$	578
270	4.712	$\frac{3}{4} = 0.750$	$b\delta = 1.089\frac{H}{v}$	579
300	5.236	$\frac{5}{6} = 0.833$	$b\delta = 1.045\frac{H}{v}$	580

The formulas for vulcanized-rubber belts $\frac{7}{32}$ inch thick (say three-ply) over cast-iron pulleys are as follows:

When $\alpha = 180°$,

Single leather-lacing,	$b = 0.0186P$;	. . . . (581)
Single rawhide-lacing,	$b = 0.0172P$;	. . . . (582)
Double leather-lacing,	$b = 0.0161P$;	. . . . (583)
Double rawhide-lacing,	$b = 0.0151P$;	. . . . (584)
Riveted joint,	$b = 0.0105P$.	. . . . (585)
Single leather-lacing,	$b = 10.208\dfrac{H}{v}$;	. . . . (586)
Single rawhide-lacing,	$b = 9.481\dfrac{H}{v}$;	. . . . (587)
Double leather-lacing,	$b = 8.850\dfrac{H}{v}$;	. . . . (588)
Double rawhide-lacing,	$b = 8.297\dfrac{H}{v}$;	. . . . (589)
Riveted joint,	$b = 5.760\dfrac{H}{v}$.	. . . . (590)

When $\alpha = 135°$,

Single leather-lacing,	$b = 0.0215P$;	. . . . (591)
Single rawhide-lacing,	$b = 0.0200P$;	. . . . (592)
Double leather-lacing,	$b = 0.0187P$;	. . . . (593)
Double rawhide-lacing,	$b = 0.0175P$;	. . . . (594)
Riveted joint,	$b = 0.0122P$.	. . . . (595)
Single leather-lacing,	$b = 11.845\dfrac{H}{v}$;	. . . . (596)
Single rawhide-lacing,	$b = 10.990\dfrac{H}{v}$;	. . . . (597)

Double leather-lacing, $b = 10.258\dfrac{H}{v}$; . . . (598)

Double rawhide-lacing, $b = 9.632\dfrac{H}{v}$; . . . (599)

Riveted joint, $b = 6.668\dfrac{H}{v}$. . . . (600)

TABLE OF WIDTHS OF VULCANIZED-RUBBER BELTS OVER CAST-IRON PULLEYS, WHEN $\alpha = 180°$ AND $\delta = \tfrac{7}{18}''$. From Formulas (581)–(585).

Width in inches.	P, single leather-lacing.	P, single rawhide-lacing.	P, double leather-lacing.	P, double rawhide-lacing.	P, riveted joints.	No.
1	53.88	58.04	62.15	66.27	95.51	1
1½	80.82	87.06	93.23	99.40	143.27	2
2	107.76	116.08	124.30	132.54	191.02	3
2½	134.70	145.10	155.38	165.67	238.78	4
3	161.64	174.11	186.45	198.81	286.53	5
3½	188.58	203.13	217.53	231.94	334.29	6
4	215.52	232.15	248.60	265.08	382.04	7
4½	242.46	261.17	279.68	298.21	429.80	8
5	269.40	290.19	310.75	331.35	477.56	9
5½	296.34	319.21	341.83	364.48	525.31	10
6	323.28	348.23	372.90	397.77	573.07	11
7	377.16	406.27	435.05	463.88	668.58	12
8	431.03	464.31	497.20	530.15	764.09	13
9	484.91	522.34	559.35	596.42	859.60	14
10	538.79	580.38	621.50	662.69	955.11	15
11	592.67	638.42	683.65	728.96	1050.62	16
12	646.55	696.46	745.80	795.23	1146.13	17
14	754.31	812.54	870.10	927.77	1337.15	18
16	862.07	928.61	994.40	1060.31	1528.18	19
18	969.83	1044.69	1118.71	1192.84	1719.20	20
20	1077.59	1160.77	1243.01	1325.38	1910.22	21
22	1185.34	1276.84	1367.31	1457.92	2101.24	22
24	1293.10	1392.92	1491.61	1590.46	2292.26	23
26	1400.86	1509.00	1615.91	1723.00	2483.29	24
28	1508.62	1625.07	1740.21	1825.53	2674.31	25
30	1616.38	1741.15	1864.51	1988.07	2865.33	26

TABLE OF WIDTHS OF VULCANIZED-RUBBER BELTS OVER CAST-IRON PULLEYS, WHEN $\alpha = 180°$ AND $\delta = \frac{7}{3\,8}''$. From Formulas (586)–(590).

Width in inches.	$\frac{H}{v}$, single leather-lacing.	$\frac{H}{v}$, single rawhide-lacing.	$\frac{H}{v}$, double leather-lacing.	$\frac{H}{v}$, double rawhide-lacing.	$\frac{H}{v}$, riveted joint.	No.
1	0.0980	0.1055	0.1130	0.1205	0.1736	1
1½	0.1469	0.1582	0.1695	0.1808	0.2604	2
2	0.1959	0.2109	0.2260	0.2410	0.3472	3
2½	0.2449	0.2637	0.2825	0.3013	0.4340	4
3	0.2939	0.3164	0.3390	0.3616	0.5208	5
3½	0.3429	0.3692	0.3955	0.4218	0.6076	6
4	0.3918	0.4219	0.4520	0.4821	0.6944	7
4½	0.4408	0.4746	0 5085	0.5424	0.7812	8
5	0.4898	0.5275	0.5650	0.6026	0.8681	9
5½	0.5388	0.5801	0.6214	0.6629	0.9549	10
6	0.5878	0.6328	0.6779	0.7231	1.0417	11
7	0.6857	0.7383	0.7909	0.8437	1.2153	12
8	0.7837	0.8438	0.9039	0.9642	1.3889	13
9	0.8817	0.9493	1.0169	1.0847	1.5625	14
10	0.9796	1.0547	1.1299	1.2052	1.7361	15
11	1.0776	1.1602	1.2429	1.3258	1.9097	16
12	1.1755	1.2657	1.3559	1.4463	2.0833	17
14	1.3715	1.4766	1.5819	1.6873	2.4306	18
16	1.5674	1.6876	1.8078	1.9284	2.7778	19
18	1.7633	1.8985	2.0338	2.1694	3.1250	20
20	1.9592	2.1095	2.2598	2.4105	3.4722	21
22	2.1552	2.3204	2.4858	2.6515	3.8194	22
24	2.3511	2.5314	2.7118	2.8926	4.1667	23
26	2.5470	2.7423	2.9377	3.1336	4.5139	24
28	2.7429	2.9532	3.1637	3.3747	4.8611	25
30	2.9389	3.1642	3.3897	3.6157	5.2083	26

TABLE OF WIDTHS OF VULCANIZED-RUBBER BELTS OVER CAST-IRON PULLEYS, WHEN $\alpha = 135°$ AND $\delta = \frac{7}{32}''$. From Formulas (591)–(595).

Width in inches.	P, single leather-lacing.	P, single rawhide-lacing.	P, double leather-lacing.	P, double rawhide-lacing.	P, riveted joint.	No.
1	46.45	50.05	53.62	57.11	82.24	1
1½	69.67	75.08	80.43	85.67	123.36	2
2	92.89	100.10	107.24	114.22	164.47	3
2½	116.12	125.13	134.05	142.78	205.59	4
3	139.34	150.15	160.86	171.33	246.71	5
3½	162.56	175.18	187.67	199.89	287.83	6
4	185.79	200.20	214.48	228.44	328.95	7
4½	209.01	225.23	241.29	257.00	370.07	8
5	232.23	250.25	268.10	285.55	411.18	9
5½	255.46	275.28	294.91	314.11	452.30	10
6	278.68	300.30	321.72	342.66	493.42	11
7	325.13	350.35	375.34	399.77	575.66	12
8	371.57	400.40	428.95	456.88	657.89	13
9	418.02	450.45	482.57	513.99	740.13	14
10	464.47	500.50	536.19	571.10	822.37	15
11	510.91	550.55	589.81	628.21	904.60	16
12	557.36	600.60	643.43	685.32	986.84	17
14	650.26	700.70	750.67	799.54	1151.32	18
16	743.15	800.80	857.91	913.76	1315.79	19
18	836.04	900.90	965.15	1027.98	1480.26	20
20	928.94	1001.00	1072.39	1142.20	1644.74	21
22	1021.83	1101.10	1179.62	1256.42	1809.21	22
24	1114.72	1201.20	1286.86	1370.64	1973.68	23
26	1207.62	1301.30	1394.10	1484.87	2138.16	24
28	1300.51	1401.40	1501.34	1599.09	2302.63	25
30	1391.40	1501.50	1608.58	1713.31	2467.10	26

TABLE OF WIDTHS OF VULCANIZED-RUBBER BELTS OVER CAST-IRON PULLEYS, WHEN $\alpha = 135°$ AND $\delta = \frac{7}{32}''$. From Formulas (596)–(600).

Width in inches.	$\frac{H}{v}$, single leather-lacing.	$\frac{H}{v}$, single rawhide-lacing.	$\frac{H}{v}$, double leather-lacing.	$\frac{H}{v}$, double rawhide-lacing.	$\frac{H}{v}$, riveted joint.	No.
1	0.0844	0.0910	0.0975	0.1038	0.1495	1
1½	0.1266	0.1365	0.1462	0.1557	0.2243	2
2	0.1689	0.1820	0.1950	0.2076	0.2990	3
2½	0.2111	0.2275	0.2437	0.2596	0.3738	4
3	0.2533	0.2730	0.2924	0.3115	0.4486	5
3½	0.2955	0.3185	0.3412	0.3634	0.5233	6
4	0.3377	0.3640	0.3899	0.4153	0.5981	7
4½	0.3799	0.4095	0.4387	0.4672	0.6728	8
5	0.4221	0.4550	0.4874	0.5191	0.7476	9
5½	0.4643	0.5005	0.5362	0.5710	0.8224	10
6	0.5066	0.5460	0.5849	0.6229	0.8971	11
7	0.5910	0.6370	0.6824	0.7267	1.0466	12
8	0.6754	0.7280	0.7799	0.8306	1.1962	13
9	0.7598	0.8189	0.8773	0.9344	1.3457	14
10	0.8443	0.9099	0.9748	1.0382	1.4952	15
11	0.9287	1.0009	1.0723	1.1420	1.6447	16
12	1.0131	1.0919	1.1698	1.2458	1.7942	17
14	1.1820	1.2739	1.3647	1.4535	2.0933	18
16	1.3508	1.4559	1.5597	1.6611	2.3923	19
18	1.5197	1.6380	1.7547	1.8688	2.6914	20
20	1.6885	1.8199	1.9496	2.0764	2.9904	21
22	1.8574	2.0019	2.1446	2.2840	3.2894	22
24	2.0262	2.1839	2.3396	2.4917	3.5885	23
26	2.1951	2.3658	2.5345	2.6993	3.8875	24
28	2.3640	2.5478	2.7295	2.9070	4.1866	25
30	2.5328	2.7298	2.9245	3.1146	4.4856	26

Example.—Required the width for a vulcanized-rubber belt ¾ inch thick which will transmit a force of 1200 pounds, the fastening being a single rawhide-lacing and the arc embraced by the belt on the smaller pulley being $\alpha = 90°$.

Formula (441) gives

$$b \times \frac{3}{4} = 0.00563 \times 1200.$$

Hence $\quad b = 0.00563 \times 1200 \times \frac{4}{3},$

or $\quad b = 9''.$

Example.—Required the width for the above belt with riveted joint instead of single rawhide-lacing.

We have from formula (489)

$$b \times \frac{3}{4} = 0.00343 \times 1200,$$

$$b = 0.00343 \times 1200 \times \frac{4}{3},$$

or $\quad b = 5.489'' = 5\frac{31}{64}''.$

Example.— A vulcanized-rubber belt $\frac{1}{4}$-inch thick embraces an arc equal to $\frac{1}{8}$ the circumference of its smaller pulley, and transmits a force of 20 horse-power at a velocity of 10 feet per second. Required the proper width for double leather-lacing.

Formula (539) gives

$$b \times \frac{1}{4} = 2.404 \times \frac{20}{10},$$

$$b = 2.404 \times 2 \times 4,$$

Example.—A three-ply vulcanized-rubber belt running over two equal pulleys transmits a force of 1275 pounds. Required the proper width for single rawhide-lacing. The table on page 151, column for single rawhide-lacing, line 22, gives, corresponding to $P = 1276.84$ pounds,

$$b = 22''.$$

Example.—Given the data $H = 20$, $v = 20$, $\alpha = 135°$, $\delta = \frac{7}{32}$ inch. Required the proper width for the belt, for single rawhide-lacing.

The table on page 154 gives, corresponding to $\frac{H}{v} = 1$, a belt-width of 11 inches. (Column for single rawhide-lacing, line 16.)

Vulcanized-rubber belts are very rarely seen running over leather or rubber covered pulleys. We may, however, take for the coefficients of friction of rubber on leather and rubber on rubber, respectively,

$$\varphi = 0.50*$$

and

$$\varphi = 0.55.$$

The general formula (50) for the cross-section of any belt for a given tension is

$$b\delta = \frac{T}{f}.$$

---

*Obviously this coefficient may be used for leather belts over rubber-covered pulleys. See Appendix I.

This may be put in the form

$$b\delta = \frac{Px}{f}, \quad \ldots \quad (601)$$

and the value of x for each special case determined from the tensions T and t, as in §§ 10 and 11. The following table gives values of x for all cases likely to occur in practice:

TABLE OF GREATEST TENSION FOR VULCANIZED RUBBER BELTS OVER LEATHER AND RUBBER-COVERED PULLEYS.

a in degrees.	x, leather-covered pulleys.	x, rubber-covered pulleys.	a in degrees.	x, leather-covered pulleys.	x, rubber-covered pulleys.
30	4.35	3.99	150	1.37	1.31
45	3.08	2.85	165	1.31	1.26
60	2.45	2.28	180	1.26	1.21
75	2.08	1.95	195	1.22	1.18
90	1.85	1.73	210	1.19	1.15
105	1.67	1.57	240	1.14	1.11
120	1.54	1.46	270	1.10	1.08
135	1.44	1.38	300	1.08	1.06

Example.—Required the proper width for a vulcanized-rubber belt $\frac{1}{4}$ inch thick, and transmitting a force of 800 pounds over leather-covered pulleys, taking the angle $\alpha = 120°$, and the fastening a single rawhide-lacing.

The table gives for the value of the variable coefficient

$$x = 1.54,$$

and the value of the safe-working stress for single rawhide-lacing is

$$f = 350.$$

Hence formula (601) becomes

$$b \times \frac{1}{4} = \frac{800 \times 1.54}{350},$$

or $\quad b = 14.08'' = 14\frac{5}{64}''.$

Example.—A vulcanized-rubber belt $\frac{1}{4}$ inch thick, running over rubber-covered pulleys, transmits a force of 25 horse-power at a velocity of 10 feet per second. Required the proper width for double rawhide-lacing, the arc embraced by the belt on the smaller pulley being 135°.

From the table, $\quad x = 1.38,$

and from page 141, $\quad f = 400.$

We also have $\quad P = 550\dfrac{H}{v}.$

Substituting these values in formula (601) gives

$$b \times \frac{1}{4} = 550 \times \frac{25}{10} \times 1.38 \div 400.$$

Hence $\quad b = \dfrac{500 \times 25 \times 1.38 \times 4}{10 \times 400},$

or $\quad b = 18.98'' = 18\frac{63}{64}''.$

Example.—A ($\frac{1}{4}$-inch thick) vulcanized-rubber belt 12 inches wide runs over leather-covered pulleys, and embraces an angle of 90° upon the smaller pulley. Required the force in pounds which may be safely transmitted by the belt with a double rawhide-lacing.

The table gives $x = 1.85$,

and we have also $f = 400$.

Hence formula (601) gives

$$12 \times \frac{1}{4} = \frac{P \times 1.85}{400}, \quad P = \frac{12 \times 0.25 \times 400}{1.85},$$

or $P = 648.65$.

§ 13. Rim, Nave, and Fixing-keys for Pulleys.*

The rim of a pulley intended to carry a flat belt is generally slightly rounded (Figs. 48 and 49), in order that the belt may remain in the centre of the pulley-face, instead of working to one side, as is the case with flat-faced pulleys. The amount of this rounding (s) may be taken equal to $\frac{1}{30}$ the width of the belt.

For isolated pulleys the face-width B is taken somewhat greater than the width of the belt (b); often we take

$$B = \frac{5}{4} b. \quad \ldots \ldots \quad (602)$$

When, however, several pulleys are placed side by side in order to receive alternately the same belt the face-width B should be taken only very slightly greater than the belt-width b.

The thickness k of the edge of the rim, or the

---

* From "Reuleaux."

thickness at the ends of the face-width, may be easily calculated from the formula

$$k = 0.08 + \frac{B}{100}. \quad \cdots \quad (603)$$

High-speed pulleys and those subjected to considerable shock and vibration are often provided with lateral flanges cast on the rims, as shown in Fig. 49, or are replaced by grooved pulleys carrying belts with circular cross-section (Fig. 50).

Example.—Required the rim dimensions for an iso-

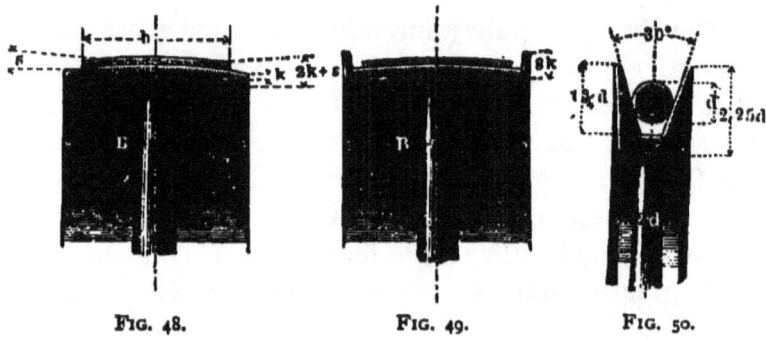

FIG. 48.   FIG. 49.   FIG. 50.

lated pulley which is to carry a belt 12 inches wide. From formula (602) we have for the face-width

$$B = \frac{5}{4} \times 12 = 15'';$$

and from formula (603), for the thickness of the rim at the edges,

$$k = 0.08 + \frac{15}{100} = 0.23''.$$

For the amount of rounding of the pulley-face, $s = \frac{1}{20}b = \frac{1}{20} \times 12 = 0.6''$. The thickness of the rim at the centre is, therefore,

$$2k + s = 2 \times 0.23 + 0.6 = 1.06''.$$

If we wish to provide the pulley with rim-flanges, as in Fig. 49, we have for the height of the flanges $8k = 8 \times 0.23 = 1.84''$, and take the thickness of the flanges equal to k.

Nave.—The thickness (w, Fig. 56) of a pulley-nave is given by the formula

$$w = 0.4 + \frac{d}{6} + \frac{R}{50}, \quad \ldots \quad (604)$$

in which d represents the diameter of the shaft upon which the pulley is keyed, and R the radius of the pulley.

The length of the nave should not be taken less than

$$L = 2.50w. \quad \ldots \quad (605)$$

Often (in idle pulleys, for example) the length L is taken equal to the face-width B of the pulley.

Example.—A pulley of 36 inches diameter is keyed upon a shaft of 4 inches diameter; required the nave dimensions. From formula (604) the thickness is

$$w = 0.4 + \frac{4}{6} + \frac{18}{50} = 1.427'',$$

and from formula (605) we have for the length of the nave

$$L = 2.50 \times 1.427 = 3.5675''.$$

In idle pulleys the interior diameter of the nave, or the eye of the pulley, is taken slightly greater than the

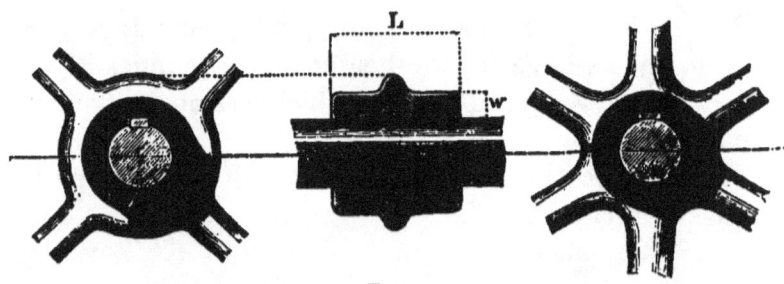

FIG. 51.

diameter of the shaft upon which the pulley is to run; often the eye of an idle pulley is furnished with a coating of bronze or white metal, in order to diminish the friction.

Keys.—There are three kinds of keys which are used to fix pulleys upon their arbors: the hollow key (Fig.

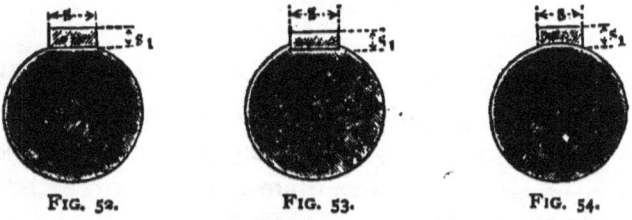

FIG. 52.   FIG. 53.   FIG. 54.

54), used for light pulleys; the flat key (Fig. 52), used for pulleys of medium size; and the countersunk key

RIM, NAVE, AND FIXING-KEYS FOR PULLEYS.

The width s and thickness s_1 of the fixing-key are given by the expressions

$$s = 0.16 + \frac{d}{5}, \quad \ldots \quad (606)$$

$$s_1 = 0.16 + \frac{d}{10}, \quad \ldots \quad (607)$$

and the inclination varies from $\frac{1}{100}$ to $\frac{1}{200}$.

Example.—Required the width and thickness of the fixing-key for the pulley of the preceding example, in which the diameter of the shaft is $d = 4''$. Formulas (606) and (607) give for the required width and thickness, respectively,

$$s = 0.16 + \frac{4}{5} = 0.96'',$$

and

$$s_1 = 0.16 + \frac{4}{10} = 0.56''.$$

FIG. 55.

Split pulleys (Fig. 55) are often used for light work. They offer the advantage of being easily put up and taken down without interfering with the shaft-hang-

dispensed with, the two parts of the pulley being pressed upon the shaft by means of the nuts *a, a*, with sufficient force to prevent slipping. For this purpose the eye of the pulley is made slightly less than the diameter of the shaft upon which the pulley is to be fastened. When the division passes through a pair of

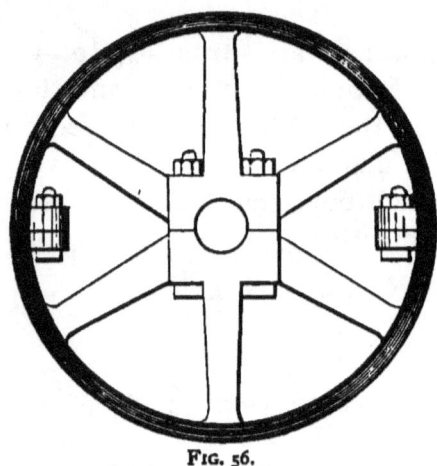

FIG. 56.

arms, as in the figure, each half of the split arm must be as strong as an entire undivided arm, and consequently of the same dimensions as the entire arms.*

Weight of Pulleys.—The weights of pulleys can evidently be calculated from one formula only approximately, since the arms, nave, etc., vary considerably in

---

* A better and stronger form of split pulley is represented in Fig. 56. In this case all the arms are entire, and the pulley presents a better appearance, as well as a simpler form. According to Unwin (see "Elements of Machine Design," § 168), the net section of the bolt at the rim should be one quarter the section of the rim plus ¼ square inch, and that of the bolt at the nave one quarter the section of the nave plus ¼ square inch.

RIM, NAVE, AND FIXING-KEYS FOR PULLEYS.

different pulleys. We may, however, calculate the weights of pulleys with sufficient accuracy for ordinary purposes from the formula

$$G = \left(0.163\frac{R}{b} + 0.015\left(\frac{R}{b}\right)^2 + 0.00309\left(\frac{R}{b}\right)^3\right)b^3, \quad (608)$$

in which G is the weight of the pulley in pounds, R and b respectively the radius of the pulley and width of the belt.

The following table gives values of $\frac{G}{b^3}$ for different values of $\frac{R}{b}$:

TABLE OF WEIGHTS OF PULLEYS.

$\frac{R}{b}$	$\frac{G}{b^3}$	$\frac{R}{b}$	$\frac{G}{b^3}$	$\frac{R}{b}$	$\frac{G}{b^3}$	$\frac{R}{b}$	$\frac{G}{b^3}$
1.0	0.181	2.5	0.550	5.0	1.579	8.25	4.111
1.1	0.202	2.6	0.580	5.2	1.691	8.50	4.378
1.2	0.223	2.7	0.612	5.4	1.807	8.75	4.657
1.3	0.244	2.8	0.642	5.6	1.929	9.00	4.947
1.4	0.266	2.9	0.675	5.8	2.057	9.25	5.250
1.5	0.289	3.0	0.708	6.0	2.190	9.50	5.567
1.6	0.312	3.2	0.777	6.2	2.329	9.75	5.895
1.7	0.335	3.4	0.850	6.4	2.473	10.00	6.237
1.8	0.360	3.6	0.926	6.6	2.623	10.25	6.592
1.9	0.385	3.8	1.007	6.8	2.780	10.50	6.961
2.0	0.411	4.0	1.089	7.0	2.943	11.00	7.742
2.1	0.437	4.2	1.180	7.25	3.155	11.50	8.581
2.2	0.464	4.4	1.273	7.50	3.378	12.00	9.482
2.3	0.492	4.6	1.370	7.75	3.611	12.50	10.446
2.4	0.520	4.8	1.472	8.00	3.856	13.00	11.475

Example.—The radius of a pulley is 16 inches, and the width of the belt which runs upon the pulley 4 inches; required the approximate weight of the pulley. Here $\frac{R}{b} = \frac{16}{4} = 4$. From formula (608),

$$G = (0.163 \times 4 + 0.015 \times 16 + 0.00309 \times 64)64,$$
$$G = (0.652 + 0.240 + 0.19776)64 = 1.08976 \times 64;$$

or, $\qquad G = 69.74$ pounds.

Example.—Required the approximate weight of a pulley for the data $R = 36''$, $b = 4\frac{1}{2}''$. In this case $\dfrac{R}{b} = \dfrac{36}{4\frac{1}{2}} = 8$, and $b^3 = 91.125$. From the table we find for $\dfrac{R}{b} = 8$,

$$\frac{G}{b^3} = 3.856.$$

Hence $\quad G = 3.856 \times 91.125 = 351.378$ pounds.

§ 14. Arms of Pulleys.*

Ordinarily the arms of pulleys have oval cross-sections, the diameter in the plane of the pulley being twice the smaller diameter. The profile of such a cross-section may be drawn by circle-arcs as shown in Fig. 57. The dotted circle is drawn on the greater diameter h_1 of the pulley-arm, and the arcs ab and $a'b'$ have their centres respectively in the points c and c'. The arcs ab and $a'b'$ are connected at their ends by small circle-arcs as shown in the figure.

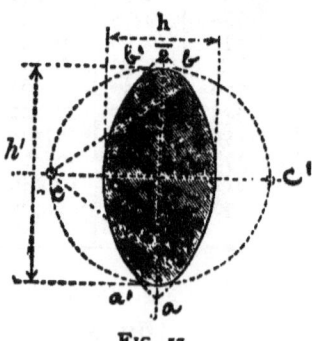

Fig. 57.

The axes of pulley-arms may be straight as in Fig.

58, curved as in Fig. 59, or double curved in the form of a letter S. Single-curved arms may be drawn in the following manner: Take (Fig. 59) the arc AE equal to $\frac{2}{3}$ the arc EF, determined by the centre s of the arms at the rim of the pulley, and draw A_1O perpendicular to AO. From the centre D draw CD perpendicular to

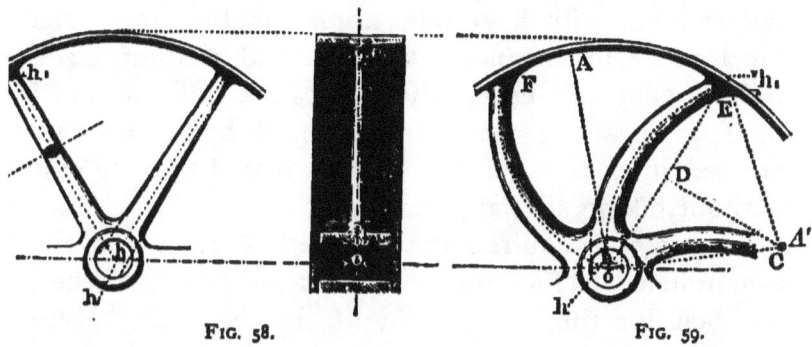

FIG. 58.   FIG. 59.

OE, and the point C of intersection of DC and OC is the centre for the curved axis of the arm.

The number of arms (N) necessary for pulleys of different sizes may be determined by means of the formula

$$N = \frac{1}{2}\left(5 + \frac{R}{b}\right), \quad \ldots \quad (609)$$

or the following table calculated from it:

The formula

$$h = 0.24 + \frac{b}{4} + \frac{R}{10N} \quad \ldots \quad (610)$$

gives the greater diameter for the pulley-arms. The diameter or width h is taken at the nave as shown in Fig. 58, and the width h_1 at the rim may be conveniently taken equal to $\frac{2}{3}h$. These expressions have been determined, with a certain approximation from the most accurate formulas; for large and medium sized pulleys they are especially applicable, but for small light pulleys the dimensions should be slightly increased in order that the pulleys may be easily cast without taking special precautions.

Example.—Required the number of arms and the arm dimensions for a pulley having a radius of 18 inches, the belt for the pulley being 6 inches wide. Here

$$\frac{R}{b} = \frac{18}{6} = 3.$$

From the above table we find the number of arms to be $N = 4$, and formula (610) gives for the width of the arms in the plane of the pulley

$$h = 0.24 + \frac{6}{4} + \frac{18}{10 \times 4} = 2.19''.$$

The width at right angles with the plane of the pulley is therefore

$$h_1 = \tfrac{2}{3} \times 2.19 = 1.46''.$$

To trace the profiles of the arms proceed as follows: Straight arms (Fig. 60).—Having drawn the diameter EOC, take $ab = cC = Cd = \frac{2}{3}h$, and draw the lines ac and bd, which give the limits of the profile. Connect ac and

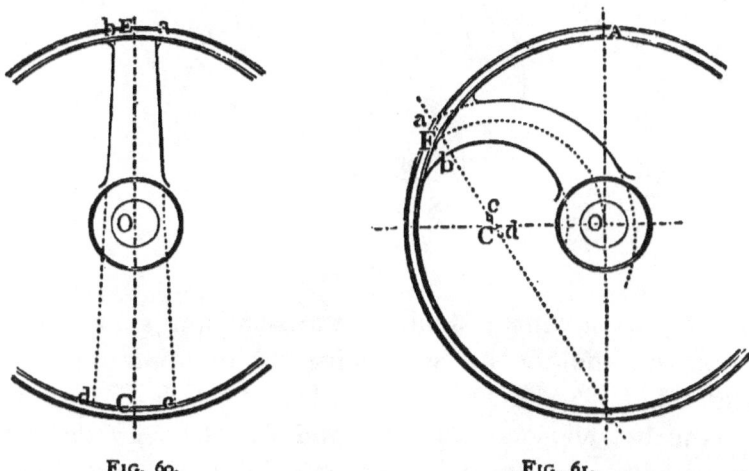

FIG. 60.   FIG. 61.

bd with the rim and nave by small circle arcs, and the profile is complete. Curved arms (Fig. 61.)—The centre C for the axis having been determined, draw the straight line ad, then take $aE = Eb = \dfrac{h}{3}$ and $Cc = Cd = \dfrac{h}{6}$; the points c and d thus determined are the centres for the arcs which limit the profile, and cb and da are the radii.

Double-curved arms.*—Fig. 62 shows a simple method for drawing double-curved arms. Draw the radial line oA, making 30° with the horizontal. Take $oc = \frac{2}{3}oA$, and through the point c draw the line pD, making 60° with the horizontal. Intersect the line

---

* From the author's "Treatise on Toothed Gearing."

pD by a horizontal line through the point A: the points D and p are respectively the centres for the arcs oc and cA, which together form the axis of the arm. Lay off the arm-widths as shown in the figure. From the

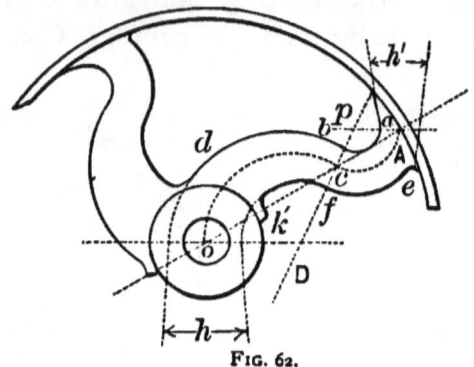

FIG. 62.

point p as a centre strike the arcs ab and ef, and find upon the line oD the centres for the remaining arcs bd and fk'.

Another very similar method for drawing double-curved arms is shown in Fig. 63. Draw the radial line

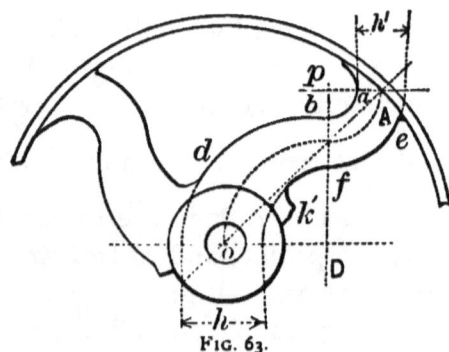

FIG. 63.

oA, making 45° with the horizontal. Take $oc = \tfrac{1}{3}oA$, and through the point c draw the vertical line pD.

Intersect the line pD by the horizontal line Ap. The points p and D are the centres for the arcs of the axis. Lay off h and h_1 as shown in the figure, and proceed, as in Fig. 62, to strike the arcs ab, ef, bd, and fk'.

§ 15. Shafts.*

When a shaft is so supported by its bearings as to be subjected to a *torsional* strain only, as is almost invariably the case in pulley-shafts (the bending strain due to the weight of the pulley and the force transmitted by the belt being ordinarily slight enough to be safely neglected), the calculation of the proper strength for the shaft may be made as follows:

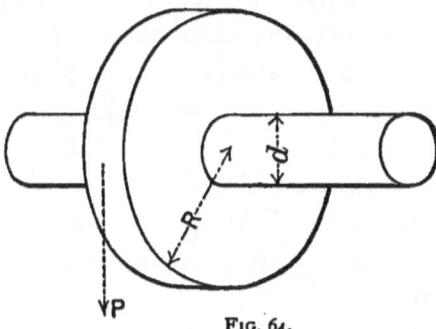

FIG. 64.

In Fig. 64, P represents the total force tending to twist the shaft, i.e., the total force transmitted by the belt; R the distance from the centre of the shaft to the point at which the force acts, i.e., the radius of the pulley; and d the diameter of the pulley-shaft. The

---

* From the author's "Treatise on Toothed Gearing."

greatest safe torsional strain which can be sustained by the shaft is given by the expression

$$P = \frac{\pi f'd^3}{16R} = 0.19635\frac{f'd^3}{R},$$

in which f' is the greatest safe shearing stress in pounds per square inch for the material of the shaft. From this,

$$d = \sqrt[3]{\frac{PR}{0.19535f'}}$$

or, $\quad\quad\quad\quad d = 1.720\sqrt[3]{\frac{PR}{f'}}.\quad\ldots\quad(611)$

RULE.—To determine the diameter of a pulley-shaft of any material multiply the total force transmitted by the belt by the radius of the pulley, divide this product by the greatest safe shearing stress in pounds per square inch for the material of the shaft, extract the cube root of the quotient thus obtained, and multiply the result by 1.720.

Example.—Required the diameter for an oak shaft upon which is a 60-inch pulley transmitting a force of 1000 pounds, taking $f' = 500$ pounds. From formula (611) we have

$$d = 1.720\sqrt[3]{\frac{1000 \times 30}{500}} = 1.720 \times 3.915 = 6.734'' = 6\tfrac{47}{64}''.$$

We propose to take for steel $f' = 12000$ pounds; for wrought-iron $f' = 8000$ pounds; and for cast-iron $f' = 4000$ pounds. These values of f' are nearly mean between those used by Stoney, Haswell, and Unwin, which differ far more than is conducive to any degree of accuracy. Substituting the above values of f' successively in formula (611) and reducing, we obtain,

For steel, $\qquad d = 0.075 \sqrt[3]{PR}. \quad \ldots \quad (612)$

For wrought-iron, $d = 0.086 \sqrt[3]{PR}. \quad \ldots \quad (613)$

For cast-iron, $\qquad d = 0.108 \sqrt[3]{PR}. \quad \ldots \quad (614)$

RULE.—To determine the diameter for a pulley-shaft of steel, wrought or cast iron, multiply the total force transmitted by the radius of the pulley, extract the cube root of the product, and multiply the result by 0.075 for steel, 0.086 for wrought-iron, and 0.108 for cast-iron.

Example.—A 48-inch pulley transmits a force of 1000 pounds. Required the diameter for a steel shaft. From formula (612) we have

$$d = 0.075 \sqrt[3]{1000 \times 24} = 0.075 \times 28.84,$$

or, $\quad d = 2.163'' = 2\tfrac{11}{64}''$ nearly.

Example.—Taking the data of the preceding example, required the diameter for a shaft of cast-iron. Formula (614) gives

$$d = 0.108 \sqrt[3]{1000 \times 24} = 0.108 \times 28.84,$$

or, $\quad d = 3.115'' = 3\tfrac{1}{8}''$ nearly.

Formulas for the diameters of pulley-shafts in terms

of the horse-power transmitted and the revolutions per minute may be obtained as follows:

As before explained, we have the expression

$$P = 63000 \frac{H}{Rn},$$

H representing the horse-power, R the radius of the pulley, and n the number of revolutions per minute. Substituting this value in formulas (611), (612), (613), and (614), and reducing, we obtain the following:

General formula, $\quad d = 68.44 \sqrt[3]{\dfrac{H}{nf^1}}. \quad \ldots \quad$ (615)

For steel, $\quad d = 2.984 \sqrt[3]{\dfrac{H}{n}}. \quad \ldots \quad$ (616)

For wrought-iron, $d = 3.422 \sqrt[3]{\dfrac{H}{n}}. \quad \ldots \quad$ (617)

For cast-iron, $\quad d = 4.297 \sqrt[3]{\dfrac{H}{n}}. \quad \ldots \quad$ (618)

RULE.—To determine the diameter for a pulley-shaft of any material from the horse-power and number of revolutions per minute, divide the horse-power by the product of the number of revolutions into the greatest safe shearing stress in pounds per square inch for the material of the shaft, extract the cube root of the quotient thus obtained, and multiply the result by 68.44.

To determine the diameter for a pulley-shaft of steel, wrought or cast iron, from the horse-power and number of revolutions per minute, divide the horse-power by the number of revolutions, extract the cube root of the quotient, and multiply the result by 2.984 for steel, 3.422 for wrought-iron, and 4.297 for cast-iron.

Example.—Required the diameter for an oak pulley-shaft which transmits a force of 10 horse-power and makes 40 revolutions per minute. If we take for the greatest safe shearing stress for oak $f' = 500$ pounds per square inch, we shall have, from formula (615),

$$d = 68.44 \sqrt[3]{\frac{10}{40 \times 500}} = 68.44 \sqrt[3]{\frac{1}{2000}} = 68.44 \times \frac{1}{12.60},$$

or, $\qquad d = 5.432'' = 5\frac{7}{16}''$ nearly.

Example.—Taking the data of the preceding example, required the diameters for shafts of steel and wrought-iron.

From formula (616),

$$d = 2.984 \sqrt[3]{\frac{10}{40}} = 2.984 \sqrt[3]{0.25} = 2.984 \times 0.62996,$$

or, for steel, $\qquad d = 1.88'' = 1\frac{57}{64}''.$

From formula (617),

$$d = 3.422 \sqrt[3]{\frac{10}{40}} = 3.422 \times 0.62996,$$

or, for wrought-iron,

$$d = 2.1557'' = 2\frac{5}{32}''.$$

Pulley-shafts are most commonly of wrought-iron; when, however, wrought-iron shafts, in order to give the necessary strength, become so large as to be inconvenient, steel shafts are used. Cast-iron shafts are, as a rule, unreliable and treacherous; they are therefore seldom used except for the transmission of slight powers and in cheap, inferior machinery. The following tables, calculated from formulas (612), (613), (616), and (617) to the nearest $\frac{1}{64}$ inch, will be found very convenient in designing pulley-shafts of steel and wrought-iron:

TABLE OF SHAFT-DIAMETERS.

PR	d for steel.	d for wrought-iron.	PR	d for steel.	d for wrought-iron.
250	$\frac{15}{16}''$	$\frac{65}{64}''$	60000	$2\frac{15}{16}''$	$3\frac{28}{64}''$
500	$\frac{19}{16}$	$1\frac{1}{4}$	70000	$3\frac{8}{64}$	$3\frac{35}{64}$
1000	$\frac{9}{8}$	$\frac{36}{64}$	80000	$3\frac{15}{64}$	$3\frac{45}{64}$
1500	$\frac{60}{64}$	$\frac{61}{64}$	90000	$3\frac{24}{64}$	$3\frac{54}{64}$
2000	$1\frac{1}{64}$	$1\frac{5}{64}$	100000	$3\frac{32}{64}$	4
2500	$1\frac{1}{16}$	$1\frac{14}{64}$	110000	$3\frac{39}{64}$	$4\frac{1}{8}$
3000	$1\frac{5}{64}$	$1\frac{12}{64}$	120000	$3\frac{45}{64}$	$4\frac{15}{64}$
3500	$1\frac{8}{64}$	$1\frac{1}{8}$	130000	$3\frac{51}{64}$	$4\frac{24}{64}$
4000	$1\frac{8}{16}$	$1\frac{25}{64}$	140000	$3\frac{57}{64}$	$4\frac{3}{8}$
4500	$1\frac{14}{64}$	$1\frac{27}{64}$	150000	$3\frac{63}{64}$	$4\frac{9}{16}$
5000	$1\frac{9}{32}$	$1\frac{15}{16}$	175000	$4\frac{13}{64}$	$4\frac{48}{64}$
6000	$1\frac{21}{64}$	$1\frac{9}{16}$	200000	$4\frac{25}{64}$	$5\frac{1}{32}$
7000	$1\frac{7}{16}$	$1\frac{41}{64}$	250000	$4\frac{48}{64}$	$5\frac{57}{64}$
8000	$1\frac{1}{2}$	$1\frac{13}{16}$	500000	$5\frac{60}{64}$	$6\frac{53}{64}$
10000	$1\frac{39}{64}$	$1\frac{55}{64}$	750000	$6\frac{7}{8}$	$7\frac{48}{64}$
12500	$1\frac{3}{4}$	2	1000000	$7\frac{1}{2}$	$8\frac{29}{64}$
15000	$1\frac{27}{32}$	$2\frac{1}{4}$	1500000	$8\frac{37}{64}$	$9\frac{57}{64}$
20000	$2\frac{3}{16}$	$2\frac{21}{64}$	2000000	$9\frac{28}{64}$	$10\frac{48}{64}$
25000	$2\frac{7}{16}$	$2\frac{33}{64}$	2500000	$10\frac{14}{64}$	$11\frac{42}{64}$
30000	$2\frac{21}{64}$	$2\frac{43}{64}$	3000000	$10\frac{52}{64}$	$12\frac{28}{64}$
35000	$2\frac{27}{64}$	$2\frac{13}{16}$	3500000	$11\frac{25}{64}$	$13\frac{1}{16}$
40000	$2\frac{9}{16}$	$2\frac{15}{16}$	4000000	$11\frac{57}{64}$	$13\frac{38}{64}$
45000	$2\frac{41}{64}$	$3\frac{1}{64}$	4500000	$12\frac{3}{8}$	$14\frac{13}{64}$
50000	$2\frac{49}{64}$	$3\frac{11}{64}$	5000000	$12\frac{52}{64}$	$14\frac{44}{64}$

SHAFTS.

TABLE OF SHAFT-DIAMETERS.

$\frac{H}{n}$	d for steel.	d for wrought-iron.	$\frac{H}{n}$	d for steel.	d for wrought-iron.
0.025	$\frac{7}{8}''$	$1''$	3.75	$4\frac{11}{32}''$	$5\frac{5}{16}''$
0.050	$1\frac{8}{32}$	$1\frac{17}{64}$	4	$4\frac{7}{16}$	$5\frac{7}{16}$
0.075	$1\frac{17}{64}$	$1\frac{7}{16}$	4.25	$4\frac{9}{16}$	$5\frac{35}{64}$
0.100	$1\frac{25}{64}$	$1\frac{19}{32}$	4.50	$4\frac{21}{32}$	$5\frac{21}{32}$
0.150	$1\frac{9}{16}$	$1\frac{13}{16}$	4.75	$5\frac{1}{32}$	$5\frac{3}{4}$
0.200	$1\frac{3}{4}$	2	5	$5\frac{3}{32}$	$5\frac{55}{64}$
0.250	$1\frac{7}{8}$	$2\frac{5}{32}$	5.50	$5\frac{7}{32}$	$6\frac{3}{64}$
0.300	2	$2\frac{9}{32}$	6	$5\frac{27}{64}$	$6\frac{7}{32}$
0.350	$2\frac{7}{64}$	$2\frac{13}{32}$	6.50	$5\frac{3}{16}$	$6\frac{25}{64}$
0.400	$2\frac{1}{4}$	$2\frac{35}{64}$	7	$5\frac{17}{32}$	$6\frac{9}{16}$
0 500	$2\frac{3}{8}$	$2\frac{23}{32}$	8	$5\frac{51}{64}$	$6\frac{47}{64}$
0.600	$2\frac{17}{32}$	$2\frac{57}{64}$	9	$6\frac{3}{64}$	$7\frac{1}{8}$
0.700	$2\frac{21}{32}$	$3\frac{1}{32}$	10	$6\frac{27}{64}$	$7\frac{7}{8}$
0.800	$2\frac{49}{64}$	$3\frac{11}{64}$	11	$6\frac{3}{4}$	$7\frac{27}{64}$
0.900	$2\frac{27}{32}$	$3\frac{5}{16}$	12	$6\frac{31}{32}$	$7\frac{47}{64}$
1.	$2\frac{31}{32}$	$3\frac{27}{64}$	14	$7\frac{3}{16}$	$8\frac{1}{4}$
1.25	$3\frac{7}{32}$	$3\frac{11}{16}$	16	$7\frac{15}{32}$	$8\frac{5}{8}$
1.50	$3\frac{27}{64}$	$3\frac{55}{64}$	18	$7\frac{13}{16}$	$8\frac{31}{32}$
1.75	$3\frac{19}{32}$	$4\frac{1}{8}$	20	$8\frac{3}{16}$	$9\frac{3}{16}$
2.	$3\frac{23}{32}$	$4\frac{5}{16}$	22	$8\frac{17}{64}$	$9\frac{27}{64}$
2.25	$3\frac{55}{64}$	$4\frac{31}{64}$	25	$8\frac{17}{32}$	10
2.50	$4\frac{1}{64}$	$4\frac{21}{32}$	27	$8\frac{11}{16}$	$10\frac{17}{64}$
2.75	$4\frac{11}{64}$	$4\frac{11}{16}$	30	$9\frac{1}{8}$	$10\frac{5}{8}$
3.	$4\frac{5}{16}$	$4\frac{15}{16}$	32	$9\frac{1}{4}$	$10\frac{55}{64}$
3.25	$4\frac{27}{64}$	$5\frac{1}{16}$	35	$9\frac{17}{32}$	$11\frac{3}{16}$
3.50	$4\frac{35}{64}$	$5\frac{3}{16}$	40	$10\frac{21}{64}$	$11\frac{27}{64}$

Example.—Required the diameter for a wrought-iron shaft for a 40-inch pulley which transmits a force of 1000 pounds. In this case

$$PR = 1000 \times 20 = 20000,$$

and from the table on page 176, the value of d for wrought-iron corresponding to $PR = 20000$ is $d = 2\frac{21}{64}$ inches.

Example.—The diameter of a wrought-iron pulley-shaft is $4\tfrac{1}{8}$ inches. Required the force which the shaft can safely transmit by means of a 24-inch pulley. From the table on page 176 the value of PR corresponding to $d = 4\tfrac{1}{8}$ inches for wrought-iron is 110,000; hence we have

$$P = \frac{110000}{R} = \frac{110000}{12} = 9167 \text{ pounds nearly.}$$

Example.—A pulley transmitting a force of 20 horse-power makes 200 revolutions per minute. Required the diameter for a shaft of steel. We have

$$\frac{H}{n} = \frac{20}{200} = \frac{1}{10} = 0.100,$$

and from the table on page 177 the value of d for steel corresponding to $\frac{H}{n} = 0.100$ is $d = 1\tfrac{25}{64}$ inches.

Example.—A 2-inch steel shaft transmits a force of 25 horse-power. It is required to determine the proper number of revolutions per minute. From the table on page 177 the value of $\frac{H}{n}$ which corresponds to $d = 2$ inches for steel is $\frac{H}{n} = 0.300$; hence we have

$$\frac{H}{n} = \frac{25}{n} = 0.300,$$

or
$$n = 83\tfrac{1}{3} \text{ revolutions per minute.}$$

§ 16. *The Tightening-Pulley.—Fast and Loose Pulleys.*

Tightening-pulleys are used to tighten loose belts, or, in other words, to increase the tension, and thus prevent slipping upon the principal pulleys. Fig. 65 represents a tightening-pulley as commonly used in the shops. *A* and *B* are the principal pulleys, and *C* the tightening-pulley, which is pressed against the belt

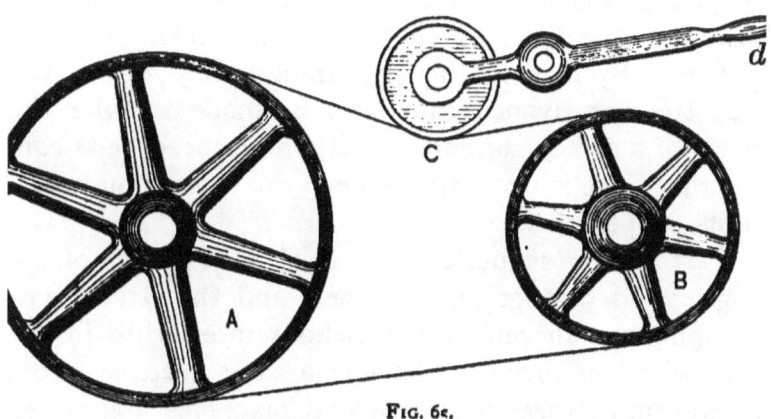

FIG. 65.

or raised off the belt by means of the lever *d*. Often the weight of the tightening-pulley is sufficient to produce the required tension; if not, extra weights are hung to the pulley, or the lever fastened up in its proper position. When the pulley *C* is lifted off the belt entirely, the belt relieved of its tension no longer runs upon the driver; the driven pulley is then at rest, or the belt is disengaged. The tightening-pulley obviates the necessity of taking up the slack caused by the stretching of the belt, for as the belt becomes longer and consequently looser upon the principal pulleys by stretching, it may be tightened by simply lowering the tightening-pulley. A glance at the figure will show that by means of this pulley the arcs of contact between the belt and the principal pulleys are increased to a considerable extent—which in itself is an important consideration. The tightening-pulley is also a valuable means of increasing the duration of a belt; for since the wear upon the belt increases with the tension to which it is subjected, it is important that the tension be no greater than is sufficient to prevent slipping, and this may be easily regulated by lifting or lowering the lever which controls the position of the pulley. By placing the tightening-pulley below the belt the contrivance may also be made to take the place of a pulley support. With high-speed belts considerable care is necessary to keep the tightening-pulley in its proper position.

Fast and loose pulleys are used as a means of engaging and disengaging the belt, and thus starting or stopping the driven pulley without interfering in any way with the driver. This is a very necessary consideration in cases where several machines are driven by a single driving-pulley, as is almost always the case in practice. Many contrivances have been from time to time devised for this purpose, but few if any have proved as simple and sure as the fast and loose pulleys seen in nearly every shop and factory in the land. Fig. 66 represents a pair of such pulleys. A is keyed fast to the shaft CC, while the pulley B runs loose upon the shaft. The belt is made to pass from one pulley to the other by means of a lever, or similar device.

When the belt is on the fast pulley *A*, the motion of the driving-pulley is transmitted to the shaft *C C*. When the belt is on the loose or idle pulley *B*, this pulley simply rotates upon the shaft without giving to it any motion. In many cases the loose pulley is placed upon the driven shaft; the belt then continues its motion when upon the loose pulley. It is preferable, however, to have the loose pulley on the driving-shaft, because when the belt is out of gear it remains mo-

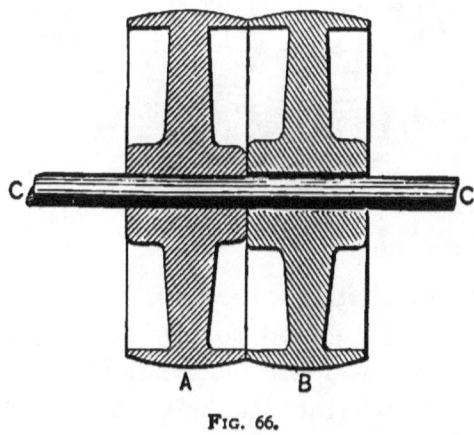

Fig. 66.

tionless, thus saving it from unnecessary wear. Often there are two loose pulleys, one on each shaft; the driving fast pulleys are then of the same face-width, while with one loose pulley the driving-pulley on the other shaft must have a face-width equal to those of the loose pulley and its neighboring fast pulley together.

A device introduced some years ago for the purpose of diminishing the tension upon a belt while upon a loose pulley is shown in Fig. 67. *A* is an ordinary pulley keyed fast to the shaft *D D*, and *B* a loose pulley, which is somewhat smaller than the fast pulley, and which carries a conical flange *C C*, the outside diameter of which is equal to that of the fast pulley *A*. When the belt passes from *A* to *B*, the tension

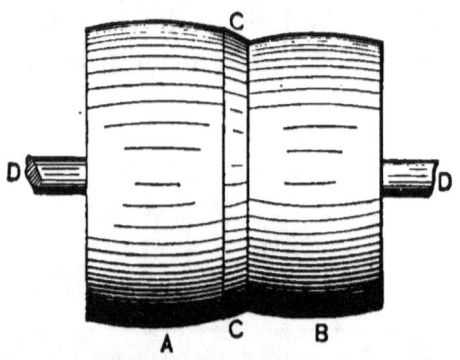

FIG. 67.

upon it is diminished, the belt slackens, and while out of work is not subjected to any considerable strain. In ordinary fast and loose pulleys the tension upon the belt is constant, whether the belt is at work or at rest.

Fig. 68 represents a common application of the principle of fast and loose pulleys, by which an alternate rotating motion in both directions is obtained from the continuous rotary motion of the driving-shaft. The pulleys *A*, *C*, *A'*, and *C'* are fast, while *B* and *B'* run loosely upon their shafts. Two belts, one open and the other crossed, are placed side by side in such a manner that one rests upon the loose pulleys, while the other runs upon one or the other pair of fast pulleys. When the belts are in the positions shown in the figure, the crossed belt is the driver, and the open belt remains motionless. By sliding the two belts over the pulley-faces the open belt is placed upon the fast pulleys A and A', and the crossed belt upon the two loose pulleys. This reverses the direction of

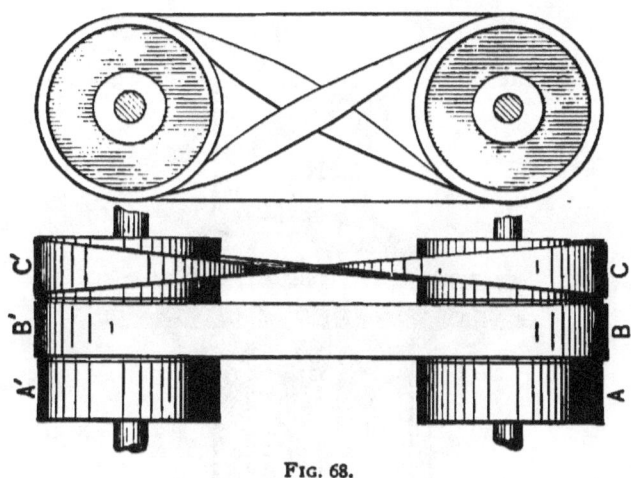

FIG. 68.

rotation of the driven shaft, and by sliding the belts back into their first positions the motion of the driven shaft is again reversed.

The most familiar example of this reversing gear is seen in the planing-machine, where the forward and backward motion of the table which carries the work is thus accomplished.

Belts with circular cross-sections, such as round leather-belts, rope-belts, etc., generally have pulleys with grooved faces. The ordinary fast and loose pulleys obviously cannot be used in such cases. Fig. 69 shows a fast and loose pulley for round belts, which seems to answer the purpose very well. The part B of the fast pulley is keyed fast to the shaft dd, and the part A may be moved away from the part B by means of the lever f. In the figure the parts of the

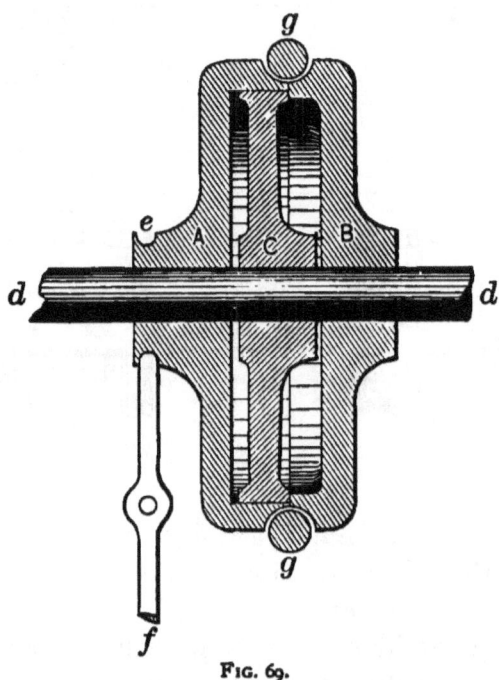

FIG. 69.

fast pulley are together, and the belt gg therefore drives the shaft. When the parts are separated the belt slides from the part B to the inside loose pulley C, which then rotates about the shaft without transmitting to it its motion. Upon sliding the part A

again into the position shown in the figure the thin rim slides under the belt and lifts it into the groove, in position for work.

Another fast and loose pulley for round belts is represented in Fig. 70. In this case the pulley runs loosely upon the shaft dd when in the position shown in the figure. The conical key B is fast to the shaft, and, when forced into the hub of the pulley by means of the lever f, bites with sufficient force to secure the pulley. A collar kk fast to the shaft prevents the pulley from sliding away from the key.

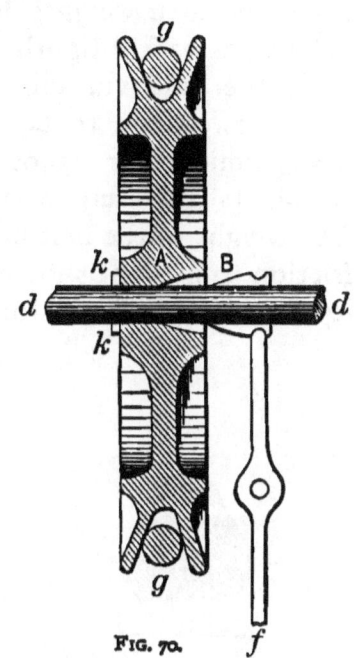

FIG. 70.

For light transmissions this pulley may work satisfactorily, but for heavy or unsteady work it can hardly be spoken of as reliable.

§ 17. Rope-Belts.

Hemp and cotton ropes are sometimes used for transmission-belts, the principal pulleys being placed from 25 to 60 feet apart. Three-strand ropes, such as is represented in section in Fig. 71, are most commonly used; the diameters vary from $\frac{3}{4}$ inch to $2\frac{1}{4}$ inches, and by placing several ropes side by side upon the principal pulleys, large powers may be transmitted.

As a general rule, rope-belts work almost entirely by means of their weights, being hung loosely upon the pulleys instead of tightly stretched over the pulleys as in leather and vulcanized-rubber belts. When only small powers are to be transmitted, the pulleys may have semicircular grooves upon their faces, and the rope-belts may run in the bottoms of the grooves. The weight of the belt in such cases furnishes sufficient friction to prevent slipping. Fig. 72 represents a pulley-rim of this kind for a single rope-belt. When,

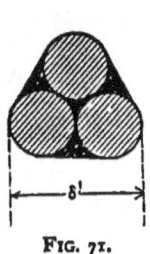

Fig. 71.

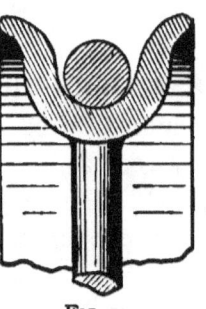

Fig. 72.

however, large powers are to be transmitted, the grooves in the pulley-faces should be V-shaped, so that the ropes may be wedged between the sides, and thus furnish the friction lost by diminishing the initial tension. A pulley-rim for four rope-belts transmitting large power is represented in Fig. 73. The dimensions of the pulley may be calculated as for ordinary pulleys, and the sides of the grooves commonly make angles of 45° with each other, as shown in the figure.

The coefficient of friction for rope-belts running in the bottoms of semicircular grooves without biting

ROPE-BELTS.

against the sides (Fig. 72) may be taken, for cast-iron pulleys,

$$\varphi = 0.30.$$

For V grooves, of which the sides are inclined at angles of 45°, as in Fig. 73,

$$\varphi = 0.70. \quad \ldots \ldots \quad (619)$$

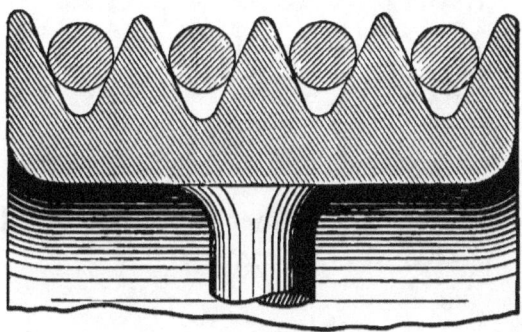

FIG. 73.

By substituting this value in formula (41), we obtain for the ratio of the tensions

$$\log \frac{T}{t} = 0.0053\alpha, \quad \ldots \quad (620)$$

in which α is expressed in degrees.

If in formula (48) we make the quantity $\dfrac{\frac{T}{t}}{\frac{T}{t}-1} = x$,

we have

The following table gives values for $\frac{T}{t}$ and x for all values of α likely to be needed in practice:

α in degrees.	α in circular measure.	α in fractions of circumference.	$\frac{T}{t}$.	x.
45	0.785	$\frac{1}{8} = 0.125$	1.732	2.37
60	1.047	$\frac{1}{6} = 0.167$	2.080	1.93
75	1.309	$\frac{5}{24} = 0.208$	2.498	1.67
90	1.571	$\frac{1}{4} = 0.250$	3.001	1.50
105	1.833	$\frac{7}{24} = 0.292$	3.602	1.38
120	2.094	$\frac{1}{3} = 0.333$	4.325	1.30
135	2.356	$\frac{3}{8} = 0.375$	5.194	1.24
180	3.142	$\frac{1}{2} = 0.500$	8.995	1.12
210	3.665	$\frac{7}{12} = 0.583$	12.97	1.08
240	4.188	$\frac{2}{3} = 0.667$	18.71	1.06

If we represent the diameter of the rope by δ', we have for the area of cross-section

$$\frac{\pi \delta'^2}{4} = 0.785 \delta'^2,$$

and this substituted for $b\delta$ in formula (50) gives

$$0.785 \delta'^2 = \frac{T}{f}.$$

The safe working stress in pounds per square inch may be taken

$$f = 1200,$$

but for greatest durability and best performance of

work this is in practice about $\frac{1}{10}$ the above value. Hence we use

$$f = 120,$$

which substituted in the above formula gives

$$0.785\delta'^2 = \frac{T}{120},$$

or
$$\delta' = 0.103 \sqrt{T},$$

and consequently

$$\delta' = 0.103 \sqrt{Px}. \quad \ldots \quad (622)$$

As before explained, we have the expression

$$P = \frac{550H}{v},$$

in which H represents the horse-power transmitted and v the velocity in feet per second. By substituting this in formula (622) we obtain

$$\delta' = 0.103 \sqrt{\frac{550H}{v} x},$$

or
$$\delta' = 2.416 \sqrt{\frac{H}{v} x}. \quad \ldots \quad (623)$$

Example.—Required the proper diameter for a rope-belt which will transmit a force of 1000 pounds over two equal V-grooved pulleys. In this case $\alpha = 180°$, and the table gives

$$x = 1.12.$$

Hence, from formula (622),

$$\delta' = 0.103\sqrt{1000 \times 1.12} = 0.103 \times 33.47,$$

or
$$\delta' = 3.447'' = 3\tfrac{29}{64}''.$$

Rope-belts as large as this are seldom used in practice. In the above example, therefore, we should use two ropes instead of one. Each rope would then transmit a force of $\tfrac{1000}{2} = 500$ pounds, and we should have
$$\delta' = 0.103\sqrt{500 \times 1.12},$$

or
$$\delta' = 2.437'' = 2\tfrac{7}{16}''.$$

Example.—A rope-belt embracing an angle of 135° upon its smaller principal pulley transmits a force of 15 horse-power at a velocity of 30 feet per second. It is required to determine the proper diameter for the belt. From the table we have

$$x = 1.24,$$

and from formula (623)

$$\delta' = 2.416\sqrt{\frac{15 \times 1.24}{30}} = 2.416 \times 0.787,$$

or
$$\delta' = 1.901'' = 1\tfrac{29}{32}''.$$

Example.—It is required to transmit a force of 800 horse-power at a velocity of 80 feet per second by means of 15 rope-belts. The arc embraced by each belt upon the smaller principal pulley is equal to $\frac{3}{8}$ the circumference. Required the diameters for the rope-belts.

It is evident that each belt must transmit a force of $\frac{800}{15} = 50$ horse-power at a velocity of 80 feet per second.

The table gives, for $\alpha = \frac{3}{8}$ the circumference,

$$x = 1.24,$$

and from formula (623) we have

$$\delta' = 2.416 \sqrt{\frac{50 \times 1.24}{80}} = 2.416 \times 0.88,$$

or δ' $2.126'' = 2\frac{1}{8}''$.

Because of the circular cross-sections of rope-belts and the character of the material generally used, it is necessary that the wear due to the bending of the ropes about the pulleys be reduced as low as possible. To this end very large principal pulleys are used—from about 7 to 15 feet in diameter commonly. It is a safe rule, that the diameter of the smaller principal pulley should not be less than thirty times the diameter of the rope, and when small ropes are used we may conveniently increase the durability by taking the diameter of the smaller pulley equal to 45 to 60 times the diameter of the rope. Thus in the three examples given above we may have for the diameters of the smaller principal pulleys $30 \times 2.44 = 73.20'' = 6\frac{1}{4}$ feet, $30 \times 1.9 = 57'' = 5$ feet nearly, and $30 \times 2.13 = 63.9'' = 5\frac{1}{3}$ feet.

The ends of rope-belts are usually spliced together by pressing them firmly together and winding about with stout small rope. The spliced part should be as long as possible in order to bend properly over the pulleys and give the necessary strength. The weight per foot of length of rope-belts is approximately given by the formula

$$G = 0.3\delta''^2. \quad \ldots \ldots \quad (624)$$

§ 18. Jointed Chain-Belts.*

Of late years numerous attempts have been made to replace ordinary leather belts by traction-bands. Among the various systems proposed we mention in the first place the chain-belt (leather) of Rouiller: this contrivance, which at first appeared destined to do good service, has not justified this hope, but has fallen into disuse because of its want of durability. Belts formed of twisted metallic wires (Godin) have produced results scarcely more satisfactory. As for leather belts covered with gutta-percha, they cannot, in reality, compete with ordinary leather belts; and at the present time there is scarcely a transmission-band, with the exception of rubber-belts with layers of hemp or cotton, which seems to be as advantageous in practice as ordinary leather belts, especially when used for the transmission of considerable forces.

---

* From Reuleaux.

JOINTED CHAIN-BELTS.

In certain special cases, for the transmission of large forces, and for unsteady work, such as in agricultural machines, the ordinary leather belt may be successfully replaced by the jointed chain-belt of Clissold (Fig. 74). In this chain the joints are bound together, two by two, by leather bands wound several times around, and bevelled at the edges to fit properly in the trapezoidal groove which forms the face of the pulley. Ångström

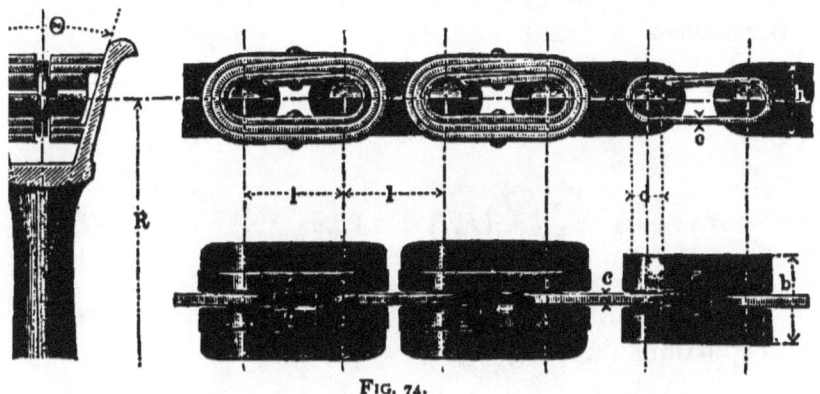

Fig. 74.

has used instead of the leather bands pieces of wood trimmed with iron.

In calculating the tensions for jointed chain-belts it is necessary to introduce the friction of the joints instead of the rigidity which figures in formulas for leather-belts. The formulas for tensions of leather-belts may be used in the present case by putting $\varphi\alpha = \dfrac{\varphi\alpha}{\sin \Theta}$, Θ representing the angle of the bevelled edges of the chain-belt.

For $\varphi = 0.24$, $\alpha = 0.8\pi$, $\Theta = 30°$, we obtain

$$\frac{t}{P} = 0.20, \quad \frac{T}{P} = 1.23, \quad \frac{T+t}{P} = 1.43, \quad \frac{t}{T} = 0.163 ; \quad (625)$$

and for $\varphi = 0.28$, $\alpha = 0.95\pi$, $\Theta = 30°$,

$$\frac{t}{P} = 0.12, \quad \frac{T}{P} = 1.15, \quad \frac{T+t}{P} = 1.27, \quad \frac{t}{T} = 0.105. \quad (626)$$

By making use of these values we may obtain for the diameter of the joint pivots (d, Fig. 74) the expressions:*

$$d = 0.0146\sqrt{P} = 3.656\sqrt{\frac{H}{nR}}; \quad \ldots \quad (627)$$

$$d = 0.0414\sqrt[3]{\frac{l}{R}(PR)} = 1.644\sqrt[3]{\frac{l}{R}\frac{H}{n}}. \quad (628)$$

We should take for jointed chain-belts the following proportions (see Fig. 74):

$$\frac{l}{d} = 3, \quad \frac{b}{d} = 2\tfrac{3}{4}, \quad \frac{c}{d} = \frac{1}{3}, \quad \frac{e}{d} = \frac{1}{5}, \quad \frac{h}{d} = 2\tfrac{1}{6}. \quad (629)$$

For small pulleys it is convenient to take

$$\frac{R}{l} \gtrless 5.$$

In practice d should not be taken less than 0.32 inch, even when a smaller diameter would be sufficient for strength. In jointed chain-belts the limit of the force

---

* P = force in pounds transmitted, H = horse-power, n = revolutions per minute.

P which may be transmitted (supposed to be applied at the circumference of the pulley) is about 500 pounds, which would require a width of about 11 inches in a simple leather belt.

Example.—Given the data $H = 20$, $n = 50$, $n_1 = 100$. Required the dimensions for a jointed chain-belt, supposing the radius of the smaller pulley to be $R_1 = 5l$. Formula (628) gives

$$d = 1.644 \sqrt[3]{\frac{1}{5} \times \frac{20}{100}}$$

$$= 1.644 \sqrt[3]{\frac{1}{25}} = \frac{1.644}{2.924} = 0.5624'' = \tfrac{9}{16}''.$$

From formula (629) then we obtain $l = 3 \times 0.5624 = 1.6872''$, $b = 2\tfrac{3}{4} \times 0.5624 = 1.5466''$, $c = 0.2''$, $e = 0.12''$, $h = 2\tfrac{1}{8} \times 0.5624 = 1.2185''$, $R_1 = 5l = 8.436''$, $R = 2 \times R_1 = 16.872''$.

Clissold has also invented a transmission by means of a thick belt with trapezoidal section. This, however, has proved poorly because of its want of durability.*

---

* The experiments of Wedding of Berlin have shown that in an angular groove, the angle being 30° (Fig. 50), the force necessary to produce slipping of the cable is twice that corresponding to a cable lying in a round groove. This confirms the preceding expressions, since $\frac{1}{\sin 30°} = \frac{1}{2}$.

TRANSMISSION BY METALLIC CABLE.

§ 19. *Tensions of Cables.*

Transmission of forces by means of metallic cables was first introduced about the year 1850, by the Hirn brothers.† The use of metallic cables, by means of which we are able to transmit great forces at distances as great as several thousand feet without notable loss, depends essentially upon the principles of transmission by belt, the principal difference being that with a metallic cable the tension is due to its own weight.

The two principal pulleys of a transmission by cable, as a general thing, have their axes parallel; also the pulleys are in the same plane, so that the cable may be driven without guides. Moreover, the axes of the principal pulleys are ordinarily in the same horizontal plane, forming what is termed a horizontal transmission. An inclination of the plane of the axes to the

---

* From Reuleaux.

† In this first application the axes of the pulleys were about 280 feet apart; the force transmitted was 42 horse-power, at 60 revolutions per minute.

surface of the ground constitutes an oblique transmission. Vertical transmissions by metallic cable are very rarely used. When the driven pulley transmits to a third pulley the force which it receives from the driver the transmission is said to be compound. In a simple transmission by cable the two pulleys are ordinarily of the same diameter.

In order to prevent the cable from touching the ground, when the height of the pulleys above the ground is insufficient and the separation of the axes great, intermediate rollers are used to support the cable. By inclining the rollers more or less they may be used for guides when the axes of the pulleys cross or intersect each other. We meet, however, very few examples of transmission by cable in which the axes of the pulleys are not parallel. When it becomes necessary to give to the cable a considerable deviation, we can place between two vertical rollers a horizontal guide; but it is preferable in such cases to rely upon a compound transmission, with pulleys placed obliquely to each other.

The inferior limit for the separation of the pulley-axes in transmissions by metallic cable should be about 50 feet.

The distances between the rollers which support the cable are determined by the flexibility of the cable and its position above the ground.

The transmission-cables ordinarily used are composed of 36 iron wires divided into six twists, each containing six wires twisted around a central core of hemp; the six twists are likewise twisted around a larger core, also of hemp (Fig. 75). When it is necessary to strengthen the cable, we may, without serious disadvantage, replace the central hempen core by a twist of iron wire similar to the six others. It has also been proposed to replace by an iron wire the smaller hempen cores of the separate twists, in order to overcome the looseness of the cable, which may tend to produce a rapid wear. The value of such an arrangement yet remains to be established. It has the dis-

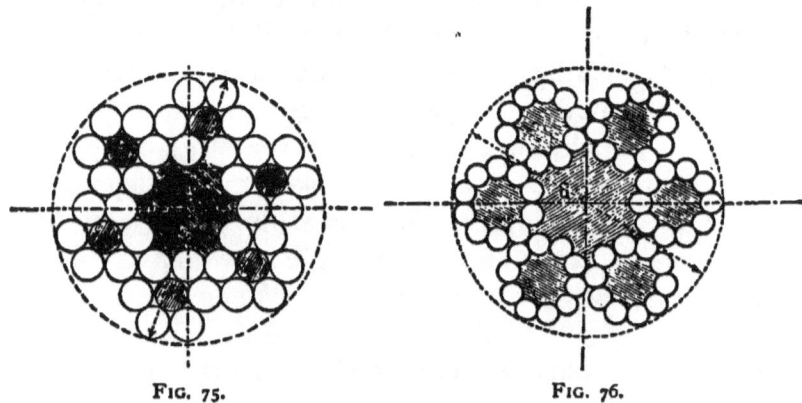

FIG. 75.   FIG. 76.

advantage of destroying the elasticity of the cable. When the cores are of hemp, it is of first importance that first quality hemp be used in their manufacture, instead of the inferior qualities which have been hitherto extensively used for this purpose. The wires composing the cable should be forced firmly together, so that the diameter of the cable is not more than eight times that of the wire.

In cables having more than 36 wires the number of twists is generally six, and the large and small cores of hemp.

While there is no absolute necessity of limiting the number of twists to six, this number is almost always used: in the different cables in use the total number of wires is therefore 36, 48, 54, 60, 66, 72, etc.

Fig. 76 represents a cross-section of a cable of 60 wires. In these different cables the relations between the external diameter d and the diameter δ of the wires are as follows:

For the number of wires—

$$i = 36 \quad 48 \quad 54 \quad 60 \quad 66 \quad 72,$$
$$\frac{d}{\delta} = 8.00 \quad 10.25 \quad 11.33 \quad 12.80 \quad 13.25 \quad 14.20.$$

In order to obtain the tensions T and t in metallic cables we make use of the formulas determined for tensions in ordinary belts. By substituting in these formulas a coefficient of friction $\varphi = 0.24$, and an arc of the pulleys equal to $\frac{1}{2}$ the circumstance, $\alpha = 180° = \pi$, we may obtain the relations

$$\frac{t}{P} = 0.97, \quad \frac{T}{P} = 2.02, \quad \frac{T+t}{P} = 2.99, \quad \frac{t}{T} = 0.48; \quad (630)$$

or, in round numbers,

$$\frac{t}{P} = 1, \quad \frac{T}{P} = 2, \quad \frac{T+t}{P} = 3, \quad \frac{t}{T} = 0.5.^{*} \quad . \quad . \quad (631)$$

---

* The loss of velocity due to the shipping of the cable does not ordinarily exceed $\frac{1}{50}$ per cent; it may therefore be neglected altogether in our calculations.

§ 20. *Calculation of Diameters of Cables.*

In a transmission by metallic cable composed of i wires the tension T in the cable corresponds to a tension S in the wires; this tension should not exceed 25601.4 pounds per square inch of section.* To determine the diameter δ of the wires the following formulas may be used:

For a resistance of P pounds acting at the circumference of the pulley,

$$\delta = 1.627\sqrt{\frac{P}{Si}} \quad \ldots \quad (632)$$

For a force of H horse-power, with a velocity of v feet per second at the circumference of the pulley,

$$\delta = 37.867\sqrt{\frac{H}{Svi}} \quad \ldots \quad (633)$$

in which v should not materially exceed 100 feet per second.

For a force of H horse-power at n revolutions of the pulleys per minute,

$$\delta = 4070.04\sqrt{\frac{H}{SRni}} \quad \ldots \quad (634)$$

If we represent by $s = 25601.4 - S$ the tension produced in the wires by the bending of the cable around the pulleys, and by (PR) the statical moment of rotation of the driven pulley, we shall have

$$\delta = 0.0057\sqrt[3]{\frac{s}{Si}(PR)}. \quad \ldots \quad (635)$$

---

* 18 kilograms per square millimetre.

CALCULATION OF DIAMETERS OF CABLES.

Finally, if in place of the moment (PR) we have the horse-power and revolutions per minute,

$$\delta = 0.227 \sqrt[3]{\frac{H}{Sni}}. \quad \ldots \quad (636)$$

It is, moreover, important that the ratio of the radius of the pulleys to the diameter of the wires be taken not less than the limit,

$$\frac{R}{\delta} = \frac{14223000}{s}. \quad \ldots \quad (637)$$

This relation serves to calculate the following table:

S	s	$\frac{R}{\delta}$	S	s	$\frac{R}{\delta}$
711.15	24890.25	571	12800.70	12800.70	1111
1422.30	24179.10	588	14223.00	11378.40	1250
2844.60	22756.80	625	15645.30	9956.10	1429
4266.90	21334.50	667	17067.60	8533.80	1667
5689.20	19912.20	714	18489.90	7111.50	2000
7111.50	18489.90	769	19912.20	5689.20	2500
8533.80	17067.60	833	21334.50	4266.90	3333
9956.10	15645.30	909	22756.80	2844.60	5000
11378.40	14223.00	1000	24179.10	1422.30	10000

For a constant value of $S + s$ the minimum value of the radius of the pulleys is given by the table by making $\frac{s}{S} = 2$.* This minimum value corresponds to

---

* We may obtain from formulas (636) and (637) $R = K\sqrt[3]{\frac{1}{s^2 S}}$. The sum $s + S$ being constant, the maximum value of the product $s^2 S$ is obtained by making $\frac{s}{S} = 2$.

$S = 8533.8$, $s = 17067.6$, $\frac{R}{\delta} = 833$. For values of $\frac{R}{\delta}$ nearly equal to 833 the numerical value of R differs very little from the minimum value; we may therefore safely give somewhat greater values to R when, by so doing, we can make use of patterns and models already on hand.

The two tables which follow have been calculated from formulas (632)–(634), and (635) and (636) respectively. In the first table we have given $1000 \frac{H}{SRn}$ in order to avoid the small numbers which result from $\frac{H}{SRn}$:

Diameter δ for number of wires $i =$					$\frac{P}{S}$	$\frac{H}{Sv}$	$1000 \frac{H}{SRn}$
36	42	48	60	72			
0.020	0.0184	0.0172	0.0156	0.0140	0.0054	0.000010	0.000088
0.024	0.0220	0.0208	0.0184	0.0168	0.0078	0.000015	0.000123
0.028	0.0260	0.0244	0.0216	0.0196	0.0107	0.000020	0.000175
0.032	0.0296	0.0276	0.0248	0.0228	0.0139	0.000026	0.000229
0.036	0.0332	0.0312	0.0280	0.0256	0.0176	0.000033	0.000281
0.040	0.0368	0.0348	0.0308	0.0284	0.0218	0.000040	0.000352
0.048	0.0444	0.0416	0.0372	0.0340	0.0313	0.000060	0.000492
0.056	0.0516	0.0484	0.0432	0.0396	0.0426	0.000079	0.000686
0.064	0.0592	0.0556	0.0484	0.0452	0.0557	0.000103	0.001072
0.072	0.0664	0.0624	0.0556	0.0508	0.0705	0.000131	0.001125
0.080	0.0740	0.0692	0.0620	0.0564	0.0870	0.000160	0.001389
0.088	0.0812	0.0764	0.0680	0.0624	0.1331	0.000195	0.001688
0.096	0.0888	0.0832	0.0744	0.0680	0.1408	0.000232	0.002004
0.104	0.0960	0.0900	0.0804	0.0736	0.1471	0.000272	0.002356
0.112	0.1036	0.0968	0.0868	0.0792	0.1586	0.000306	0.002725
0.120	0.1108	0.1040	0.0928	0.0848	0.1958	0.000364	0.003329

In metallic transmission-cables, wires of less than 0.02 inch or more than 0.08 inch diameter are very seldom used. The values of δ given in these two tables, in the second to the fifth columns, are taken from values contained in the first column, and should in practice be taken in round numbers. The quality of the metal used for transmission-cables is of first importance, from the fact that only superior qualities can withstand for any length of time the rapid wear to which the cables are subjected. Swedish iron, which possesses at the same time a remarkable tenacity and great strength, is especially adapted for the wires of transmission-cables. In order to reduce as much as possible the number of joints, only long wires should be used. Experience has shown that for transmission-cables wires of steel offer no advantages over those of good iron.

Diameter of wire δ for number of wires $i =$					$\dfrac{s}{S}(PR)$	$\dfrac{s}{S}\dfrac{H}{n}$
36	42	48	60	72		
0.020	0.0188	0.0180	0.0168	0.0160	1554	0.025
0.024	0.0228	0.0220	0.0204	0.0192	2685	0.043
0.028	0.0264	0.0256	0.0236	0.0224	4264	0.068
0.032	0.0304	0.0292	0.0268	0.0252	6365	0.101
0.036	0.0340	0.0328	0.0304	0.0284	9062	0.144
0.040	0.0380	0.0364	0.0336	0.0316	12431	0.197
0.048	0.0456	0.0436	0.0404	0.0380	21481	0.341
0.056	0.0532	0.0508	0.0472	0.0444	34112	0.542
0.064	0.0608	0.0580	0.0540	0.0508	50919	0.894
0.072	0.0684	0.0656	0.0608	0.0572	72499	1.152
0.080	0.0764	0.0728	0.0676	0.0636	99451	1.580
0.088	0.0836	0.0800	0.0744	0.0700	132369	2.103
0.096	0.0912	0.0872	0.0808	0.0760	171851	2.730
0.104	0.0988	0.0944	0.0876	0.0824	218493	3.471
0.112	0.1064	0.1016	0.0944	0.0888	272892	4.335
0.120	0.1140	0.1092	0.1012	0.0952	335646	5.332

In the formulas (632)–(634) the radius R of the pulleys is supposed to be known; the values of δ given by them are admissible only when the ratio $\frac{R}{\delta}$ gives for the tension s a value which, added to S, does not exceed 25601.4 pounds. In the case where $s + S$ exceeds this limit, it is convenient to begin the calculation by giving to R a greater value. To make use of the preceding formulas and tables, we must begin by fixing upon a value for the tension S. This may easily be done with the aid of the considerations contained in the following paragraph, and in the examples which we now give we shall suppose this preliminary operation already accomplished.

Example.—It is proposed to transmit, by means of a metallic cable running over pulleys 9.84 feet in diameter, a force of 550 pounds: required the proper diameter for the wires of the cable, supposing the number to be $i = 36$.

If we take $S = 9956.1$, we shall have $\frac{P}{S} = \frac{550}{9956.1} = 0.0552$, which in the first table (column 6, line 9) corresponds to a diameter of $\delta = 0.064$ inch. From this we obtain $\frac{R}{\delta} = \frac{59.04}{0.064} = 922$, which, in the table on page 201, corresponds nearly to $S = 9956.10$, and is therefore admissible. If we had taken $R = 48$ inches, we should have had $\frac{R}{\delta} = \frac{48}{0.064} = 750$—a value less than the limit mentioned above, and it would therefore be necessary to increase the value of R.

Example.—The force transmitted by a metallic cable is 300 horse-power, and the velocity $v = 82$ feet per

CALCULATION OF DIAMETERS OF CABLES. 205

second; taking $S = 11378.4$, and consequently $s = 25601.4 - 11378.4 = 14223$, we shall have $\frac{H}{Sv} = \frac{300}{11378.4 \times 82} = 0.000322$. In the first table the nearest value of $\frac{H}{Sv}$ is 0.000306 (column 7, line 15). The diameter for the wires is therefore $\delta = 0.112$ inch for $i = 36$, $\delta = 0.0868$ inch for $i = 60$. For the value $s = 14223$, we have, for the radius of the pulleys, $R = \frac{14223000 \times 0.0848}{14223} = 84.8$ inches. The expression $v = \frac{2\pi R n}{12 \times 60}$ gives for the number of revolutions per minute

$$n = \frac{82 \times 12 \times 60}{6.28 \times 84.8} = 111.$$

Example.—It is required to calculate the horse-power which may be transmitted by a cable of thirty-six wires, the diameter of the wires being 0.08 inch, the diameter of the pulleys 9.84 feet, and the number of revolutions per minute 90. In this case we have $\frac{R}{\delta} = \frac{59.04}{0.08} = 738$, which, from formula (637), gives $s = \frac{14223000}{738} = 19272.3$ and $S = 6329.1$. For $\delta = 0.08$ and $i = 36$, the first table furnishes the value $1000\frac{H}{SRn} = 0.001389$; hence

$$H = \frac{0.001389}{1000} SRn = \frac{0.001389 \times 6329.1 \times 59.04 \times 90}{1000}$$

$= 46.71$ horse-power. With a pulley of 8 feet diameter

we would have $\frac{R}{\delta} = \frac{48}{0.08} = 600$, $s = \frac{14223000}{600} = 23705$, $S = 1896.4$. Consequently
$$H = \frac{0.001389 \times 1896.4 \times 48 \times 90}{1000} = 11.40 \text{ horse-power.}$$

Example.—Upon the driven arbor of a transmission by cable a resistance of 110 pounds acts continuously with a lever arm of 40 inches. Required the proper diameter for the 36 wires of the cable, supposing we give to the pulleys the smallest admissible radius. In order to satisfy this last condition, we ought to take (from what precedes) $s = 17067.60$ and $S = 8533.80$, which gives $\frac{s}{S}(PR) = 2 \times 110 \times 40 = 8800$. In the second table (column 6, line 5) we find, for the nearest value of $\frac{s}{S}(PR)$, $\delta = 0.036$ inch. From the table on page 201, therefore, we obtain $\frac{R}{\delta} = 833$, $R = 833 \times 0.036 = 30$ inches.

Example.—A cable of 42 wires transmits a force of 30 horse-power at a velocity of 100 revolutions per minute. Required the proper diameter for the wires of the cable, taking $S = 8533.80$. In this case $s = 17067.60$, and $\frac{s}{S}\frac{H}{n} = \frac{17067.60}{8533.80} \times \frac{30}{100} = 0.6$. The second table gives, for the nearest value of $\frac{s}{S}\frac{H}{n}$ to 0.6, $\delta = 0.056$ inch. From formula (637), then, we have for the radius of the pulleys $R = 0.056 \times \frac{14223000}{17067.60} = 833 \times 0.056 = 46.65$ inches.

§ 21. Deflections in the Cable of a Horizontal Transmission.

In order that, in the two parts of a transmission-cable, the tensions T and t have proper values (not too small, for then the cable will slip on its pulleys; nor too great, because the wear is then great), the deflection which we give to each part, in a state of repose, must be a determined quantity. It is equally necessary that we know the deflections which are produced during the motion of the cable, in order to leave sufficient room for the passage of the cable. The deflection of a cable depends upon the tension of its wires.

Let us represent by

A the separation of the pulleys of a horizontal transmission in feet; h the deflection of the cable in feet (h_1 for the driving part, h_2 for the driven part, and h_0 for the state of repose); S the tension per square inch in the wires (S_1 for the driving part, S_2 for the driven part, and S_0 for the state of repose).

For a metallic cable of any number of wires we have the relations

$$\frac{h}{A} = 0.3535 \left[0.369 \frac{S}{A} - \sqrt{\left(0.369 \frac{S}{A}\right)^2 - 1} \right] \quad (638)$$

and

$$\frac{S}{A} = 3.8029 \left(\frac{h}{A} + \frac{A}{8h} \right). \quad \ldots \quad (639)$$

By means of these formulas the following table has

been calculated. As a first approximation we may take simply

$$\frac{h}{A} = 0.4755 \frac{A}{S} \quad \ldots \quad (640)$$

In order to make use of the table, we begin by determining from the given quantities the ratio $\frac{A}{S}$ of the separation of the pulleys to the tension developed in the wires, and then find in the table the number nearest to this ratio. From this we obtain the value of $\frac{h}{A}$, which gives the amount of deflection h. The tension S_0 of the cable in a state of repose is not the arithmetical mean between S_1 and S_2; we may, by a more complicated calculation, however, determine it from the length of the two cable parts. The value which we need to know is the deflection h_0 in the two parts of the cable for a state of repose, and we have approximately

$$h_0 = \sqrt{\frac{h_2^2 + h_1^2}{2}} = 0.67 h_2 + 0.28 h_1 \quad . \quad (641)$$

This expression gives for h_0 a value slightly too great, but which approaches more nearly the true value as the tensions S_1 and S_2 become less. The error may be still farther decreased by using, instead of exact values of h_1 and h_2, those furnished by formula (640).

The driving part of the cable does not necessarily

occupy the higher position, as is the case in Fig. 77: it may be placed in the lower position, as in Fig. 78. In the latter, the space required by the deflection of

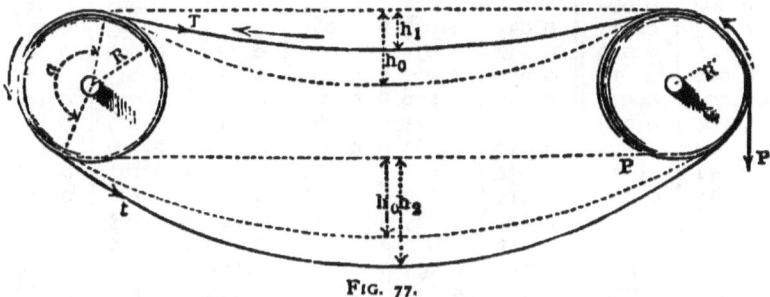

FIG. 77.

the cable is considerably less than in the former. The two parts of the cable do not intersect each other as long as $h_2 - h_1 < 2R$. With a cable in motion, we may place, at the lowest point of the curve, a graduated rule, by means of which we may observe at any instant the tensions. The graduation of the rule may, moreover, be such as to give directly the tension S.

14

Table of Deflections in Metallic Cables.

$\dfrac{h}{A}$	$\dfrac{A}{S}$	$\dfrac{h}{A}$	$\dfrac{A}{S}$	$\dfrac{h}{A}$	$\dfrac{A}{S}$	$\dfrac{h}{A}$	$\dfrac{A}{S}$
0.003	0.006	0.033	0.069	0.063	0.128	0.093	0.183
0.004	0.008	0.034	0.071	0.064	0.130	0.094	0.185
0.005	0.011	0.035	0.073	9.065	0.132	0.095	0.186
0.006	0.013	0.036	0.075	0.066	0.134	0.096	0.188
0.007	0.015	0.037	0.077	0.067	0.136	0.097	0.190
0.008	0.017	0.038	0.079	0.068	0.138	0.098	0.191
0.009	0.019	0.039	0.081	0.069	0.140	0.099	0.193
0.010	0.021	0.040	0.083	0.070	0.142	0.100	0.195
0.011	0.023	0.041	0.085	0.071	0.144	0.101	0.196
0.012	0.025	0.042	0.087	0.072	0.145	0.102	0.198
0.013	0.027	0.043	0.089	0.073	0.147	0.105	0.203
0.014	0.029	0.044	0.091	0.074	0.149	0.110	0.211
0.015	0.031	0.045	0.093	0 075	0.151	0.115	0.219
0.016	0.034	0.046	0.095	0 076	0.153	0.120	0.226
0.017	0.036	0.047	0.097	0.077	0 155	0.125	0.234
0.018	0.038	0.048	0.099	0.078	0.156	0.130	0.241
0.019	0.040	0.049	0.101	0.079	0.158	0.135	0.248
0.020	0.042	0.050	0.103	0.080	0.160	0.140	0.255
0.021	0.044	0.051	0.105	0.081	0.162	0.145	0.261
0.022	0.046	0.052	0.107	0.082	0.164	0.150	0.267
0.023	0.048	0.053	0.109	0.083	0.165	0.155	0.274
0.024	0.050	0.054	0.111	0.084	0.167	0.160	0.279
0.025	0.052	0.055	0.113	0.085	0.169	0.165	0.285
0.026	0.054	0.056	0.115	0.086	0.171	0.170	0.291
0.027	0.056	0.057	0.117	0.087	0.173	0.175	0.296
0.028	0.059	0.058	0.119	0.088	0.174	0.180	0.301
0.029	0.061	0.059	0.121	0.089	0.176	0.185	0.305
0.030	0.063	0.060	0.123	0.090	0.178	0.190	0.310
0.031	0.065	0.061	0.125	0.091	0.179	0.195	0.315
0.032	0.067	0.062	0.127	0.092	0.181	0.200	0.319

Example.—In the last example of § 20 the separation A of the pulleys is 360.8 feet, and we take the tension $S_1 = 8533.8$ pounds per square inch. Required the deflections in the parts of the cable. For the driving part of the cable the relation $\dfrac{A}{S} = \dfrac{360.8}{8533.8} = 0.0423$

corresponds in the table (column 2, line 18) to the value $\frac{h}{A} = 0.02$. Hence we have $h_1 = 360.8 \times 0.02 = 7.216$ feet. For the driven part of the cable we have from formula (631) $S = \frac{8533.8}{2} = 4266.9$, and consequently $\frac{A}{S} = \frac{360.8}{4266.9} = 0.0845$. For this value of $\frac{A}{S}$ the table gives (column 4, line 9) $\frac{h}{A} = 0.041$, and we have $h_2 = 360.8 \times 0.041 = 14.79$ feet. From formula (641) the deflection of the cable in a state of repose is $h_0 =$

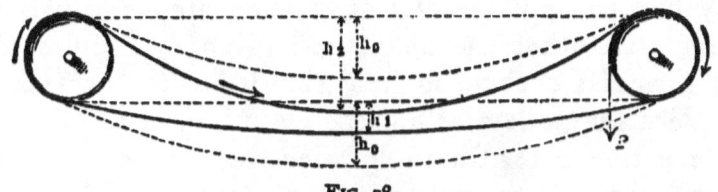

Fig. 78.

$0.67 \times 14.79 + 0.28 \times 7.216 = 11.93$ feet. We have also $h_2 - h_1 = 14.79 - 7.216 = 7.574$ and $2R = 2 \times 3.8875 = 7.7750$ feet. Since $2R > h_2 - h_1$, we may if necessary make use of the disposition of Fig. 78. (See first example of § 22.)

Example.—In the third example of § 20 the distance below the line of centres of the pulleys is 9.84 feet; it is required to determine the proper distance between the pulley-centres. Assuming that we can make use of the disposition represented in Fig. 78, the greatest admissible value for the distance of separation of the pulleys may be calculated from the deflection of the cable while in a state of repose. Making use of the approximate formula (640), and remembering the value

$S_1 = 6642.141$ pounds per square inch, we shall have
$h_1 = 0.4755\dfrac{A^2}{6642.141}$ and $h_2 = 2h_1$. Formula (641) then gives

$h_0 = 9.84 = \dfrac{(0.67 \times 2 + 0.28)A^2 \times 0.4755}{6642.141}$,

$A = \sqrt{\dfrac{9.84 \times 6642.141}{0.4755(0.67 \times 2 + 0.28)}} = \sqrt{84847.23} = 291.3$ feet.

§ 22. *Transmission by Cable with Increased Tension.*

When the pulleys of transmission are very distant from each other the deflections given by the preceding formulas become so great that it is often necessary to place the pulleys at a great elevation, or to provide a deep trench for the cable when we wish to dispense with intermediate pulleys and guides (see § 28). In a great many cases we may arrive at the same result by simply giving to the cable a greater tension than is necessary to prevent slipping, and taking care to give to the cable a diameter sufficient to withstand the additional strain. This artifice may be employed all the more easily when the transmission is to be used for moderate forces, and consequently a small diameter of the cable is sufficient. It is only necessary to examine carefully the rules which follow, to be convinced that a rational use of this method presents in reality little or no difficulty.

A transmission by cable, established under the above conditions, constitutes, by way of distinction from ordinary cable-transmission, what we term a transmission with increased tension. We may distinguish it from ordinary transmissions by giving the sign s to the forces and dimensions connected with it (T_s, t_s, S_s, δ_s instead of T, t, S, and δ). The tension T, in the ordinary mode of transmission, ought not to be less than $2P$; in a transmission with increased tension the tension ought to be increased by a certain factor which we shall designate by m. We shall therefore have

$$T_s = mT, \qquad t_s = (2m-1)t, \qquad \frac{t_s}{T_s} = \frac{2m-1}{2m}. \quad (642)$$

The tension S_1 in the driving part of the cable is not changed, but in the driven part the tension S_{2s} is no longer equal to $\frac{S_1}{2}$. We take instead

$$S_{2s} = S_1 \frac{2m-1}{2m}. \quad \ldots \quad (643)$$

The diameter δ_s of the wire is deduced from the diameter δ given by one of the formulas (632) to (634), by means of the relation

$$\delta_s = \delta \sqrt{m}. \quad \ldots \quad (644)$$

If, however, δ is calculated from formula (636) or (638), we must take

$$\delta_s = \delta^s\sqrt{m}. \quad \ldots \quad (645)$$

From these formulas the following table has been calculated. It is important to remark, that in cables with increased tension the strain in the wires is no greater than in ordinary cables, because they have a proportionately greater diameter. The cable is heavier in the former than in the latter case, and should therefore be strained more firmly over the pulleys in order to reduce the deflection in the driven part.

$m = \dfrac{T_2}{T}$	$\dfrac{T_2}{P}$	$\dfrac{t_2}{t} = \dfrac{t_2}{P} = \dfrac{S_{22}}{S_2}$	$\dfrac{S_{22}}{S_1} = \dfrac{t_2}{T_2}$	$\dfrac{\delta_2}{\delta} = \sqrt{m}$	$\dfrac{\delta_2}{\delta} = \sqrt[3]{m}$
1.2	2.4	1.4	0.58	1.10	1.06
1.4	2.8	1.8	0.64	1.18	1.12
1.6	3.2	2.2	0.69	1.26	1.17
1.8	3.6	2.6	0.72	1.34	1.22
2.0	4.0	3.0	0.75	1.41	1.26
2.2	4.4	3.4	0.77	1.48	1.30
2.4	4.8	3.8	0.79	1.55	1.34
2.6	5.2	4.2	0.81	1.61	1.38
2.8	5.6	4.6	0.82	1.67	1.41
3.0	6.0	5.0	0.83	1.73	1.44
3.2	6.4	5.4	0.84	1.79	1.47
3.4	6.8	5.8	0.85	1.84	1.50
3.6	7.2	6.2	0.86	1.90	1.53
3.8	7.6	6.6	0.87	1.95	1.56
4.0	8.0	7.0	0.88	2.00	1.59
4.2	8.4	7.4	0.88	2.05	1.61
4.4	8.8	7.8	0.89	2.10	1.64
4.6	9.2	8.2	0.89	2.14	1.66
4.8	9.6	8.6	0.90	2.19	1.69
5.0	10.0	9.0	0.90	2.24	1.71
5.5	11.0	10.0	0.91	2.36	1.75
6.0	12.0	11.0	0.92	2.45	1.82
6.5	13.0	12.0	0.92	2.55	1.87
7.0	14.0	13.0	0.93	2.65	1.91
7.5	15.0	14.0	0.93	2.74	1.96
8.0	16.0	15.0	0.94	2.83	2.00

Example.—In the first example of §21 the driven part of the cable has a deflection of $h_2 = 11.76$ feet, and the diameter of the wire is 0.056 inch. If we wish to diminish the value of h_2 by using a cable with increased tension, the value of δ must be increased accordingly. If we take $m = 2$, the table gives (column 4, line 5) $\frac{S_{23}}{S_1} = 0.75$, $S_{23} = 0.75 \times 8533.8 = 6400.35$ pounds. Consequently $\frac{A}{S_{23}} = \frac{360.8}{6400.35} = 0.056$, which, in the table of § 21, corresponds to $\frac{h}{A} = 0.027$ or $h = 0.027 \times 360.8 = 9.74$ feet. The tension of deflection s has the same value as if for an ordinary cable; the quotient $\frac{s}{S_1} \cdot \frac{H}{n}$ does not change its value, and consequently δ may be determined by means of formula (636). The preceding table gives, then, $\delta_s = 1.26\delta = 1.26 \times 0.56 = 0.07$ inch.

When, in calculating the diameter δ for an ordinary cable of 36 wires, we obtain a very small value, the cable itself may have such a small diameter that its manufacture involves as great an expense as for a cable of larger diameter. In such a case we cannot recommend too highly the use of a transmission by cable with increased tension, which has the advantage of reducing the deflection in the driven part of the cable without appreciably increasing the expense of manufacture. As a general rule, we should never make use of wires of a less diameter than 0.04 inch, so that the minimum diameter of cable may be 0.32 inch.

Example.—For a transmission by cable, we have given $H = 5.5$, $n = 100$, and $A = 590.4$. If we assume $S_1 = 14223$ and $s = 11378.4$, we have $\frac{s}{S_1} \cdot \frac{H}{n} = \frac{11378.4}{14223} \times \frac{5.5}{100} = 0.044$, which, for $i = 36$ (table on page 203) gives, for the diameter of the wire $\delta = 0.024$

inch. We have also $\frac{A}{S_1} = \frac{590.4}{14223} = 0.0415$, $\frac{A}{S_2} = \frac{590.4}{711.51} = 0.0830$, and consequently, from the table of page 210, $h_1 = 0.0198 \times 590.4 = 11.69$ feet, $h_2 = 0.04 \times 590.4 = 23.616$ feet, $h_2 - h_1 = 23.616 - 11.69 = 11.926$ feet. But since $R = \frac{14223000}{11378.4}\delta = 1250 \times 0.024 = 30$ inches, $h_2 - h_1$ is greater than $2R$. In this case, therefore, we cannot place the driven part of the cable above the driving part, and the axes of the pulleys must have a height above the ground at least equal to $R + h_2 = 2.5 + 23.62 = 26.12$ feet. Suppose now we take for the cable diameter 0.32 inch, instead of $8 \times 0.024 = 0.192$ inch; that is, we take 0.04 inch for the diameter of the wires. We have then $\frac{\delta_s}{\delta} = \frac{0.04}{0.024} = 1.67$, and the preceding table gives (columns 6 and 4, line 18) $S_{2s} = 14223 \times 0.89 = 13058.47$. Consequently $\frac{A}{S_{2s}} = \frac{590.4}{13058.47} = 0.0452$ and $h_{2s} = 0.0228 \times 590.4 = 13.46$ feet, $h_{2s} - h_1 = 13.46 - 11.69 = 1.77$ feet. As before, $R = 1250 \times \delta_s = 50$ inches and $2R = 8.33$ feet: the inequality $h_{2s} - h_1 < 2R$ is now satisfied, and we may give to the cable the desired arrangement. The maximum deflection in this case corresponds to the state of repose, for which we have, from formula (641), $h_{0s} = 12.28$ feet. The height of the pulley-axes above the ground must be at least $h_{0s} + R = 12.28 + 4.165 = 16.445$ feet; that is, less by nearly 10 feet than for the first calculated cable.

§ 23. *Transmission by Inclined Cable.*

Of the various transmissions by metallic cable, the one which has met with the greatest development corresponds to the case in which the pulleys are not on the same level, one being higher than the other, and constitutes, therefore, what we call an inclined transmission. We give here the rules necessary for such transmissions. In the cable BCD, Fig. 79, which rep-

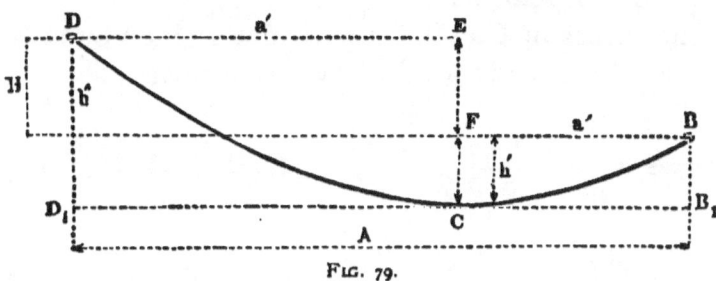

FIG. 79.

resents a part of an inclined transmission, the summit of the curved axis is not in the middle of the distance between the points of suspension, and the deflections are therefore different from those in the cable of a horizontal transmission. The deflections may, however, be easily determined in functions of the elements of a horizontal transmission, having the same separation of pulleys and sensibly the same tensions.

Let us represent by

h and A, respectively, the deflection of the cable and the separation of the pulleys of a horizontal transmission;

S the tension corresponding to the point of suspension of the part of the cable under consideration;

h' and h'', respectively, the smallest and greatest deflection (FC and EC) in an inclined transmission, in which the separation of the pulleys measured horizontally is equal to A;

a' and a'', respectively, the distances CB_1 and CD_1 of the summit of the curve from verticals through the points of suspension;

S' and S'', the tensions (at B and D) at the lower and higher points of suspension respectively;

H the difference between the levels (EF) of the points of suspension.

The values of h and S may be determined by means of the rules already given. We have then

$$h' = h\left(1 + \frac{1}{16}\frac{H^2}{h^2}\right) - \frac{H}{2}, \qquad h'' = H + h'; \quad (646)$$

$$a' = \frac{A}{2}\left(1 - \frac{1}{4}\frac{H}{h}\right), \qquad a'' = A - a'; \quad (647)$$

$$S' = S - 3.804(h - h''), \quad S'' = S + 3.804(h'' - h),$$
$$S'' - S' = 3.804H. \quad . \quad . \quad (648)$$

In certain cases the value of a' may be negative; the summit of the curve of the cable prolonged is then situated beyond the lower pulley. The tension of flection s, and consequently the diameter of the pulleys, are determined when we have obtained the value of the tension S'', which very often does not differ materially from S. The difference between the two tensions becomes important only in cases where several inclined transmissions are taken from a single higher pulley.

Example.—A transmission by cable, the data of which are the same as in the fifth example of § 20, has its pulleys placed at different heights; taking for the difference in the levels of the pulleys $H = 16.4$ feet, it is required to determine the deflections and the positions of the curve-summits.

For the driving part of the cable we have

$S_1 = 8533.8$, $h_1 = 7.216$ feet, $H = 16.4$ feet, $A = 360.8$ feet.

Starting at the lower pulley, we have, from formula (646),

$$h'_1 = 7.216\left(1 + \frac{1}{16}\frac{16.4^2}{7.216^2}\right) - \frac{16.4}{2} = 1.35 \text{ feet},$$
$$h''_1 = 7.216 + 1.35 = 8.566 \text{ feet};$$
$$a'_1 = \frac{360.8}{2}\left(1 - \frac{1}{4}\frac{16.4}{7.216}\right) = 180.4 \times 0.432 = 77.93 \text{ feet},$$
$$a''_1 = 360.8 + 77.93 = 382.87 \text{ feet}.$$

For the driven part of the cable,

$$S_2 = 4266.9, \quad h_2 = 14.79 \text{ feet};$$

consequently

$$h'_2 = 14.79\left(1 + \frac{1}{16}\frac{16.4^2}{14.79^2}\right) - \frac{16.4}{2} = 7.73 \text{ feet},$$
$$h''_2 = 16.4 + 7.73 = 24.13 \text{ feet}.$$

For the state of repose,

$$h_0 = 0.67 \times 14.79 + 0.28 \times 7.216 = 12.05 \text{ feet};$$

hence

$$h'_0 = 12.05\left(1 + \frac{1}{16}\frac{16.4^2}{12.05^2}\right) - \frac{16.4}{2} = 5.24 \text{ feet},$$
$$h''_0 = 16.4 + 5.24 = 21.64 \text{ feet};$$
$$a'_0 = \frac{360.8}{2}\left(1 - \frac{1}{4}\frac{16.4}{12.05}\right) = 119.06 \text{ feet},$$
$$a''_0 = 360.8 - 119.06 = 241.74 \text{ feet}.$$

The tensions in the driving part of the cable are as follows: $S'_1 = 8533.8 - (7.216 - 1.35)3.804 = 8511.5$, $S''_1 = 8533.8 + (8.566 - 7.216)3.804 = 8538.94$; the values of S'_1 and S''_1 differing so slightly from S_1 that we may neglect the difference.

The heights which the calculations furnish for the deflections of an inclined transmission should be laid out in the drawing to a scale three or five times that of the horizontal lines; we then trace the curve of the cable as an arc of a parabola (see the following paragraph), and try if the conditions of the ground will permit us to use the curve obtained. If this prove not the case, we must recommence the calculation by adopting new values for the tension until we have obtained a curve which will satisfy the conditions. With a little practice, it is easy to determine by the eye the proper values to be adopted, and the calculation may then be made without difficulty.

§ 24. Method of Tracing the Curves of Cables.

The curve of a cable may be drawn with sufficient accuracy for ordinary purposes by assuming it to be an arc of a parabola. After having determined the summit C of the part of the cable BCD, Fig. 80, as explained in the preceding section, divide into two equal parts, at the points C_1 and C_2, the two distances B_1C and D_1C (B_1D_1 being tangent to the curve of its summit), and through the points C_1 and C_2 draw the lines BC_1 and DC_2, which give the directions in which the cable

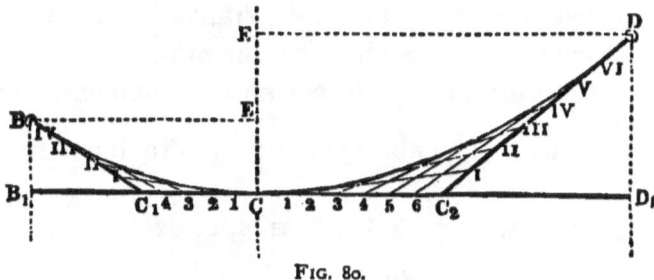

FIG. 80.

leaves the pulleys. Divide the distances CC_1 and C_1B into a certain number of small equal parts at the points 1, 2, 3, etc., and I, II, III, etc.; by joining 1I, 2II, 3III, etc., we obtain a series of lines tangent to the required parabola. By a similar method with CC_2D we obtain the other part of the curve. When the summit C of the curve falls outside of the pulleys, on the side of the pulley which occupies the lower level, a part of the parabola near the summit cannot be made use of, but the construction is still the same.

§ 25. *Transmission by Cable with Pulleys near together.*

When the distance between the pulleys of a transmission by cable is small, it is necessary, first of all, that the deflections have not too small values, in order that the cable may run properly upon the pulleys, and also that we may be able to shorten the cable without seriously increasing the tension. We adopt then for S_1 a very small value, and thus determine upon a value for the deflection; then, by means of formula (638) and the table calculated from it, obtain S_1; i and R are then calculated as we have already indicated. For a small tangential resistance and a small separation of the pulleys, transmissions by cable may still be used with satisfactory results.

Example.—A metallic cable transmits a force of 6 horse-power at 150 revolutions per minute; the separation of the pulleys is 65.6 feet and the deflection in the driven part of the cable 3.28 feet. We have then $\frac{h}{A} = 0.05$, which, from § 21, corresponds to $\frac{A}{S} = 0.103$, and we obtain $S_1 = \frac{65.6}{0.103} = 637$. In order to find the value of δ, we must know that of s. Assuming that $s + S_1$ is still equal to 25601.4, we have $s = 25601.4 - 637 = 24964.4$, which gives $\frac{s}{S_1}\frac{H}{n} = \frac{24964.4}{637}\frac{6}{150} = 1.57$. The second table of § 20 gives (column 7, line 11), therefore, $\delta = 0.08$ inch, for $i = 36$. From formula (637) we have for the radius of the pulleys $R =$

$0.08 \dfrac{14223000}{24964.4} = 45.6$ inches. From what precedes, we find that these values of δ and R are perfectly admissible. If we wish to take for the diameter of the cable, $d = 8\delta = 0.48$ inch, that is, δ is reduced to 0.06 inch, it is only necessary to give to R a smaller value. In this case the table of §20 gives (column 7, lines 8 and 9) $\dfrac{s}{S_1}\dfrac{H}{n} = 0.718$, hence $s = 0.718 S_1, \dfrac{n}{H} = 0.718 \times 637\dfrac{150}{6} = 11434.15$, and formula (637) gives $R = 0.06\dfrac{14223000}{11434.15} = 74$ inches. In some cases pulleys of large radii cannot be conveniently used, and we are obliged to use pulleys of different radii in order to make the deflections great enough. For the transmission of considerable forces, we obtain good results only on the condition of giving to the pulleys a certain velocity of rotation, the limits for which are indicated at the end of the following paragraph.

§ 26. Rim of Cable-pulleys.

When first used, the rims of cable-pulleys were made of wood covered with leather, but practice soon demonstrated the fact that rims of metal are preferable, and at the present time the latter are used almost exclusively in all cases where durability forms an important factor. Figs. 81 and 82 represent two cast-iron rims, single and double. The sides of the groove in the single rim are inclined at an angle of 30° with the middle plane of the pulley. In the double rim such an inclination would necessitate too great a weight for the projection between the two grooves; the inclination of the sides of this projection is therefore less than 30°. In Fig. 82 (which represents a portion of a large pulley) this inclination is 15°. All the dimensions indicated in the figures are in terms of the diameter d

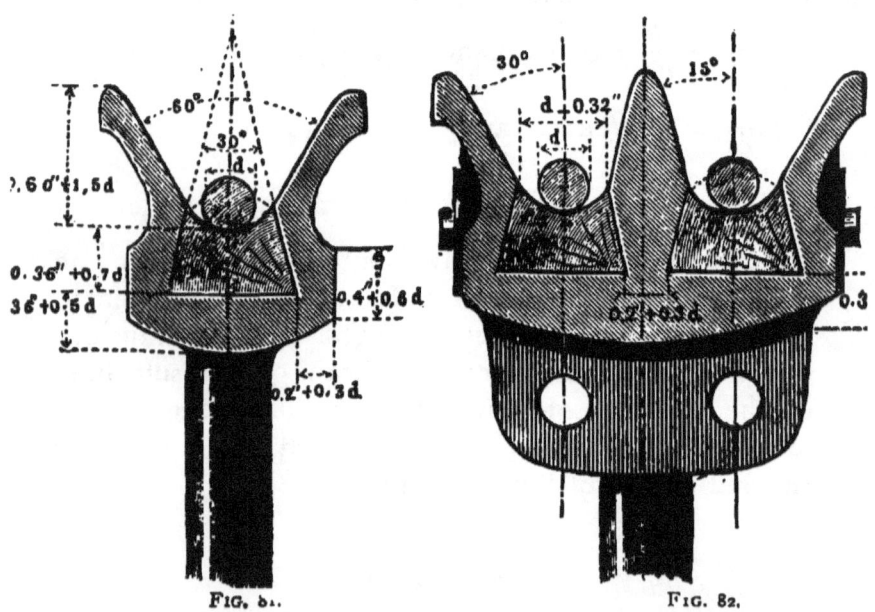

Fig. 81.　　　　　　Fig. 82.

of the cable. Since cables of less than 0.4 inch diameter are seldom used, we may consider the value of $d = 0.4$ inch as the inferior limit of the unit for the construction of cable-pulleys. The grooves in the faces of the pulleys are bottomed with gutta-percha driven into the dovetails, as shown in the figures; or small pieces of wood, which are introduced into the dovetails through openings in the side of the rim. Fig. 82 shows two openings of this kind covered up by pieces which are bolted in after the insertion of the wooden pieces. Of late years grooves with leather bottoms have come into use for very heavy cables; to this end old belts cut into strips and wedged into the dovetails may be advantageously used. Professor Fink has successfully employed bottoms formed by winding twine tightly around in the dovetails; bottoms thus made give great resistance to slipping. Bottoms of cork have also been used, but while they offer the advantage of being inexpensive, they have not been tested sufficiently in practice to determine their utility for transmission by cables where there is danger of slipping. When we wish to make use of bottoms of twine, the depth of the dovetails need not be so great as that indicated in the figures. In the first three modes of furnishing the grooves with bottoms which present more resistance to slipping than cast-iron (gutta-percha, wood, and leather), the profile of the groove upon which the cable rests may be hollowed out after the introduction of the material into the dovetails. Pulleys of 12 to 15 feet in diameter are ordinarily cast in two pieces, which makes them easier to handle and transport; projections are cast upon the inside of the rim by means of which the two parts may be bolted together.

In order that no harm may come to the rim through excessive centrifugal force, the velocity of rotation of the rim should not exceed 100 feet per second. The velocity of about 90 feet per second, which is now commonly given to metallic cables, may be considered as without disadvantages in ordinary practice.

§ 27. Arms and Nave of Cable-pulleys.

The body and rim of a cable-pulley are ordinarily of cast-iron, as is often the case with the entire pulley. We however sometimes find arms of wrought-iron set into cast-iron rims (see Fig. 96). In any case the number of arms A is determined from the expression

$$A = 4 + \frac{1}{40}\frac{R}{d}. \quad \ldots \quad (649)$$

The cross-sections of cast-iron arms are oval or flanged; in either case the width in the plane of the pulley is given by the formula

$$h = 4d + \frac{1}{4}\frac{R}{A}. \quad \ldots \quad (650)$$

In a flanged cross-section the thickness of the principal flange (in the plane of the pulley) is $e = \frac{h}{5}$, and that of the secondary flange $e' = \frac{2}{3}e$. In an oval cross-section the thickness is one half the width, as in pulleys for transmission by belt. The width at the rim may be taken equal to $\frac{2}{3}$ the width at the nave.

Arms with flanged cross-sections are generally straight (Fig. 83), and eight in number, while those having oval cross-sections are curved, either single, as explained in § 14, or double, as in Fig. 84.

To draw double-curved arms for cable-pulleys, we begin by striking a circle with a radius $OA = \frac{R}{2}$, then take upon the circle the lengths AB and BC, corresponding to the division by the arms. Draw the arc OE representing one portion of the double curve, in the same manner as for single-curved arms. Through the centre of curvature C of this arc (which, for eight arms, is on the circumference ABC) draw the line CED,

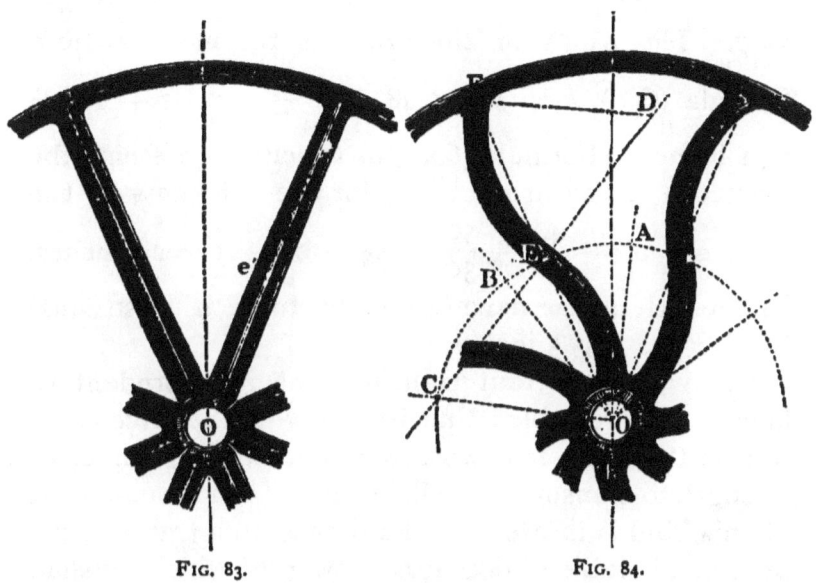

Fig. 83. Fig. 84.

and taking $ED = EC$, obtain the radius of curvature corresponding to the part EF of the arm. To draw the curves which limit the profile, it is necessary only to follow the method of § 14, remarking that the centres for the arcs are found upon the line CD.

When straight arms are used the nave is sometimes cast with grooves, into which iron rings are afterwards placed; by putting on the rings hot, and allowing them to cool, they are very firmly fixed, and add greatly to the strength of the pulley. The dimensions of the nave are determined, as already explained for pulleys for transmission by belt, in § 13.

Example.—In a transmission by cable the radius of the pulleys is 50 inches, the diameter of the arbor is 4.8 inches, and that of the cable 0.48 inch; it is required to determine dimensions of the pulley. From formula (649) the number of arms is $A = 4 + \frac{1}{40}\frac{50}{0.48} = 7$. The width of the arms at the nave is, from formula (650), $h = 4 \times 0.48 + \frac{1}{4}\frac{50}{7} = 1.92 + 1.8 = 3.72$ inches. Formula (604), in which d represents the diameter of the arbor, gives for the thickness of the nave $w = 0.4 + \frac{4.8}{6} + \frac{50}{50} = 0.4 + 0.8 + 1 = 2.2$ inches. The length of the nave (L) ought to be at least equal to $2\frac{1}{2} \times 2.2 = 5.5$ inches.

For very important transmissions it is prudent to have a reserve cable; that is, to divide the force to be transmitted between two cables, each having sufficient strength to transmit the whole force. An arrangement of this kind is in use at Schaffhouse, in a transmission by metallic cable of 600 horse-power, of which we shall have occasion to speak farther on. In this transmission the two pulleys are placed upon one driving arbor, as shown in Fig. 85. The pulleys which run loosely upon the arbor are fixed to the two gear-wheels B and D, which engage with the intermediate gears A and C. The latter gears run loosely upon their journals, which form a part of and rotate with the driving arbor. By means of this arrangement each cable is made to transmit an equal share of the total force. If one of the cables breaks, the pulley over which it ran is free to rotate in the opposite direction, and the gears are thus put in motion. In order to prevent too rapid motion in the pulley, which by the breaking of a cable may become loose upon the arbor, the transmission at Schaffhouse is provided with a powerful brake, by means of which the motion of the motive turbine-wheel may

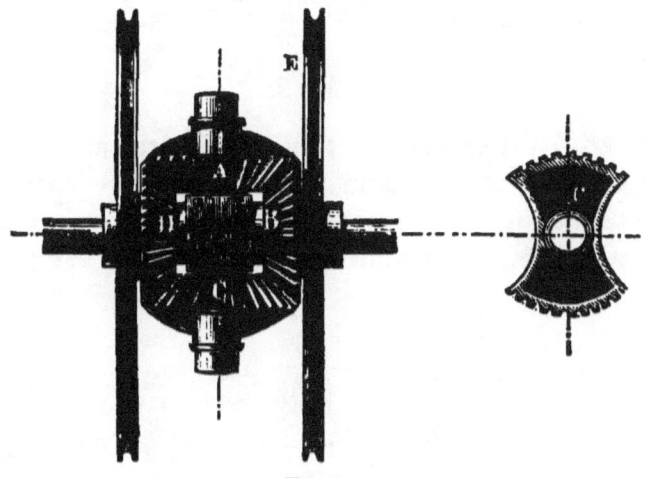

FIG. 85.

be almost instantaneously arrested. Instead of the intermediate gears A and C, simple sectors, such as are represented in the figure on the right, might be used in this transmission. In this case as soon as a break in one of the cables occurred, the sectors would be put in motion, and when the toothless parts came opposite the gears D and B the motion of the pulleys would be stopped, and danger of further accident avoided.

§ 28. Pulley-Supports and Intermediate Pulleys

When the principal pulleys of a transmission by cable are placed far apart, and especially when they are not high above the ground, it is often necessary to support the cable by other pulleys. In certain cases it is sufficient to support at a single point the driven part of the cable while the driving part is left free, as shown in

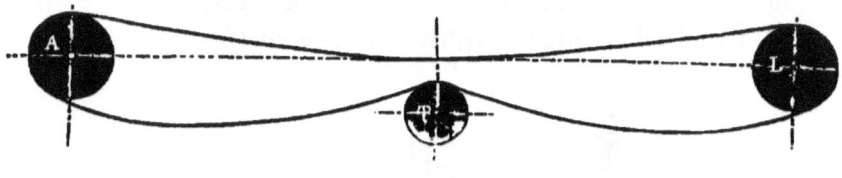

Fig. 86.

Fig. 86. When several pulley-supports are necessary, the driving part is also supplied with at least one, as shown in Fig. 87. In other cases the number of pulley-supports is the same for both parts of the cable; it

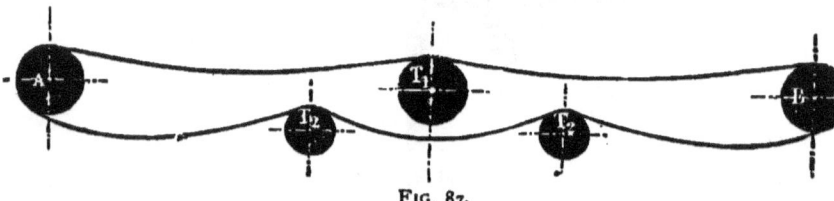

Fig. 87.

is then best to place the pulleys of the driving part directly over those of the driven part, instead of juxtapositing them, as has been several times attempted, and which causes rapid wear of the cable, consequently produces a wearing friction upon the pulley-grooves, and also tends to make the cable run off the pulleys.

In the arrangement represented in Fig. 88 the pulley-supports of the driving part are placed under those of the driven part in order to gain space above the ground.

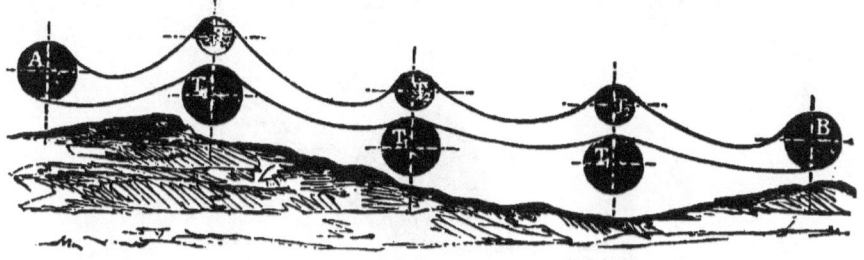

Fig. 88.

In most cases when the distance between the principal pulleys makes a great number of pulley-supports necessary, this arrangement may be advantageously replaced by a series of successive transmissions (Ziegler), Fig. 89. The pulley-supports of Fig. 88 are then replaced by intermediate double-grooved pulleys placed at as near the same distances apart as possible, so that

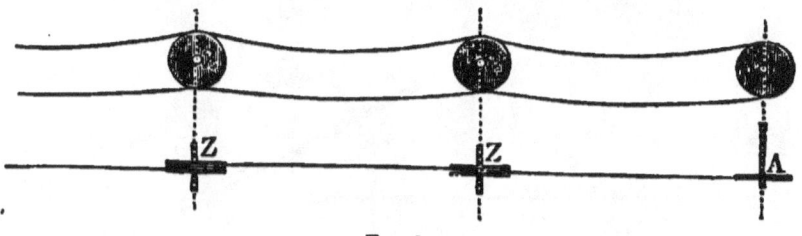

Fig. 89.

in case of breakage in any of the cables a single reserve cable may be used to replace it.*

---

*This has been done by Ziegler at Frankfort-on-the-Main, where a force of 100 horse power is transmitted at a distance of 984 metres—nearly ⅔ of a mile.

The different points at which a cable is supported are called stations; those which correspond to the principal pulleys of the transmission are called the stations at the extremities and the others intermediate

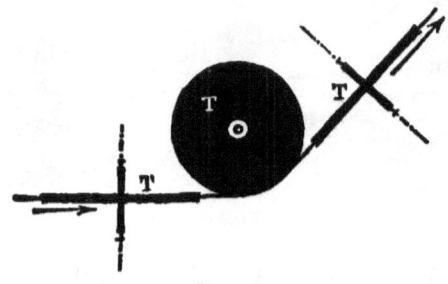

Fig. 90.

stations. Sometimes it is necessary to change the directions of the cable at an intermediate station; Hirn has proposed to accomplish this change of direction by means of a horizontal pulley, Fig. 90, while it has also been suggested to use a pair of bevel gears, Fig. 91.

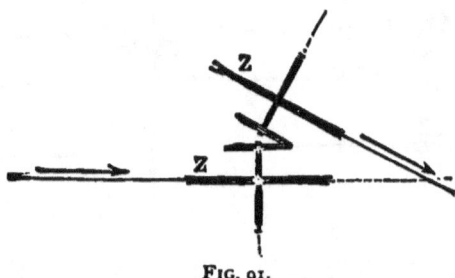

Fig. 91.

The use of transmissions by cable is very convenient when we wish to divide between several establishments, belonging to different proprietors, the force derived from a single motor: to do this we have simply to make the intermediate stations the starting-points or stations at one extremity of supplementary transmissions. Stations of this kind are called division-stations.

Pulley-supports are also used in the special case in which the driven arbor is placed almost vertically above or below the driving-arbor. There would be serious difficulty in making use of an inclined cable, connecting directly the two pulleys A and B, Figs. 92 and 93; it is preferable by far to use the pulley-supports T, T, placed in such a manner that one part of the cable, TA or TB, may be horizontal. It is then sufficient to

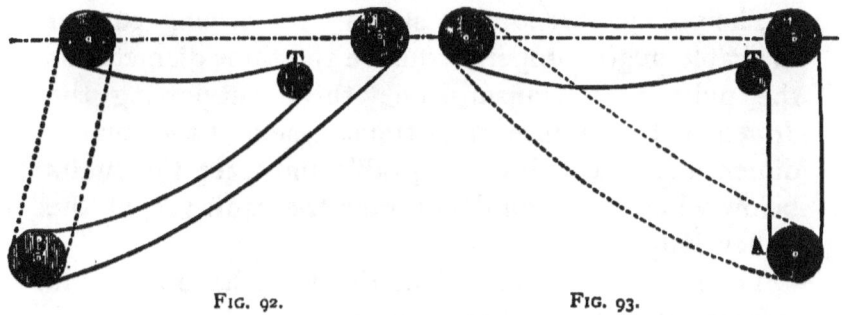

Fig. 92.   Fig. 93.

determine, by means of the preceding rules, the proper tensions to give to the horizontal part of the transmission without reference to the inclined part.

The use of cables for the transmission of forces to great depths—into the shafts of mines, for example—is still in a period of development. We may say, however, from attempts already made in this direction, that satisfactory results have been obtained.*

---

* Review of Society of German Engineers, 1866, p. 371. Werner, "Use of transmissions by metallic cables for the shafts of mines."

234   BELTS AND PULLEYS.

We meet with a remarkable example of this mode of transmission in the arrangement at Schaffhouse, where a force of about 600 horse-power, taken from the current of the Rhine, is received by turbines at the left bank, and is intended to be transmitted across the river to the right bank, there to be divided among several factories. This important application, credit for which is due to the Society of Hydraulic Engineers of Schaffhouse, is very nearly completed, and affords, in all its details, information of the greatest interest to engineers.

§ 29. Dimensions of Pulley-supports.

The pulleys intended to support the driving part of the cable ought properly to have the same diameter as the pulleys of transmission; those supporting the driven part may, in normal transmissions, have smaller dimensions. The following table indicates the limits below which we should not take the radius R_0 of the pulley-supports.

The numbers contained in the table have been calculated by means of the formula

$$\frac{R_0}{\delta} = \frac{28446000}{51202.8 - S_1} \quad \ldots \quad (651)$$

S_1	s	$\frac{R_0}{\delta}$	S_1	s	$\frac{R_0}{\delta}$
711.15	24890.25	563	12800.70	12800.70	741
1422.30	24179.10	571	14223.00	11378.40	769
2844.60	22756.80	588	15645.30	9956.10	800
4266.90	21334.50	606	17067.60	8533.80	833
5689.20	19912.20	625	18489.90	7111.50	870
7111.50	18489.90	645	19912.20	5689.20	909
8533.80	17067.60	667	21334.50	4266.90	952
9956.10	15645.30	690	22756.80	2844.60	1000
11378.40	14223.00	714	24197.10	1422.30	1053

The values contained in the table furnish excellent dimensions for R_0 principally for large values of S_1. In transmissions with increased tension (see § 21) the difference between R_0 and R is so small that we may take, without disadvantage, $R = R_0$. In compound transmssions (see § 28) there is no difference in size between the principal pulleys at the extremities and the intermediate pulleys.

§ 30. *Pressure upon the Axes of Pulley-supports.*

In a transmission by cables, which we have taken care to calculate for its entire length, we should know the tensions at each station, and (from the curves of

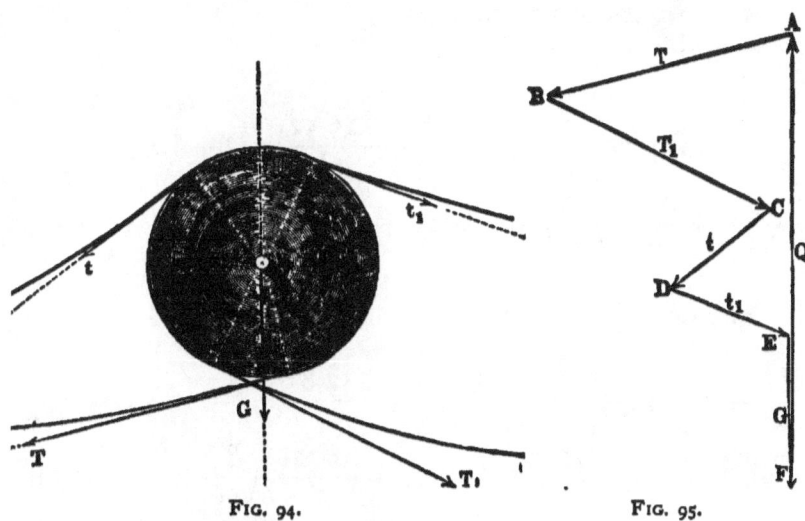

FIG. 94.   FIG. 95.

the cables traced according to § 23) the directions of the different parts which are to be supported by intermediate pulleys. For example, in Fig. 94, for an intermediate pulley we should know the values of T,

t, T_1, and t_1, and their directions. We can then determine by means of formulas already given the approximate weight of the pulley, which allows us to trace graphically (Fig. 95) the resultant Q of the different forces. To accomplish this we draw the lines AB, BC, CD, DE, and EF respectively equal and parallel to T, T_1, t, t_1, and G. The line AF, which completes the polygon, represents in amount and direction the resultant Q.

Pulley-supports are ordinarily in construction identical with the principal pulleys for the same diameter of cable. By virtue of the rules of §§ 26 and 27, the following formulas may be obtained for the approximate weights of the pulleys:

For single-grooved pulleys,

$$\frac{G}{d^3} = 0.034375 \left[\left(45 + \frac{145.6}{d} + \frac{115.52}{d^2}\right)\left(\frac{R}{d}\right) + \left(0.33 + \frac{0.464}{d} + \frac{0.115}{d^2}\right)\left(\frac{R}{d}\right)^2 + \left(0.005 + \frac{0.0028}{d}\right)\left(\frac{R}{d}\right)^3 \right] . \quad (652)$$

For double-grooved pulleys,

$$\frac{G}{d^3} = 0.034375 \left[\left(84 + \frac{265.6}{d} + \frac{212.8}{d^2}\right)\left(\frac{R}{d}\right) + \left(0.33 + \frac{0.464}{d} + \frac{0.115}{d^2}\right)\left(\frac{R}{d}\right)^2 + \left(0.005 + \frac{0.0028}{d}\right)\left(\frac{R}{d}\right)^3 \right] . \quad (653)$$

Example.—In the fourth example of § 20 for a radius of 30 inches the diameter of the wires (of which there are 36) is 0.036 inch. The diameter of the cable itself is therefore $d = 8 \times 0.036 = 0.288$ inch, which

PRESSURE ON PULLEY-SUPPORT AXES.

gives $\dfrac{R}{d} = \dfrac{30}{0.288} = 104$. The weight of the pulley for a single groove is, from formula (652), $G = 0.024 \times$

FIG. 96.

$$0.034375\left[\left(45 + \dfrac{145.6}{0.288} + \dfrac{115.52}{0.083}\right)104 + \left(0.33 + \dfrac{0.464}{0.288} + \dfrac{0.115}{0.083}\right)10816 + \left(0.005 + \dfrac{0.0028}{0.288}\right)1124864\right] = 204$$

pounds.

238 BELTS AND PULLEYS.

Example.—For the transmission of 300 horse-power of the second example of § 20 we have $\delta = 0.087$, which for a cable of 60 wires gives $d = 12.8 \times 0.087 = 1.11$ inches, $R = 85$ inches. Consequently $\dfrac{R}{d} = \dfrac{85}{1.11} = 77$. The weight of the pulley for double grooves is therefore $G = 1.37 \times 0.034375 \left[\left(84 + \dfrac{265.6}{1.11} + \dfrac{212.8}{1.23}\right) 77 + \left(0.33 + \dfrac{0.464}{1.11} + \dfrac{0.115}{1.23}\right) 5929 + \left(0.005 + \dfrac{0.0028}{1.11}\right) 456533 \right] = 2193$ pounds.

For very large transmission-pulleys the weights become important considerations, as may be seen by the last example. For this reason engineers have sought, by modifying the system of construction, to reduce the weights. By adopting the arrangement represented in Fig. 96, in which the arms are formed by two series of inclined rods meeting in pairs at the rim of the pulley, the weights may be reduced to about three quarters those given by the preceding formulas. In Sweden, where transmission by cable has already been firmly established, pulleys constructed of sheet-iron have been successfully employed.*

§ 31. Station Pillars.

Fig. 96 represents the arrangement of a station for the intermediate pulleys of a compound transmission. To support the pedestals for the axle of a pulley of this kind we may with propriety build up a frame-work

---

* See Annals of the Society of German Engineers, 1868, p. 591.

STATION PILLARS. 239

of wood; it is, however, preferable to use a solid pier of brick or stone, upon which are fixed either low pedestals, as in the figure, or high pedestals, such as

Fig. 97.

Figs. 97 or 98, which are especially advantageous when the height of the pulley-axes above the ground is great.

The pedestal-plates are fastened to the pier by means

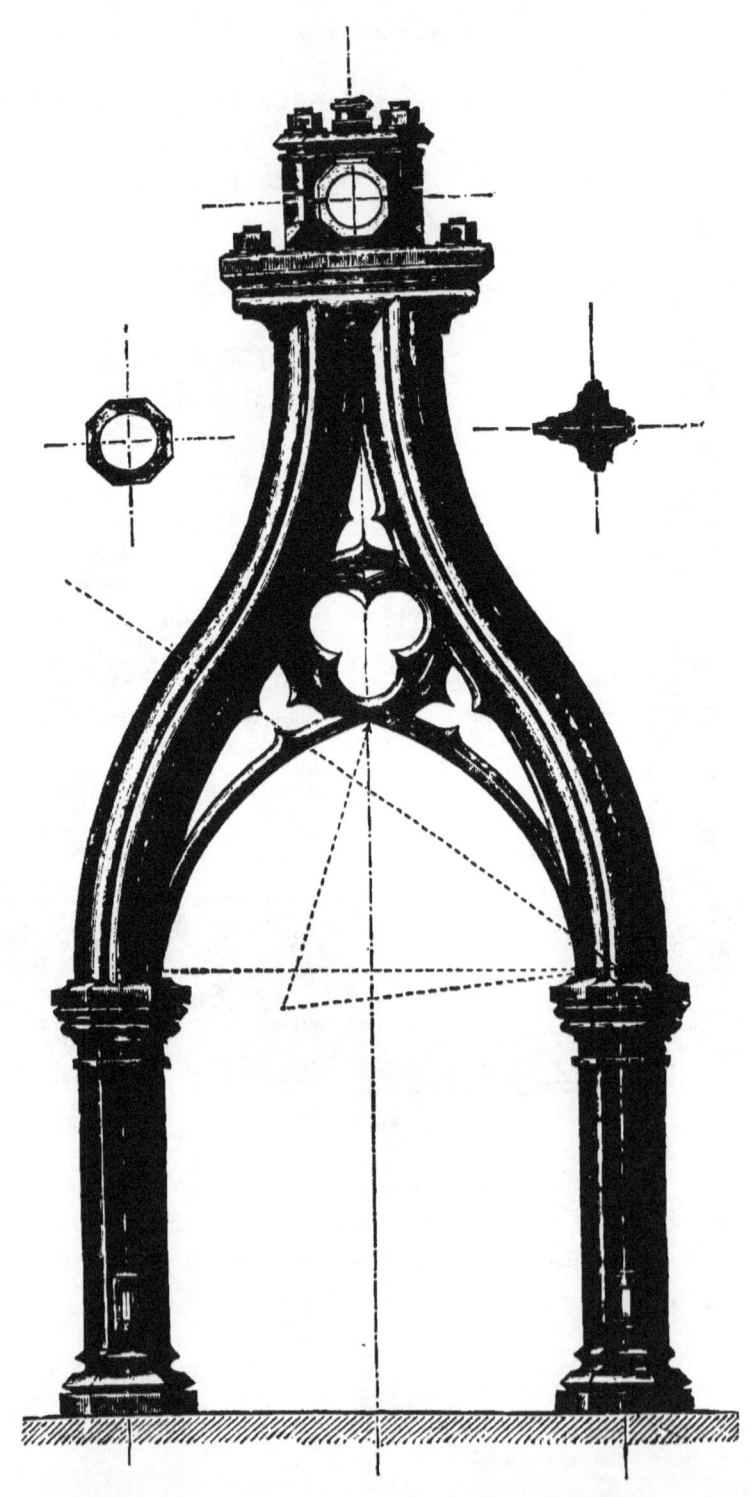

of four strong anchor-bolts passing through the pier and into the foundation. The length of the axle between the centres of the journals is generally taken equal to the radius of the pulley. In stations for two pulleys the pier is divided to a greater depth, and the axle of the upper pulley is supported by high pedestals. In certain cases the two pulleys are placed side by side, as indicated by the dotted lines in Fig. 96—

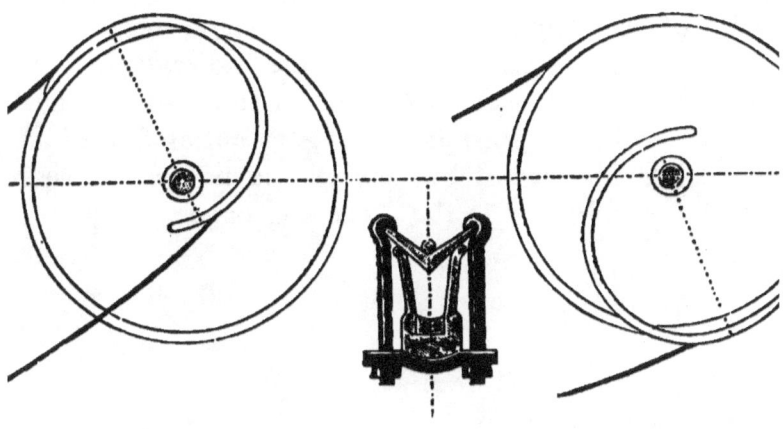

FIG. 99.

an arrangement especially convenient for putting on the cable. Because of the weight of metallic cables this operation is by no means simple; to accomplish it Ziegler has employed an arrangement similar to Herland's tool for putting on belts. Fig. 99 represents the arrangement, which consists of a curved piece of angle-iron, fixed in the groove of one of the pulleys by means of hooked bolts (see figure in centre). In the left-hand figure the cable is at the side of the pulley;

in the right-hand figure it rests in the groove of the pulley.

Although throughout this entire chapter we have assumed that the two pulleys of transmission have the same diameter, it does not follow that we may not use transmission-pulleys of different diameters. Indeed it may sometimes be necessary to have such an inequality of pulleys. In all cases of this kind it is best to confine ourselves to the determination of the dimensions of the smaller pulley and the corresponding diameter of the cable; taking care, however, not to lose sight of the fact that, in order to obtain the best results from our transmission, it is essential, first of all, that the diameters of our pulleys be no smaller than the limits indicated in the preceding pages.

APPENDIX.

I.

ACTUATED by a desire to obtain, by experiment with the belts and pulleys in ordinary practical use, the coefficient of friction which should be used in belt-calculations, the author provided himself with apparatus, and, before making use of the coefficient value $\varphi = 0.40$ in this work, very carefully proved this value as the mean of a number of trials. The apparatus consisted of the following arrangement:

Fig. 100. A pulley A securely fastened by the pins x, x, so that it could not move in any direction; a belt B, B passed around the pulley, and its ends attached to the levers abc and $a'b'c'$; two weights $w = 20$ pounds and $W = 40$ pounds, the latter being arranged so that it could be moved along the lever-arm bc at will. Belts and pulleys which had been used for some time—not, however, badly worn or injured—were purposely chosen in order to obtain more practical results.

The fulcrums b and b' were metallic knife-edges, and the friction between them and their levers therefore practically nothing. The weight $w = 20$ pounds was fixed upon the lever $a'b'c'$, the arms being $a'b' = 4$ inches and $b'c' = 12$ inches. The tension t was therefore, from the principles of the simple lever, $20 \times \frac{12}{4} = 60$ pounds. In each experiment the arm ab was 4 inches long and the weight W was moved along the lever-arm bc until the tension T was such that the belt was just on the point of slipping; the corresponding

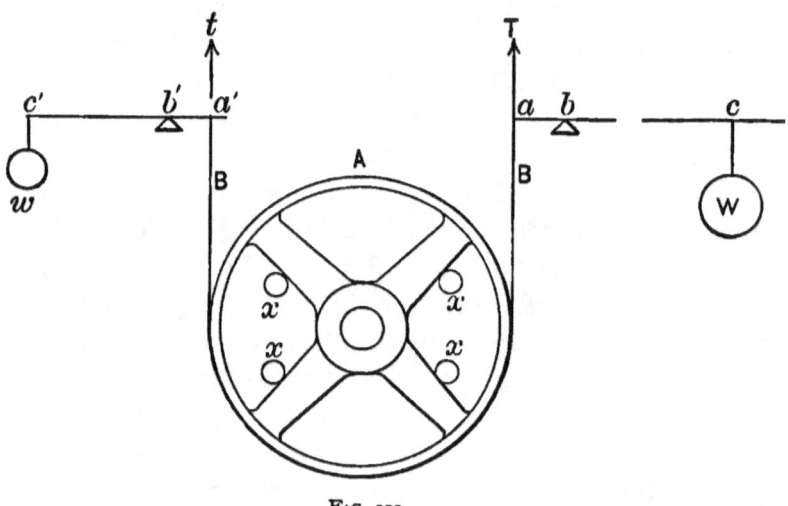

FIG. 100.

arm was then carefully measured with an accurate hundredth rule, and the tension T calculated as above for t.

Experiment 1.—The angle embraced by the belt was $\alpha = 180$ degrees, the tension $t = 60$, and the lever-arm $bc = 22.50$ inches. The tension T was therefore $T = \frac{22.50}{4} \times 40 = 225$ pounds. Hence $\frac{T}{t} = \frac{225}{60} = 3.75$,

$\log \dfrac{T}{t} = \log 3.75 = 0.57403$. From formula (41), by transposing, we obtain for the coefficient of friction the expression $\varphi = \log \dfrac{T}{t} \div 0.007578\alpha$, which in the present case becomes $\varphi = \dfrac{0.57403}{0.007578 \times 180} = \dfrac{0.57403}{1.36404}$ or $\varphi = 0.42083$.

In this experiment, although tried with five different

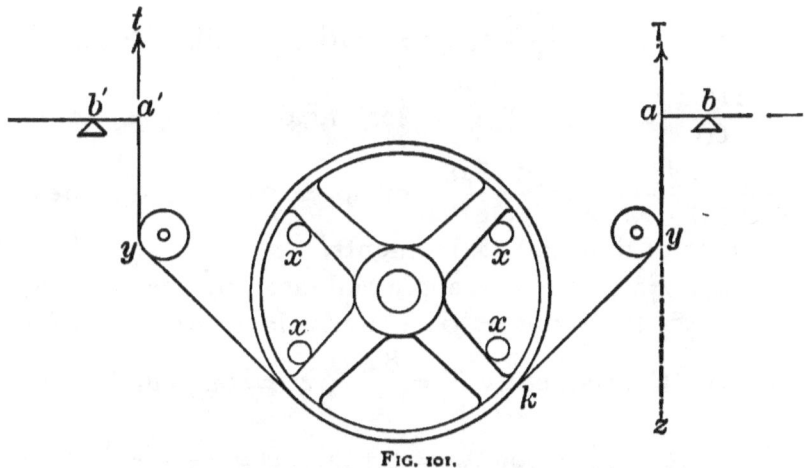

FIG. 101.

pulleys and as many different belts, the greatest value obtained for the coefficient was $\varphi = 0.4248$, and the smallest $\varphi = 0.41997$. The value determined above was nearest to the average of the different experiments.

Experiment 2.—The angle embraced by the belt was $\alpha = 90°$. The arrangement of apparatus for this experiment is shown in Fig. 101, being the same as in Experiment 1, except that the belt was held away from the pulley by means of two small rollers y, y, in order to obtain the required value for the angle α. The friction of the rollers was so small that when used for an angle $\alpha = 180°$, with the belt and pulley which gave the mean result in Experiment 1, and with the same angle of deviation (kyz, Fig. 101), made a difference of only 0.00197 in the results—practically none at all.

The tension t was as before $t = 60$ pounds, and the lever-arm $bc = 11.64$ inches. The greater tension was therefore $T = \dfrac{11.64}{4} \times 40 = 116.4$ pounds. Hence $\dfrac{T}{t} = \dfrac{116.4}{60} = 1.94$, $\log \dfrac{T}{t} = \log 1.94 = 0.28780$, $\varphi = \dfrac{0.28780}{0.007578 \times 90} = \dfrac{0.28780}{0.68202}$ or $\varphi = 0.42198$—nearest average of different experiments.

Experiment 3.—The angle embraced by the belt was $\alpha = 45°$, tension $t = 60$ pounds, lever-arm $bc = 8.4$ inches. Consequently $T = \dfrac{8.4}{4} \times 40 = 84$ pounds, $\dfrac{T}{t} = \dfrac{84}{60} = 1.4$, $\log \dfrac{T}{t} = \log 1.4 = 0.14613$, $\varphi = \dfrac{0.14613}{0.007578 \times 45} = \dfrac{0.14613}{0.34101}$, or $\varphi = 0.42852$—nearest average value.

In this experiment the angle of deviation (kyz, Fig. 101) was so great that the friction of the rollers y, y must have had an appreciable effect, which probably accounts for the increased value of φ.

Experiment 4.—The angle embraced by the belt was 210°; the arrangement of apparatus in order to obtain

APPENDIX. 247

this angle is shown in Fig. 102. Tension $t = 60$ pounds, and the lever-arm $bc = 28.4$ inches. Therefore the greater tension was $T = \dfrac{28.4}{4} \times 40 = 284$ pounds, and $\dfrac{T}{t} = \dfrac{284}{60} = 4.733$. The logarithm of this ratio is 0.67514, and we have, for the coefficient,

$$\varphi = \dfrac{0.67514}{0.007578 \times 210} = \dfrac{0.67514}{1.59138} = 0.42425\text{—nearest}$$

average value.

Example 5.—The angle embraced by the belt was

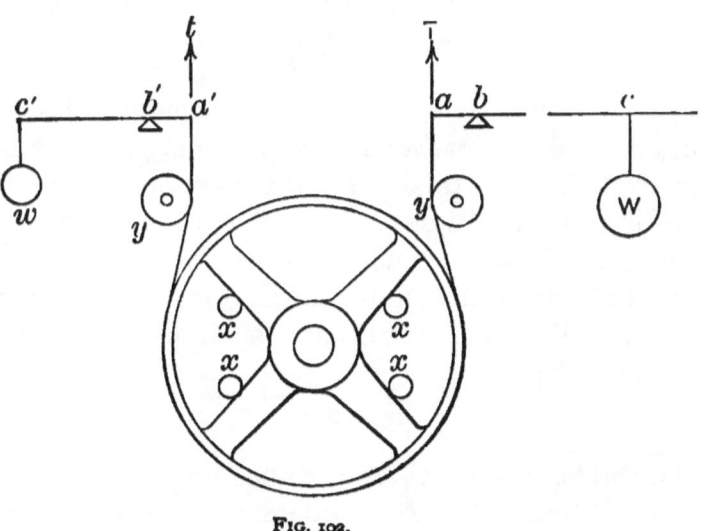

Fig. 102.

$\alpha = 250°$, tension $t = 60$ pounds, and the lever-arm bc 39.15 inches long. The greater tension was therefore $T = \dfrac{39.15}{4} \times 40 = 391.5$ pounds, $\dfrac{T}{t} = \dfrac{391.5}{60} =$

6.525, $\log \dfrac{T}{t} = 0.81458$. Hence $\varphi = \dfrac{0.81458}{0.007578 \times 250} = \dfrac{0.81458}{1.8945} = 0.42997$—nearest average value.

In each of these experiments five trials were made with different belts and pulleys, the values worked out above being about mean for each separate experiment. A mean between the five values given above is therefore a mean value determined by twenty-five very careful experiments, and may be relied upon for practical calculations. This gives for us our coefficient of friction between leather belts and iron pulleys * $\varphi = 0.42507$. Since in this coefficient there is not the same need of a factor of safety as in calculations with proof-strengths and to prevent breakage, we may take very nearly the full value without running risk of any serious accident. We have taken, and shall use throughout this work, the value

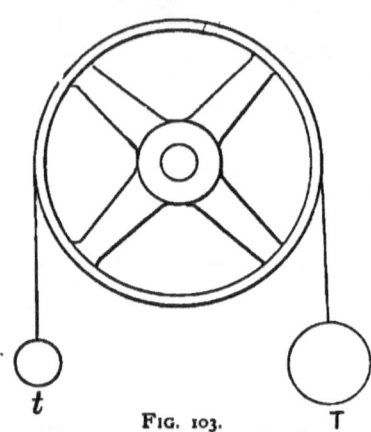

Fig. 103.

$$\varphi = 0.40.$$

All the belts with which the above experiments were made had been oiled to a moderate extent with castor-oil.

---

* This value practically agrees with the results of the experiments of Messrs. Briggs and Towne, as given in *Journal of the Franklin Institute*, January, 1868.

APPENDIX.

A series of 18 experiments with new dry leather belts hung over a fixed pulley and weighted at each end (see Fig. 103) gave an average value of

$$\varphi = 0.304.$$

The angle embraced by the belt in each case was 180°, the weights on the ends varying from 10 and $25\frac{1}{2}$ pounds to 90 and 229 pounds.

The author also tried 21 experiments with some old, gummy leather belting which had lain in a dry room for nearly two years, and to his astonishment found an average value of $\varphi = 0.61$ for the coefficient of friction. These belts, which were 2 inches wide and $\frac{3}{16}$ inch thick, broke through the solid parts when tested for strength, at an average strain of 1088 pounds. This would give for the ultimate strength $1088 \times \frac{8}{3}$, or about 2900 pounds per square inch—very little if any below that of ordinary belt-leather.

Leather over Leather-covered Pulleys.—Using the belting and pulleys of the first five experiments mentioned in this Appendix, the author tried the following experiments with leather-covered pulleys:

Experiment 1.—With apparatus of Fig. 100. $\alpha = 180°$, $t = 60$ pounds. The lever-arm bc was 26.15 inches long when the belt began to slip. Hence $T = \frac{26.15}{4} \times 40 = 261.5$ pounds, $\log \frac{T}{t} = \log \frac{261.5}{60} = \log 4.358 = 0.63929$. Consequently $\varphi = \frac{0.63929}{0.007578 \times 180} = \frac{0.63929}{1.36404} = 0.4687$.

Experiment 2.—With apparatus of Fig. 101. $\alpha = 90$, $t = 60$ pounds. The lever-arm bc was 12.61 inches long. Hence $T = \dfrac{12.61}{4} \times 40 = 126.1$, $\log \dfrac{T}{t} = \log \dfrac{126.1}{60} = \log 2.102 = 0.32263$, and $\varphi = \dfrac{0.32263}{0.007578 \times 90} = \dfrac{0.32263}{0.68202} = 0.473$.

Experiment 3.—With apparatus of Fig. 101. $\alpha = 45°$, $t = 60$ pounds. The lever-arm bc was 8.75 inches long. Hence $T = \dfrac{8.75}{4} \times 40 = 87.5$ pounds, $\log \dfrac{T}{t} = \log \dfrac{87.5}{60} = \log 1.458 = 0.16376$, and $\varphi = \dfrac{0.16376}{0.007578 \times 45} = \dfrac{0.16376}{0.34101} = 0.4802$.

Experiment 4.—With apparatus of Fig. 102. $\alpha = 210°$, $t = 60$ pounds. The lever-arm bc was 34.99 inches long. Hence $T = \dfrac{34.99}{4} \times 40 = 349.9$ pounds, $\log \dfrac{T}{t} = \log \dfrac{349.9}{60} = \log 5.832 = 0.76582$, and $\varphi = \dfrac{0.76582}{0.007578 \times 210} = \dfrac{0.76582}{1.59138} = 0.4812$.

Experiment 5.—With apparatus of Fig. 102. $\alpha = 250°$, $t = 60$ pounds. The lever-arm bc was 49.77 inches long. Consequently $T = \dfrac{49.77}{4} \times 40 = 497.7$ pounds, $\log \dfrac{T}{t} = \log \dfrac{497.7}{60} = \log 8.295 = 0.91882$, and $\varphi = \dfrac{0.91882}{0.007578 \times 250} = \dfrac{0.91882}{1.8945} = 0.485$.

Each of the above experiments is the one **giving the nearest average value of** φ out of five tests. **The average** of these five experiments is therefore **the average of twenty-five carefully-made trials.** This **average** value is $\varphi = 0.4776$, which permits us, **after making** fair allowances for the friction of the rollers y, y used in the apparatus, to use, for the coefficient of friction of leather over leather-covered pulleys, the **value**

$$\varphi = 0.45.$$

Experiments tried with new dry leather over pulleys covered with the same gave for the **coefficient of** friction

$$\varphi = 0.348.$$

Vulcanized-rubber Belts. — The author has made nearly sixty different trials with vulcanized-rubber belts over cast-iron pulleys, the belts and **pulleys having** been used to a moderate extent for **practical purposes**; the mean value for the ratio of **the tensions for** $\alpha = 180°$ was found to be

$$\frac{T}{t} = 4.55.$$

From this we have

$$\log \frac{T}{t} = \log 4.55 = .0658011,$$

and consequently

$$\varphi = \frac{0.658011}{0.007578 \times 180} = \frac{0.658011}{1.36404} = 0.4824.$$

This value is slightly greater than that obtained for oiled leather belts over leather-covered pulleys; for reasons given in § 12, however, we take the coefficient of friction for vulcanized-rubber belts over cast-iron pulleys, the same as for leather over leather-covered pulleys, i.e.,

$$\varphi = 0.45.$$

II.

The principles of the endless belt and pulleys, as applied for numerous different purposes of the shops and factories, have developed from time to time a vast number of ingenious contrivances by means of which many motions other than that of simple, continuous rotation may be easily obtained. Thus, while the fundamental mechanism itself has remained essentially unchanged from the forgotten ages which gave it birth to the present time, instead of the simple band transmitting the motion of one pulley to another parallel and equal pulley, we have now devices by means of which we may transmit the motion of the driver to one or more shafts oblique in almost any direction to that of the motive pulley; to increase and decrease the speeds of the various pulleys at will; to reverse and change the directions of rotation of any or all of the driven pulleys; to almost instantly impart or arrest their motions; and to transform the continuous, rotary motion of the driver into rectilinear, reciprocating, intermittent, and intricate compound motions. Indeed it is not so far from the truth as is sometimes suspected, that "almost anything can be accomplished with a room full of pulleys and belts."

Some of the most common of the many devices made use of to obtain the different motions necessary for the various kinds of work known to the artisan have been gathered together and explained, as briefly as is consistent with a clear understanding of the mechanisms, in the following pages.

Fig. 104 represents an arrangement of pulleys by means of which the motion of the driving-pulley A

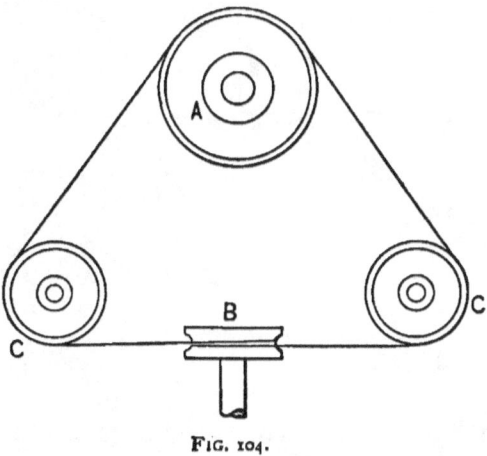

FIG. 104.

may be transmitted to the pulley B, at right angles with the driver. The guides C, C hold the band in such positions that it runs easily upon the driven pulley, about which it makes one entire turn.

Fig. 105 represents a device for transforming a rectilinear into a reciprocating rotary or oscillating motion. A rocking motion is given to the arm E by means of the connecting-rod A and the motive-piece

F. The required motion is then transmitted to the two pulleys *C* and *D* by means of the half-pulley *B* and the belt *gg*. Inversely, by giving an oscillating motion to one of the pulleys *C* and *D* a reciprocating rectilinear motion may be given to the piece *F*.

In the combination of pulleys represented in Fig. 106, the uniform rotary motion of the driver *A* gives to the pulleys *B*, *C*, and *D* uniform rotary motions at different speeds, according to their diameters, as ex-

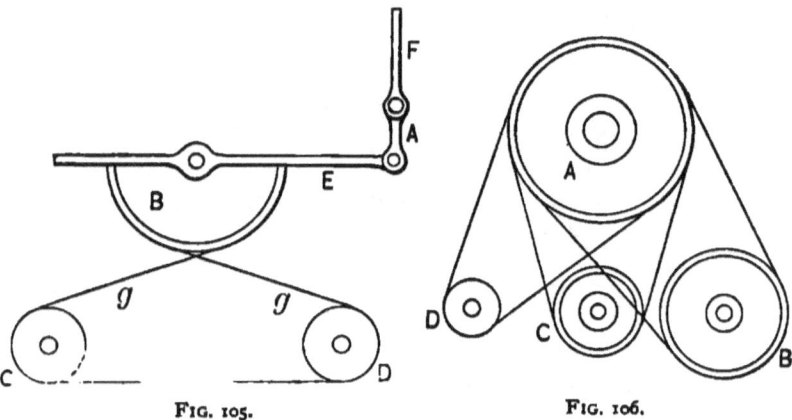

FIG. 105.   FIG. 106.

plained in § 2. The driven pulleys are in different planes, and the face-width of the driver is great enough to carry the several belts without interfering with each other.

The contrivance shown in Fig. 107 is intended to give two rotary motions in contrary directions to two coincident shafts. The pulley *A* is the driver, and carries a crossed belt running to the pulley *B*, and also an open belt running to the pulley *C*. The latter pulleys consequently rotate in opposite directions at the

APPENDIX.

same or at different speeds, according as their diameters are equal or different.

Fig. 108 represents an arrangement by means of which a great increase of friction between the band and principal pulleys may be obtained. The band passes several times around the principal pulleys, A and B, and is properly guided by means of the small rollers b and c, as shown in the figure. Let us suppose that

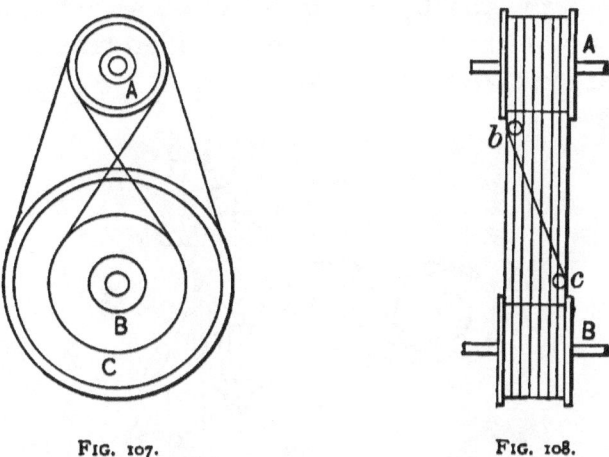

Fig. 107.   Fig. 108.

the band passes four times around the pulleys: the arc embraced is then $\alpha = 360 \times 4 = 1440°$. If we take for the coefficient of friction $\varphi = 0.30$, we shall have for the ratio of the tensions [see formula (41)],

$$\log \frac{T}{t} = 0.007578 \times 0.30 \times 1440 = 3.2737,$$

If the band passed only ½ times around the pulleys, we should have $\alpha = 180°$, and consequently

$$\log \frac{T}{t} = 0.007578 \times 0.30 \times 180 = 0.4092,$$

or $\quad \dfrac{T}{t} = 2.566.$

In other words, by means of the above arrangement the ratio of the greater to the smaller tension is increased over *seven hundred-fold*.

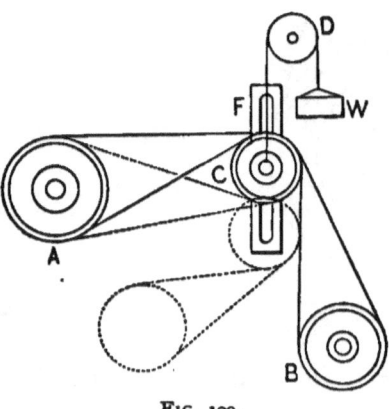

FIG. 109.

An ingenious device for transmitting a rotary motion to a movable pulley by means of an ordinary belt is represented in Fig. 109. A is the driver and B the movable driven pulley. The intermediate pulley C is suspended by means of a cord passing over the roller D and the weight W; it is thus free to move up and down in the frame F, and the pulley B may be moved through considerable distances without interfering with the motion of the belt, as is indicated by the dotted lines.

Fig. 110 represents an arrangement of pulleys for transmitting two different speeds from the driving shaft AA to the driven shaft BB. Each shaft carries two fast pulleys (C, C, C', and E) and two loose pulleys (F, F, F', and G), and the two belts xx and yy are moved together, backward and forward, across the pulley-faces. When the belts are in the positions shown in the figure, the belt xx is at work and yy at rest. When the belts are moved to the pulleys F, F and C', E, the belt xx is at rest and the belt yy transmits to the driven shaft a fast motion because of the small diameters of the pulleys G and E.

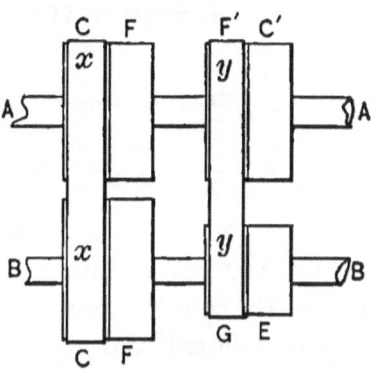

FIG. 110.

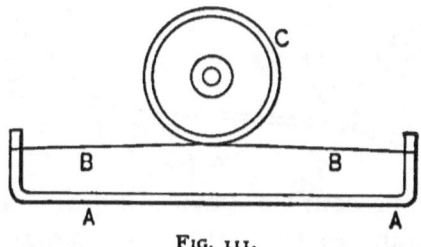

FIG. 111.

A mode of transforming a reciprocating rectilinear motion into an alternating rotary motion is shown in Fig. 111. To the piece AA a cord, which also passes

17

around the pulley *C*, is attached, and by moving the piece *AA* backward and forward, the required motion of *C* is obtained. Inversely, by giving an oscillating motion to the pulley *C*, a reciprocating rectilinear motion may be given to the piece *AA*.

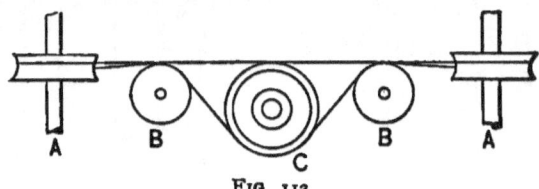

FIG. 112.

Fig. 112 represents an arrangement by means of which the continuous rotary motion of the driver *C* may be transmitted to two pulleys *A, A* at right angles with the motive-pulley. A portion of the band is horizontal, and runs without difficulty upon the pulleys *A, A*; the other part is guided by the intermediate pulleys *B, B*, as shown in the figure.

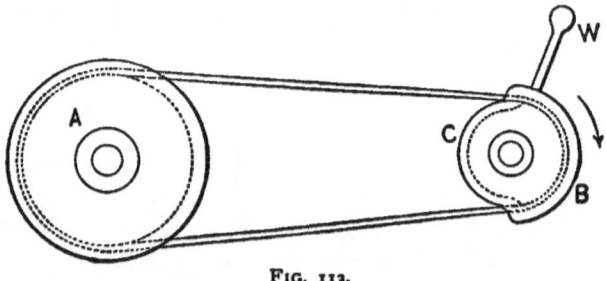

FIG. 113.

Fig. 113 represents a device by means of which a variable motion for the driven shaft may be obtained from the uniform motion of the driver. The pulley *A* is the driver, and bears upon its face a deep groove, as shown by the dotted circle. The pulley *B* is mutilated, one part having a greater radius than the other, and also has a deeply grooved face. When the pulleys are in the positions shown in the figure, the belt is tight, and drives uniformly the pulley *B*. When, however, the smaller part of the pulley *B* comes opposite the belt, the tension is greatly lessened and the weight *W* jerks the pulley quickly around until the belt again becomes tight, when the operation is repeated.

In Fig. 114, the arm *C* bearing the pulley *B*, when moved up and down in treadle motion, transmits a rotary motion to the shaft *S* by means of the belt and eccentric pulley *A*. By making the pulley *A* the driver, the pulley *B* may be given a rotary motion, and at the same time an oscillating motion about the point *D*.

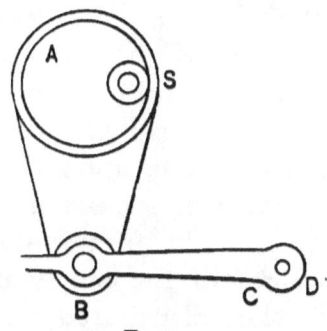

FIG. 114.

Fig. 115 represents a device for transmitting a continuous rotary motion to a movable shaft. The pulley *A* is the driver, and the driven pulley *B* may be moved about in the frame *C*, as shown by the dotted lines, without interfering with the motion of the belt. The radius of curvature of the axis of the frame is equal to the distance between the centres of the pulleys.

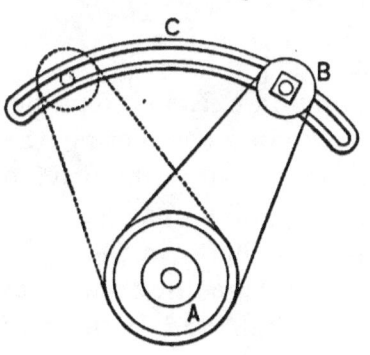

FIG. 115.

Another mode of transmitting a rotary motion to a movable pulley is shown in Fig. 116. *A* is the driving-pulley and carries an elastic belt of india-rubber.

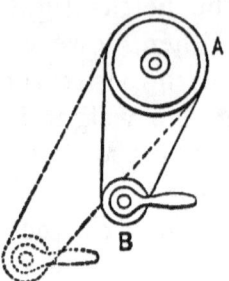

FIG. 116.

By stretching the belt, the driven pulley B may be moved about in almost any direction, as indicated by the dotted lines. This device is used extensively in hair-cutting and clipping machines, and dental apparatus for boring and drilling.

Fig. 117 represents a device known to artisans as the "frictionless bearing," or "anti-friction bearing. The shaft b of the pulley A, instead of turning in an ordinary pedestal or hanger, rests upon the circumferences of six small rollers, c, c, etc. The friction due to the weight of the pulley and shaft is thus distributed among the six rollers, and, since the shaft rolls upon the rollers instead of sliding around in the pedestal as with common bearings, the friction of sliding is eliminated.

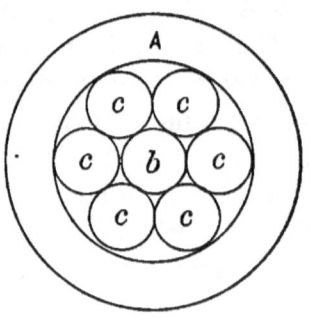

FIG. 117.

Considerable difference of opinion exists among mechanical men as to the best method of connecting the various shafts in shops and mills with the driving drum or pulley. Some engineers claim that but one belt should be used to drive all the shafts in the mill; that this method is the most advantageous, because of the great duration of the driving-belt and because of the simplicity of the arrangement. Others suggest two belts—one connecting the driving-pulley with the first shop-shaft, and the other passing from the first shop-shaft to all the other shafts; while by many it is claimed that each principal shaft should have its own belt connecting it, either directly or indirectly, with the driving-pulley.

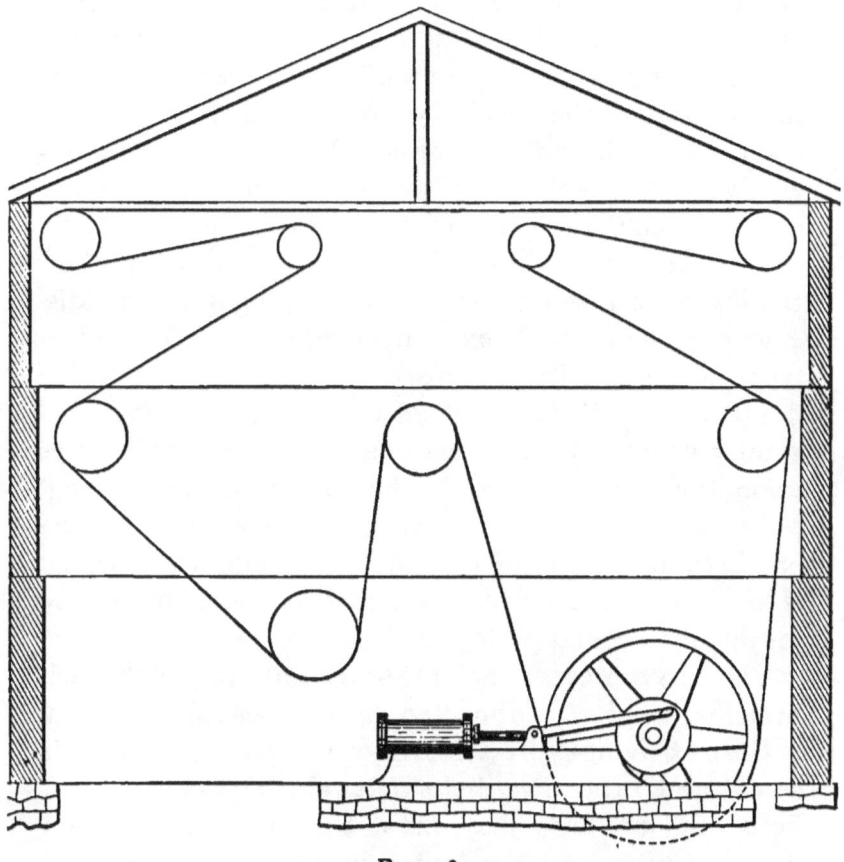

Fig. 118.

Fig. 118 represents a section of a three-story mill, the shafts of which are driven by means of a single belt. The arrangement of the various pulleys is sufficiently clear in the figure without further explanation. The objections offered to this method of transmitting to the different shafts the power of the motor are the following: the belt must necessarily be very long—often nearly or quite 500 feet; it must be very strong, and consequently wide and heavy, since it must transmit the entire power of the mill; the expense is therefore great, and the tendency to stretch greater than in a short belt; because of the weight and length the operation of shortening and tightening the belt is much more difficult than in ordinary cases; since the belt cannot be easily slipped from one pulley to another, the use of fast and loose pulleys for engaging and disengaging the shafts is extremely difficult. The advantages are simplicity, supposed long wear (we however doubt very much the truth of this, since the belt is constantly bent in both directions and run on both sides upon the various pulleys), the fact that the driving-pulley need be no wider than is necessary to carry the one belt, and economy of pulleys, the number of which is less than if the power of each shaft was obtained by means of a second pulley from its nearest neighbor.

Fig. 119 represents a three-story mill, in which each principal shaft is connected by its own belt directly with the driving-pulley. Disadvantages: the shop is so cut up by the many belts that valuable space is sacrificed; the driving-pulley must be wide enough upon its face to carry all the belts—in the figure there are seven belts; if they average six inches wide and we allow one quarter of an inch between each two belts, the face of the driver must be over three and one half feet wide; the use of fast and loose pulleys for the shafts is rendered difficult. Advantages: each belt transmits the force of one shaft only, and the belts may therefore be light; if any one belt breaks it may be removed and

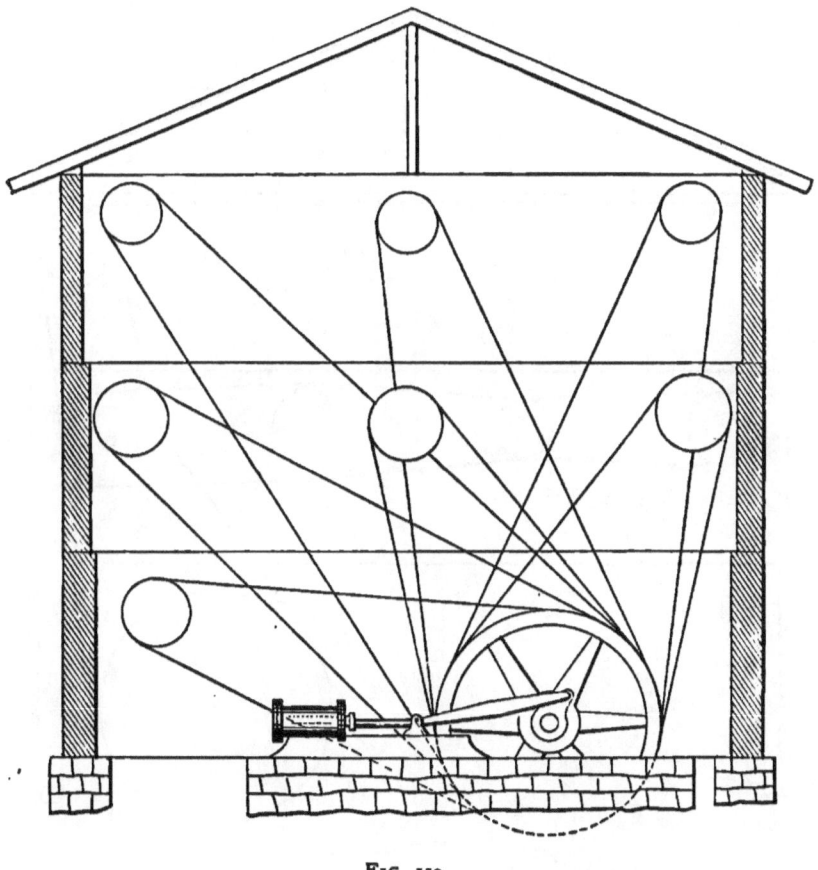

Fig. 119.

the remaining shafts driven as if no accident had occurred; each belt may be made large or small, according as it has heavy or light work to perform.

264   BELTS AND PULLEYS.

In Fig. 120, we show a section of a three-story mill driven in the manner most common at the present time throughout this country. A main driving-belt, heavy

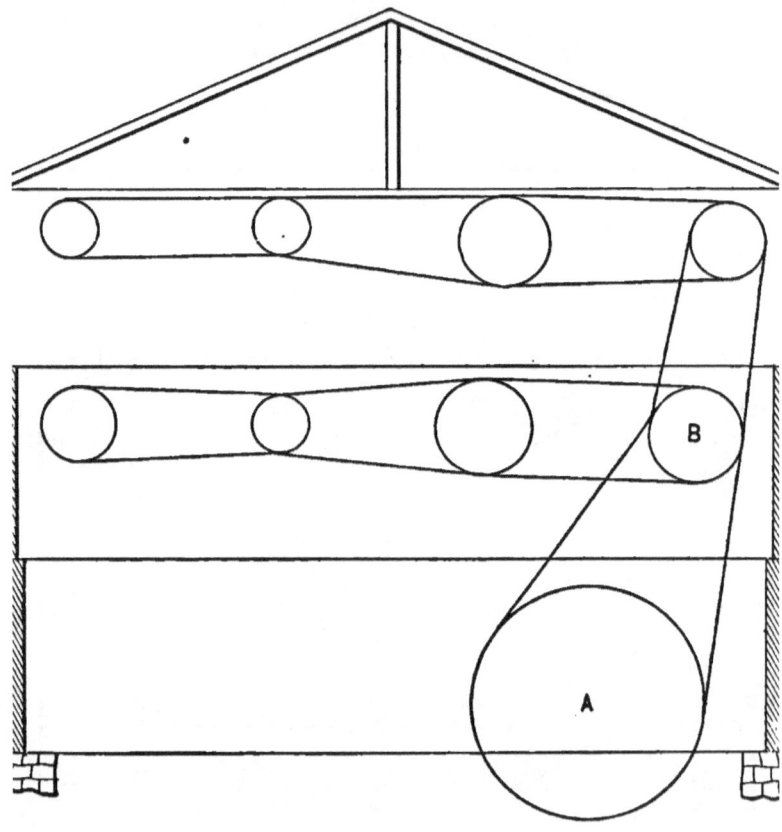

FIG. 120.

enough to transmit the entire work of the mill, runs from the motive-pulley A to the nearest shop-shaft B. From the latter shaft to the third-story main shaft runs a belt sufficiently strong to transmit the work of the third story. The other shafts on each story are connected by separate belts each with its nearest neighbor, as shown in the figure. In this arrangement the belts are all overhead and out of the way, except two which run close to the ends of the building. Thus no valuable space is used up by the belts. Fast and loose pulleys may easily be used, because none of the belts (except the driver) pass over the driving-pulley. This mode of transmitting power is open to the objection that the breakage of one of the principal belts causes a stoppage of several shafts,—for instance if the horizontal belt from the pulley B breaks, the entire second story is thrown out of gear; but its other advantages more than compensate for this risk, and it has therefore come to be the favorite in most of our shops and factories.

INDEX.

A

	PAGE
Absence of early records	1
Age of the belt and pulley	3
"American Machinist"	60
Angle between middle planes	31
— between shafts	31
Anti-friction bearing	260
Arc embraced by belt	83
Arms, curved	167
—, examples of	168
—, formulas for	167
—, method of drawing	169
—, of cable-pulleys	226
—, profiles of	169
—, of pulleys	166
—, straight	167
Arnold's rule	v
"Arts and Sciences of the Ancients"	2
Axes	28

B

	PAGE
Babylon	9
Base of Naperian Logarithms	84
Belt buckle	74
— hooks	71
Belts, canvas	66
—, Clissold's	193
—, crossed	7
—, double	66
—, flax	66
—, gut	66
—, half-crossed	31
—, hemp	66
—, leather	65
—, metallic	192

	PAGE
Belts, open	11
— over covered pulleys	116
—, rawhide	66
—, rubber	259
—, sheet-iron	67
—, vulcanized-rubber	66
— without guides	29
— with pulley-guides	32
Bending strain	171
Binomial formula	80
Briggs and Towne	248
Breaking strength of leather	92
— of rawhide	66
— of rope-belts	188
— of vulcanized rubber	141
Broken joints	66

C

	PAGE
Cables, deflections of	207
—, diameter of	200
—, examples of	204
—, formulas for	200
—, metallic	196
—, number of strands of	197
—, number of wires of	197
—, rules for	197
—, strength of	200
—, tables for	201–203
—, tensions of	196
Cast-iron shafts	176
Circumference	11
—, examples of	25
—, formulas for	11
—, rules for	11
Circumferential velocity	13

INDEX.

	PAGE
Cleat-fastening	74
Clissold's belt	193
Coefficient of friction of cables	199
— of jointed chain-belts	193
— of leather over cast-iron	86
— of leather over leather	116
— of rope-belts	187
— of rubber over cast-iron	142
— of rubber over leather	156
— of rubber over rubber	156
Coinciding axes	28
Common logarithms	85
Comparison of formulas	vii
— of leather and rubber	67
Conditions necessary for maintaining belt on pulleys	28
Continuous motion	7
— speed cones	62
Cooper, J. W.	71
Cores of metallic cables	198
Cork	225
Covered pulleys	116
Crossed axes	28
Crossed belt	7
Curved arms	167

D

Decreasing pulley-train	22
Deflections in cables	207
Device for changing motion	254
— for increasing speed	257
— for increasing tension	255
— for obtaining intermittent motion	258
— for obtaining opposite motions	255
— for obtaining variable motion	259
— for putting on cables	241
Diameter, examples of	25
—, formulas for	12
— of cables	202
— of shafts	176
Difficulties found in belting	76
Dimensions of pulley-supports	234
Direction of rotation	11
Distance between pulleys	31
— between pulley-supports	231
Double belts	66
— curved arms	169

	PAGE
Double lacing	71
Dynamometer	77

E

Elasticity of cables	198
Engaging and disengaging	180
Entire simplicity impossible	viii
Enbank, Thomas	1
Examples of arms	168
— of circumference	25
Examples of continuous speed cones	64
— of deflection	209
— of diameter	25
— of diameter of cables	204
— of diameter of shafts	172
— of greatest tensions	90
— of horse-power	27
— of inclined transmission	219
— of increased tension	214
— of jointed chain-belt	194
— of keys	163
— of length of belts	49
— of nave	161
— of power	27
— of pulley-train	26
— of radius	25
— of revolutions	25
— of rim	160
— of rope-belts	189
— of speed-cones	55
— of transmission with pulleys near together	222
Examples of velocities	26
— of weight of pulleys	165
— of weight of principal pulleys	236
— of width of leather belts over cast-iron pulleys	93
Examples of width of leather belts over leather-covered pulleys	118
Examples of width of rubber belts over cast-iron pulleys	154
Examples of width of rubber belts over leather-covered pulleys	157
Expense of belting	iii
Experiments with leather over iron	243
— with leather over leather	249
— with rubber over iron	251

INDEX.

Experiments with rubber over leather.................. 252
Extracts from letters............... iv

F

Fast and loose pulleys............. 179
Fastenings....................... 68
Fireless period................... 4
Fire-machine..................... 4
First human necessity............. 4
— machine....................... 4
— transformation................. 5
Fixing-keys...................... 162
Flax belts....................... 66
Foot-pound...................... 23
Formulas for arms................ 167
— for arms of cable-pulleys....... 226
— for cable diameters............. 200
— for circumference............... 11
— for deflections................. 207
— for diameter................... 12
— for distance between pulleys.... 31
— for face-width.................. 159
— for fixing-keys................. 163
— for horse-power................ 24
— for inclined transmission....... 219
— for increased tension........... 213
— for jointed chain-belts......... 193
— for length of belts............. 47
— for nave....................... 161
— for power...................... 20
— for pressure on axes............ 236
— for pulley-supports............. 234
— for radius..................... 12
— for ratio of powers............. 22
— for ratio of revolutions........ 14
— for ratio of velocities......... 18
— for revolutions................ 14
— for rim........................ 160
— for rope-belts................. 187
— for shafts..................... 172
— for speed-cones................ 54
— for tensions................... 84
— for tensions in cables......... 199
— for velocities................. 15
— for weight of pulleys.......... 165
— for weight of principal pulleys... 236

Formulas for width of leather belts.........................93-114
— for width of rubber belts....... 150

G

Godin's belt..................... 192
Graphical method................. 60
Greatest tension................. 88
Gum.............................. 116
Gut belts........................ 66
Gutta percha.................... 224

H

Half-crossed belts............... 31
Haswell's rule................... vii
Height of cable above ground..... 212
Hemp belts....................... 66
Herland's tool................... 241
Hirn brothers.................... 196
Holes for lacing................. 68
Horizontal transmissions......... 207
Horse-power..................... 23
"Hydraulics and Mechanics"...... 1
Hyperbolic logarithms............ 23

I

Inclined transmissions........... 217
Increased tension................ 212
Increasing pulley-train.......... 22
Inferior limit of separation of pulleys........................ 197
Integral calculus................ 84
Intermediate pulleys............. 230
— stations...................... 232
Intersecting axes................ 28
Intestines for belts............. 66

J

Jointed chain-belts.............. 192
"Journal of Franklin Institute"... 246

K

Kenedy's translation............. 4
Keys............................. 162
Kilogram......................... 200
"Kinematics of Machinery"....... 4

L

	PAGE
Lacing	68
Lack of knowledge of belting	iv
— of space	43
Leather belts	65
—, examples of	93
—, formulas for	93-114
—, tables of	88-138
Leather-covered pulleys	115
Logarithms, common	85
—, Naperian	84
Long belts	262

M

Material of belting	65
Median line	28
Metallic belts	192
— cables	196
Middle plane	28
Methods of arranging pulleys	260
Method of tracing cable-curves	221
Middle plane	28
Mill-shafts	260
Mutilated pulley	258

N

Naperian logarithms	84
Nave of cable-pulleys	226
— of pulleys	161
Nineveh	8
Nystrom's formula	vi

O

Open belt	7
Origin of belt and pulley	3
Oscillating motion	5

P

Parallel axes	28
Pedestals	239
Permissible deviation	44
Power, examples of	27
—, formulas for	20
—, ratio of	22
Pressure on axes	235
Primitive lathe, drill, etc.	5
— water-wheel	8
Probable origin of pulley	5
Profiles of arms	169

	PAGE
Proper disposition of pulleys	28
Pulley arms	166
—, cable	226
—, flanged	160
— nave	161
— rim	159
—, rounding of	159
—, split	163
— supports	230
— train	21
— with light arms	238

R

Radius, examples of	25
—, formulas for	12
Ratio of circumferences	12
— of power	22
— of revolutions	14
— of velocities	19
Rawhide belts	66
Reserve cables	228
Resistance to slipping	75
Reuleaux, Prof.	vi, 28
Reversing	182
Revolutions	14
Rim of cable-pulleys	203
— of pulleys	159
Robertson	2
Rollin	2
Rope-belts	185
Rosin	116
Rotation	11
Rouiller's belt	192
Rounded fillies	28
Rules for arms	167
— for belts with pulley-guides	32
— for circumference	11
— for diameter	11
— for distance between pulleys	31
— for horse-power	24
— for power	20
— for proper disposition of pulleys	28
— for radius	12
— for ratio of circumferences	12
— for ratio of powers	22
— for ratio of velocities	19
— for revolutions	14
— for shaft-diameters	172

S

	PAGE
Safe shearing stress	142
— working stress, leather	92
— working stress, rubber	141
Scale for cable-curves	220
Schaffhouse	228
Shafts	171
— of mines	233
Sheet-iron pulleys	238
Shop-shafts	260
Shortening	68
Single lacing	69
Size of pulleys	24
Slipping	45
Slow growth of belting	6
Smith, C. A.	60
Speed-cones	51
Spinning-mills	44
Split pulleys	163
Stations	232
Station pillars	238
Steel cables	203
— shafts	176
Stepped cones	65
Strength of gut	66
— of leather	75
— of rawhide	66
— of vulcanized rubber	141
Swedish iron	203

T

	PAGE
Table, deflections	210
—, dimensions of pulley-supports	234
—, formulas for leather belts	96–129
—, formulas for rubber belts	142–149
—, greatest tensions	90, 118, 157
—, increased tension	214
Table, metallic cables	210
—, number of arms	167
—, shaft-diameters	176
—, tensions for leather	88, 117
—, tensions for metallic cables	201
—, tensions for rope-belts	188
—, weight of pulleys	165
—, widths of leather belts	110, 135
—, widths of rubber belts	151
Tensions in cable-wires	200
— in belts	79
— in inclined transmissions	220
Thickness of rubber belts	140
Tightening-pulley	179
Torsional strain	171
Tower of Babel	9
Transmission by cable with pulleys near together	222
Transmission with inclined cable	217
"Treatise on Toothed Gearing"	169

U

Uncertain origin of belt and pulley	3
Unwin's formula	vi

V

Velocities	13
Vulcanized-rubber belts	66

W

Weakest part of belt	92
Weight of pulleys	164
Wrought-iron shafts	176

Z

Zeigler's machine for putting on metallic cables	241

www.ingramcontent.com/pod-product-compliance
Lightning Source LLC
Chambersburg PA
CBHW032102220426
43664CB00008B/1109